Acing
Administrative Law

A Checklist Approach to Solving Administrative Law Problems

Second Edition

Linda D. Jellum
Professor of Law
University of Idaho College of Law

Series Editor
A. Benjamin Spencer

ACING SERIES®

WEST ACADEMIC

860 Blue Gentian Road, Suite 350
Eagan, MN 55121
1-877-888-1330

Published in the United States of America

ISBN: 979-8-89209-461-0

To Dave, the best maid of honor and brother a girl could have. Love you, Bro!

Preface

Your Administrative Law course is a class that covers the procedures federal agencies must follow for their actions to be upheld if challenged. In short, agencies must jump through multiple hoops, and they must jump through those hoops properly. If you represent someone challenging an agency, your goal is either to make the agency start back at the beginning of the hoop-jumping process or to slow the hoop-jumping process down. Why slow it down? If you are lucky, a new administration (or president) who is more sympathetic to your client's point of view may come to office. If you represent an agency, your goal is to help it jump through the hoops properly so that if someone later challenges the agency, it is not told to start over, and if a new president comes to office, the rule is already in place and so will be much harder to repeal. This book will help you learn the hoops agencies must jump through so you can ace your Administrative Law final exam.

Why use this book to help you prepare for your exam in Administrative Law as opposed to all the other study aids that are available? When I was in law school, we used commercial outlines and hornbooks to help us study for exams. From those sources (and of course from our notes as well), we distilled hundreds of hours of classes and tremendous amounts of substantive material into digestible, short outlines. "Short" differed in length depending upon the author; however, each of us tried to draft an outline that would be useful to us as we took our exams, whatever "useful" meant. Longer outlines were more useful for open-book exams because they served as cheat sheets for when we forgot the exact wording; shorter outlines were more useful for closed-book exams because they helped us memorize the most important material.

While creating an outline may have helped us memorize the material and learn discrete topics within a particular subject, I am pretty sure that creating an outline did not help anyone learn the material as a coherent whole. What I mean is that outlining did not help us learn how the material we studied at the end of the semester related to the material we studied in the very first class.

The Acing Law series addresses this deficiency. The books in this series are designed to make you think about how a course works as a whole. You are directed to start at the beginning: What is the first question you should ask when faced with a family law, torts law, constitutional law, tax law, or administrative law issue? Once you have answered that question, what question do you ask next? And so on until you ask the last question you should ask. The books in this series are designed to help you approach your exams in an organized and logical manner, something outlines really do not do.

In closing, let me thank my research assistants, Coyleen Greenwell, J.D. 2025, Hayden Zywina, J.D. 2025, and Michael Bicksel. This edition is better for their help.

LINDA D. JELLUM

July 2024

Table of Contents

Acing
Administrative Law

A Checklist Approach to Solving Administrative Law Problems

Second Edition

Introduction

This book, Acing Administrative Law, will prepare you to take exams in Administrative Law (or even Leg/Reg). I have focused on the seven topics that you will most likely encounter on an essay exam. Because I could not cover every possible topic, I have chosen to focus on the topics on which you are most likely to be tested.

I have started differently than your law school course likely started. The first question I recommend you ask before every Administrative Law based exam question is: "What kind of agency action is at issue?" The answer to that question is important because the proper analysis of any administrative law issue flows from the type of action at issue.

For example, if the agency engaged in rulemaking, you should ask whether the delegated authority violates the non-delegation doctrine; whether formal rulemaking procedures were necessary; whether notice-and-comment procedures were required or could be avoided; whether appropriate rulemaking procedures were followed; whether, during the rulemaking process, the agency decided a question of policy, fact, or law; and whether judicial review is available. If instead the agency engaged in adjudication, then you should ask whether the authority delegated violates the very confusing public-private rights distinction; whether formal or informal adjudication was required; whether appropriate adjudication procedures were followed; whether, during the adjudication, the agency decided a question of fact, policy, or law; and whether judicial review is available.

Whether you have a rulemaking or adjudication question, you will have one more question you will need to answer. That question is, "What is the appropriate standard of review?" I anticipate that your professor will ask you a standard of review question because this area of the law has fluctuated a lot in recent years. So pay particular attention to this section of the text. It is also the section that has changed the most in this edition of the text.

Each chapter follows the series format. First, there is a brief (very brief) overview of the law in the area; followed by a chapter checklist; followed by two hypothetical problems, which are resolved using the chapter's checklist. Finally, each chapter concludes with a

"Points to Remember" section to help remind you of the most important points in that chapter. However, this book differs from others in the series in that the final chapter is a master checklist followed by a comprehensive exam question, which is resolved using the master checklist. This unique feature of this Acing Book accomplishes exactly what I identified above: a way of understanding the course as a coherent whole.

As I conclude, let me caution that this book is not a substitute for thoroughly understanding the material. Rather, it is meant to help you organize the complex and overwhelming material you will need to learn in a way that may prove useful to you as you attempt to answer an exam question in this area. Most importantly, your professor may have a unique focus or understanding of Administrative Law, particularly those areas that are unsettled. When there is conflict between us: your professor wins.

CHAPTER 1

Is There Agency Action?

Agencies regulate private conduct, administer entitlement programs, collect taxes, deport aliens, issue permits, run the space program, manage the national parks, and so on. Simply put, agencies run the functions we think of as government, whether state or federal. Of more interest to us is how agencies do what they do, which the Administrative Procedure Act (APA)[1] governs.

The APA identifies an agency's procedural law, which we call *administrative law*. Pursuant to the APA and other laws, agencies must employ specified procedures to act legally. In essence, agencies must jump through the required hoops. If the agency misses a hoop, jumps through the wrong hoop, or fails to jump at all, the agency has not used proper procedures and must generally begin its process again. Hence, here are the first three questions you must ask yourself as you approach an administrative law exam (or problem in practice): (1) is the actor a federal *agency*, (2) did the agency act, fail to act, or delay action, and (3) did the agency act via rulemaking, adjudication, or inspection/investigation. In other words, has an *agency* issued a *rule* through rulemaking, an *order* through adjudication, or a subpoena or request for information?

REVIEW

A. What Is an Agency?

The APA applies only to federal agencies. Hence, you must first confirm that the entity that acted was indeed a federal *agency*. The APA broadly defines *agency* as "each authority of the Government of the United States . . . not includ[ing Congress, the courts, state governments, etc.]."[2] Thus, the term "agency" includes all governmental authorities including administrations (*e.g.*, the Small

---

[1] 5 U.S.C. § 551 *et. seq.* (hereinafter "APA").

[2] APA §§ 551(1) & 701.

Business Administration), commissions (*e.g.*, the Commodity Futures Trading Commission), corporations (*e.g.*, the Federal Deposit Insurance Corporation), boards (National Transportation Safety Board), departments (*e.g.*, the U.S. Department of Education), divisions (*e.g.*, the NWRS Division of Refuge Law Enforcement), and agencies (*e.g.*, the Defense Health Agency). While the definition is broad, the president is not an agency.[3]

There are two types of agencies: independent agencies and executive agencies. Independent agencies are believed to be less subject to the president's influence because they are usually headed by multimember groups[4] from both political parties, who serve specific terms and can typically only be removed for cause. Examples of independent agencies include the Securities and Exchange Commission, the Federal Trade Commission, the Federal Election Commission, the Equal Opportunity Commission, and the National Labor Relations Board.

In contrast, executive agencies are headed by individuals (generally called secretaries), whom the president appoints with the advice and consent of the Senate, and who serve at the discretion of the president. Examples include the Department of Defense, the Homeland Security Administration, and the Department of Education. The largest and most influential executive agencies are called departments; departments contain a host of sub-agencies. The heads of the departments are known collectively as the cabinet.

All agencies must follow the same procedures when they promulgate a rule or when they issue an order regardless of whether they are independent or executive. Thus, the type of agency is irrelevant for purposes of this chapter; however, you may have to address the constitutionality of an independent agency's structure, including appointment and removal. We will address this issue further in Chapter 2.

B. Did the Agency Act?

After determining that the actor is an agency, you should ensure that the agency acted in some way. Often, agency action is easy to identify: a rule is promulgated, an order is entered, or an inspection takes place. But sometimes action is more difficult to identify. For example, an agency might unreasonably delay acting or fail to act at all when legally required to act. Both behaviors are defined as

---

3 Franklin v. Massachusetts, 505 U.S. 788, 796 (1992).

4 There are a few exceptions; for example, a single individual heads the Consumer Financial Protection Bureau, yet it is an independent agency. A divided D.C. Court of Appeals held that this structure does not violate the Appointments Clause of the U.S. Constitution. PHH Corp. v. CFPB, 881 F.3d 75, 110 (D.C. Cir. 2018).

"actions" under the APA. The APA defines *agency action* to include "the failure to act"[5] when action is required.[6] Also, a court can "compel agency action unlawfully withheld or unreasonably delayed."[7]

C. What Type of Agency Action Is at Issue?

Assuming the agency acted, failed to act, or unreasonably delayed acting, your next step is to determine what kind of action the agency took. Agencies act in three ways: by rulemaking, by adjudicating, and by gathering and disseminating information. Agencies act like legislatures when they make rules through rulemaking, like courts when they issue orders through adjudication, and like the police when they gather and disclose information through investigation and disclosure. Depending on the type of action, different procedural requirements apply.

The APA requires agencies to use different procedures for rulemaking, adjudication, and investigation. Hence, correctly classifying any given agency action is essential. Usually, you will have little difficulty identifying the correct category; however, sometimes this determination will be more difficult. When in doubt, you should begin with the idea that if the action is more like what a legislature does, then the action is likely rulemaking culminating in a rule. Instead, if the action is more like what a court does, then the action is likely an adjudication culminating in an order. Less likely on an exam, if the action is more like what the police do, then the action is likely investigation and disclosure. To confirm your gut reaction, apply the APA's definitions of *rule* and *order*, which are arguably somewhat circular.

1. *Agency Rulemaking & Adjudication*

Typically, if you have difficulty identifying agency action, the choice is either rulemaking or adjudication. The APA defines *adjudication* as the "agency process for the formulation of an *order*."[8] An *order* is defined as "the whole or a part of a final disposition . . . of

---

[5] APA § 551(13) (" '[A]gency action' includes the whole or a part of an agency rule, order, license, sanction, relief, or the equivalent or denial thereof, or failure to act . . . .").

[6] *See, e.g.*, Massachusetts v. EPA, 549 U.S. 497, 517 (2007).

[7] APA § 706(1). Typically, unreasonable-delay challenges relate to an agency's failure to act on a rulemaking petition as APA § 553(e) requires. To determine whether the agency's delay was reasonable, a reviewing court will apply the TRAC factors. Telecomms. Rsch. & Action Ctr. v. FCC, 750 F.2d 70, 76 (D.C. Cir. 1984) (identifying the following factors: [1] whether the applicable statute contains a timetable, [2] whether delay would impact human welfare, [3] how forcing a decision would affect higher agency priorities, and [4] how all the interests would be affected).

[8] APA § 551(7).

an agency in a matter other than *rulemaking*, but including licensing."[9] *Rulemaking* is defined as the "agency process for formulating, amending, or repealing a *rule*."[10] A *rule* is defined as "an agency statement of general . . . applicability and future effect designed to implement, interpret, or prescribe law or policy."[11] Pursuant to these definitions, rules—like statutes—are general laws that apply prospectively to multiple people and entities, while adjudications are specific laws that apply retroactively to the parties. Years ago, I had a student submit a drawing to depict the difference between an order and a rule. For rulemaking, the student drew a bus heading down the freeway with all the passengers looking forward. For adjudication, the student drew a Volkswagen bug, stopped on the road with its driver looking backward. It is a good visual of the differences: rulemaking affects many and is forward looking, while adjudication affects few and is backwards looking.

Let's be clear about one thing: agencies may choose to regulate using either procedure. So long as an agency has authority to act using both processes (you must check the enabling act to determine which authority was delegated), the decision whether to proceed through rulemaking or adjudication is vested, primarily, in the informed discretion of the agency. In *Chenery II*, the Supreme Court recognized that, although an agency should consider making policy as much as possible using rulemaking, agencies must have flexibility to deal with regulatory problems in the manner they deem most appropriate.[12]

Although the decision whether to proceed by rulemaking or adjudication is primarily vested in the informed discretion of the agency, courts may set aside an agency's order if the agency's decision to use adjudication was an abuse of discretion. For example, were an agency to impose a substantial penalty or liability on a person or business for violating a legal principle that had not been previously announced, the agency's order could be set aside.[13]

---

[9] APA § 551(6).

[10] APA § 551(5).

[11] APA § 551(4).

[12] SEC v. Chenery Corp., 332 U.S. 194, 202–03 (1947) (saying that an agency "may not have had sufficient experience with a particular problem to warrant rigidifying its tentative judgment into a hard and fast rule. Or the problem may be so specialized and varying in nature as to be impossible of capture within the boundaries of a general rule.").

[13] *See, e.g.*, NLRB v. Bell Aerospace Co. Div. of Textron Inc., 416 U.S. 267, 295 (1974). A regulated person's or entity's substantial reliance on the agency's prior practice may, in some cases, also warrant the setting aside of an agency order.

2. *Agency Investigation*

The final possible type of agency action that may be at issue I will call *investigation*. These actions include the following: an inspection, a request to an entity to voluntarily provide information, and a demand to an entity to produce information. They also include disclosures, including providing information to the public, holding open meetings, and allowing public access to certain information.

To effectively regulate, agencies need information and lots of it. To believe that its government is acting legitimately, the public demands transparency. Hence, information flows in two directions: from the regulated entities (people and business agencies regulate) to the agency and from the agency to the public.

Perhaps surprisingly, the APA does not address an agency's authority to seek information from those it regulates. Rather, the agency's enabling act and the United States Constitution regulate this area.[14] Similarly, the APA does not address an agency's duty to provide information to the public. Rather, other statutes do so, such as the Freedom of Information Act,[15] the Government in Sunshine Act,[16] the Federal Advisory Act,[17] the Privacy Act,[18] among others. If your issue relates to an investigation, then you need to determine whether the agency is seeking information from a regulated entity or whether the public is seeking information from the agency to determine which law to apply.

After you have identified that *an agency* has acted or failed to act and the type of agency action, you can proceed to the steps in the next chapter.

AGENCY ACTION CHECKLIST

A. ***Agency* Action**—Is the actor an authority of the United States government, such as an administration, commission, corporation, board, department, division, or agency?

1. **No**—If no, then the actor is not an agency, and the APA does not apply. The president, Congress, a federal court, a state or territorial government, a military commission or

---

14 Specifically, the Fourth and Fifth Amendments apply.

15 APA § 552.

16 *Id.*

17 5 U.S.C. app. § 2.

18 APA § 552a.

court martial, and specifically exempted authorities under APA §§ 551(1)(A)–(H) are not agencies. But if this is an essay question, this answer is likely wrong. Stop here.

2. **Yes**—If yes, then the actor is a federal agency, and administrative law applies. Proceed to B. below.

B. Agency *Action*—Did the agency act, fail to act, or unreasonably delay acting?

1. **No**—If the agency did not act and was not required to act or if the agency did not unreasonably delay acting, then the APA does not apply. Stop here.

2. **Yes**—If the agency unreasonably delayed acting, then the APA applies. To determine whether the agency's delay was reasonable, a reviewing court will apply the TRAC factors: [1] whether the applicable statute contains a timetable, [2] whether delay will impact human welfare, [3] how forcing a decision would affect higher agency priorities, and [4] how all the interests are affected. Stop here.

3. **Yes**—If the agency acted or failed to act when legally required, the APA applies. Proceed to C. below.

C. Agency *Action*—How did the agency act?

1. **Rulemaking**—Did the agency promulgate a general rule with future application?

   a. **No**—If no, then the agency may have acted using adjudicatory or investigative powers. Proceed to C.2. below.

   b. **Yes**—If yes, then the agency acted via rulemaking, and the APA applies. Proceed to Chapter 2.

2. **Adjudication**—Did the agency issue an order that applies to specific parties and their past actions?

   a. **No**—If no, then the agency may have acted using investigative powers. Proceed to C.3. below.

   b. **Yes**—If yes, then the agency acted using adjudication, and the APA applies. Ask whether a party was substantially penalized for abiding by prior policy.

      i. **Yes**—If yes, then the agency's choice to use adjudication is invalid, and any order should be set aside. Stop here.

ii. **No**—If no, then the agency's choice is valid. <u>Proceed to Chapter 2</u>.

3. **Investigation and Disclosure**—Did the agency seek information through an inspection, through a request for information, or through a subpoena?

   a. **No**—If no, then you have reached a wrong answer at some point in your analysis. <u>Start over</u>.

   b. **Yes**—If yes, then the agency acted using executive power and administrative law applies (such as FOIA), but the APA does not apply. <u>Proceed to Chapter 2</u>.

ILLUSTRATIVE PROBLEMS

■ PROBLEM 1.1 ■

Assume that the Federal Housing Authority (FHA) decides to stop insuring Capital Mortgage, Inc.'s single-family home mortgages because of alleged irregularities in Capital Mortgage's accounting practices. You work for Capital Mortgage. You want to know whether the FHA can make this decision. How do you proceed based on the checklist above?

Analysis

You first want to determine whether the FHA is an agency and whether the FHA's action was rulemaking or adjudication. Using Section A in the checklist above, you should ask first whether the FHA is an authority of the United States government under APA § 551(1). The answer: it is.

You should determine next how the agency acted using Section C in the checklist above. Here, FHA's rule does have prospective effect; however, the rule applies only to one company and is based on that company's prior actions. Hence, the FHA issued an order through adjudication and must follow the requirements in the APA for adjudication and, as you will learn, the Constitution's Due Process clause.

Finally, you should determine whether the agency's choice to act using adjudication rather than rulemaking in this case was an abuse of discretion. If Capital Mortgage were substantially penalized for abiding by prior policy, then the agency's choice would be invalid, and any order should be set aside. *NLRB v. Bell Aerospace Co. Div. of Textron Inc.*, 416 U.S. 267 (1974). Based on the limited facts provided, the FHA's action was not an abuse of discretion.

■ PROBLEM 1.2 ■

Assume that the automobile industry petitions the Department of Transportation (DOT) to amend a rule pertaining to use of airbags in self-driving vehicles and that the industry files a formal, written petition requesting the rule modification. You work as general counsel for DOT, which does not want to act on the petition at all or wants to delay immediate action. How would you advise DOT to respond to the petition, if at all, using the checklist above?

Analysis

First, you should confirm that the DOT is an agency using Section A in the checklist above.

Next, you want to determine whether the agency can ignore the petition or delay responding. Using Section B in the checklist above, you should determine whether the agency is required to act. The APA defines *agency action* as including an agency's failure to act and allows a court to "compel agency action unlawfully withheld or unreasonably delayed." APA §§ 551(13), 706(1). Thus, the DOT must act and cannot unreasonably delay its response.

However, the APA does not set forth how quickly an agency must act on a petition. To determine how quickly the DOT must act, look at Section B.2. in the checklist. A reviewing court will apply the TRAC factors to determine whether the agency's delay is unreasonable. *Telecommunications Research & Action Ctr. v. FCC*, 750 F.2d 70, 76 (D.C. Cir. 1984). Those factors include the following: (1) whether the applicable statute contains a timetable, (2) whether delay will impact human welfare, (3) how forcing a decision would affect higher agency priorities, and (4) how all the interests are affected.

Applying these four factors to your case, you should check the relevant enabling act to see if Congress provided a timetable (usually not), explain why delay will not negatively impact human health (which may be difficult for airbag safety especially in self-driving cars), detail the DOT's other priorities (perhaps explain other rulemakings the agency is involved in), and downplay the impact on the automobile industry and general public (again hard given the importance of airbags).

POINTS TO REMEMBER

- Administrative agencies include administrations, commissions (excluding military commissions), corporations, boards, departments, divisions, and agencies. No branch of government is an agency.

- Administrative law, and specifically the APA, governs the procedures agencies must use when they promulgate rules via rulemaking or orders via adjudication. If an agency is not the actor, the APA does not apply.
- Agencies act like legislatures when they promulgate general rules with future applicability. They act like courts when they issue orders that apply to specific parties based on their past conduct. They act like police when they investigate and seek or disclose information.
- So long as Congress authorizes agencies to act both by rulemaking and by adjudication in the enabling act, agencies have the discretion to choose to create policy using either procedure; however, courts serve as a check to ensure agencies do not abuse their discretion.
- The procedures an agency must follow according to the APA depend on whether the agency is promulgating a rule or issuing an order. Therefore, determining what action the agency is taking is the first step in determining what procedures the agency must follow.
- Agencies may not fail to act nor unreasonably delay acting when required to act.

CHAPTER 2

Does the Agency Have Authority to Act?

After determining that the entity acting was an agency and determining the type of action the agency used, the next step is to determine whether the agency acting had authority to act in the way it did. To answer this question, we will look at whether the agency had statutory and constitutional power to act. And we will look at limits on that power. Additionally, we will look at a second issue related to constitutional authority: the appointment and removal of agency personnel.

REVIEW

Agencies have no inherent power to act. For an agency to have power to act, Congress must first enact an act that both creates the agency (if it does not already exist) and identifies the agency's powers and regulatory agenda. This authorizing act is known as the *enabling*, or organic, act (or statute). Your first step should be to check to be sure that Congress actually delegated authority to the agency to act as it did; in other words, did Congress give the agency authority to conduct rulemakings, adjudications, and inspections? If the enabling act does not include such authority, another act might. For example, the Environmental Protection Agency (EPA) was established through Reorganization Plan No. 3, an executive order President Richard Nixon issued, which Congress later enacted into law. Thus, this Act created the EPA; however, other acts authorize the EPA to regulate specific topics. For example, the Clean Air Act, the Clean Water Act, and the Toxic Substances Control Act all authorize the EPA to engage in rulemaking to increase the safety of air, water, and toxic substances. Thus, the power for an agency to act comes from legislation, either the agency's enabling act or another act. In addition, some acts and executive orders limit an agency's exercise of its delegated authority. We will explore some of these limiting laws below.

Lastly, and most importantly, the Constitution and its principle of separation of powers places limits on Congress's ability to delegate legislative and judicial powers. The Constitution places limits both on what can be delegated and to whom Congress can delegate. The latter limits are found in the appointment clause. Hence, after you have determined that an agency acted using either rulemaking or adjudication, you must next determine whether Congress legitimately delegated that specific power to that agency and whether the officials from that agency were constitutionally appointed. The next sections explore the non-constitutional and constitutional constraints on agency power.

A. Non-Constitutional Constraints on an Agency's Power to Act

1. *Legislative Constraints on an Agency's Power to Act*

While Congress can limit any type of agency activity, Congress typically focuses on retaining control over agency rulemaking. For example, in 1996, Congress enacted the Congressional Review Act, under which agencies must send all new rules to the Comptroller General.[1] Major rules are stayed for sixty days. A major rule is one whose annual economic impact is greater than $100 million. If desired, Congress can use a fast-track process to pass a joint resolution disapproving the rule, which the president must sign. Until 2017, Congress had "vetoed" only one agency regulation (a 2001 Clinton-era OSHA ergonomics regulation); however, since the 2016 election in which Republicans took control of Congress and the White House, Congress used this procedure to roll back fourteen Obama-era regulations. Democrats, in turn, rolled back three Trump-era regulations.

Other statutes with procedural requirements include the Regulatory Flexibility Act, which requires agencies to create a Regulatory Flexibility Analysis for any proposed rule that will significantly impact a substantial number of small businesses, organizations, or governments.[2] Also, the Unfunded Mandates Reform Act requires agencies to prepare a statement assessing the effect of any proposed regulation that will cause state, local, or tribal governments to incur more than $100 million annually.[3]

Sometimes, the Supreme Court strikes down these creative legislative control attempts as unconstitutional. For example, the

---

1 5 U.S.C. §§ 801–08.

2 5 U.S.C. § 601 *et seq.*

3 2 U.S.C. § 1501 *et seq.*

Court struck down legislative veto provisions in *INS v. Chadha.*[4] The legislative veto allowed Congress to delegate lawmaking authority to the executive, but reserved, either to a single chamber of Congress or to a committee from a single chamber, the power to oversee and veto the executive's use of this delegated authority.[5] Because legislative veto provisions allowed one chamber of Congress to unilaterally amend legislation and thereby avoid constitutionally required bicameral passage and presentment, the Court held that these provisions were unconstitutional.[6] The Congressional Review Act replaced the legislative veto.

While it is unlikely that you will be expected to memorize the particulars of any of these acts, you will be expected to be aware that acts other than the enabling act exist and place additional procedural requirements on agencies, typically when they wish to promulgate a rule.

2. *Executive Constraints on an Agency's Power to Act*

In addition to the acts identified above, another limiting source you should consider is executive orders (E.O.). Presidents issue executive orders to tell agencies how to implement laws during their administration and for other purposes.

One well-known executive order is E.O. 12,866. This executive order was initially issued by President Reagan, who campaigned on a platform of deregulation in the 1980s. E.O. 12,291 (its original number),[7] directed all executive agencies to perform a regulatory analysis assessing the costs and benefits of any "major" proposed regulations.[8] One of Reagan's purposes for issuing this executive order was to limit unnecessary regulation. However, each president since Reagan has reissued this order, albeit with slight changes. Today, it is known as E.O. 12,866.

E.O. 12,866 provides that agencies may promulgate regulations only when they are "required by law," "necessary to interpret the law," or "are made necessary by compelling public need, such as material failures of private markets to protect or improve the health and safety of the public, the environment, or the well-being of the American people."[9] Agencies must follow specific procedural steps

---

4 462 U.S. 919, 954–55 (1983).

5 *Id.* at 954.

6 *Id.* at 954–55.

7 Exec. Order No. 12,866 § 1, 58 Fed. Reg. 51735 (October 4, 1993).

8 Exec. Order No. 12,291, 3 C.F.R. § 127 (1982).

9 Exec. Order No. 12,866 § 1(a), 58 Fed. Reg. 51735 (October 4, 1993).

when developing regulatory priorities.[10] Specifically, when deciding whether a regulation is necessary, agencies must assess the costs and benefits of the regulatory alternatives, "including the alternative of not regulating."[11] The Office of Information and Regulatory Affairs (OIRA), which is located within the Office of Management and Budget (OMB), will review the proposed rule and analysis to ensure compliance with E.O. 12,866.

Other important E.O.s include the Emancipation Proclamation (freeing enslaved people in Confederate states), E.O. 8,807 (creating a new agency to oversee the development of a top-secret nuclear weapons program known as the Manhattan Project), E.O. 9,066 (ordering the mass incarceration of Japanese Americans), E.O. 10,730 (authorizing the military to help enforce desegregation of Little Rock's public schools), Proclamation 4,311 (pardoning former President Nixon), E.O. 13,228 (creating the Department of Homeland Security after 9/11), and E.O. 13,780 (the second so-called Muslim ban).

Thus, the first step in analyzing whether the agency had the power to do what it did is to check the enabling and other relevant acts and E.O.s.

B. Constitutional Constraints on Appointment & Removal

1. *Overview*

Before you consider the constitutionality of what an agency did, you must first consider whether the agency's structure is constitutional. When Congress creates an agency, one structural issue Congress must consider is how the agency officials will be appointed and removed.

---

[10] These procedures include (1) identifying the problem the regulation was intended to address, including "the failures of private markets or public institutions that warrant new agency action;" (2) determining whether the problem could be addressed through modifications to existing regulations or laws; (3) assessing alternatives to regulation, such as economic incentives; (4) considering "the degree and nature of the risks posed by various substances or activities" within the agency's jurisdiction; (5) fashioning regulations "in the most cost-effective manner;" (6) assessing the costs and benefits, such that benefits justify the costs; (7) basing decisions "on the best reasonably obtainable scientific, technical, economic, and other information;" (8) recommending performance-based solutions rather than behavioral ones, when possible; (9) consulting with state, local, and tribal governments and assessing the impacts of regulations on these local governments; (10) avoiding duplications and inconsistencies among federal agencies; (11) minimizing the burdens; (12) considering the cumulative costs of regulation; and (13) writing all regulations in language that the general public can easily understand. Exec. Order No. 12,866 §§ 1(b)(1)–(12), 58 Fed. Reg. 51735 (October 4, 1993).

[11] Exec. Order No. 12,866 § 1(a), 58 Fed. Reg. 51735 (October 4, 1993).

In Chapter 1, you learned that one difference between independent and executive agencies is that independent agencies are often headed by multimember boards, each of whom is appointed with the advice and consent of the Senate[12] and removable only for cause. In contrast, the heads of executive agencies, who are also appointed with the advice and consent of the Senate, generally serve at the president's pleasure, meaning they are removable at will. For this reason, one issue you should consider is whether the appointment and removal provisions of an enabling act are constitutional. Appointment and removal challenges often occur together and are increasingly common. Appointment and removal challenges challenge the agency's structure. As such, they are not subject to an administrative exhaustion requirement.[13]

Let's start with appointments. Under the U.S. Constitution's Appointments Clause, Congress shares the appointment power with the president in two relevant ways. First, while the president can appoint whomever he or she pleases, the Senate must confirm presidential appointments of *principal officers*, including heads of agencies, before they can serve.[14] Second, Congress has the power to vest the appointment power of *inferior officers* in the president, the courts of law, or in heads of departments.[15] Under the U.S. Constitution, Congress cannot by itself appoint any officer of the United States.[16]

The U.S. Constitution distinguishes between (1) principal officers and inferior officers, and (2) inferior officers and employees. These distinctions are relevant to both appointment and removal issues. Unfortunately, the Supreme Court has not offered clear and consistent guidance on the difference between principal officers, inferior officers, and employees. The Court's test has changed with each case it has heard.

While the U.S. Constitution explicitly provides for the appointment[17] of principal and inferior officers, it does not explicitly

---

12 U.S. CONST. art. II, § 2, cl. 2.

13 Carr v. Saul, 593 U.S. 83, 95–96 (2021) ("[T]he inquisitorial features of [administrative] proceedings, the constitutional character of petitioners' claims, and the unavailability of any remedy make clear that adversarial development of the Appointments Clause issue simply did not exist (and could not exist) in petitioners' [administrative] proceedings." (internal quotations omitted). For a discussion of the exhaustion doctrine, see Chapter 6.

14 *Id.* at 86.

15 U.S. CONST. art. II, § 2, cl. 2; Lucia v. SEC, 585 U.S. 237, 244 n.3 (2018).

16 Buckley v. Valeo, 424 U.S. 1, 143 (1976).

17 The Constitution provides that "[t]he executive Power shall be vested in a President of the United States of America." U.S. CONST. art. II, § 1, cl. 1. As Madison stated on the floor of the First Congress, "if any power whatsoever is in its nature

address their removal.[18] The Supreme Court has held that the Constitution vests removal power in the president *implicitly* because that power was not " 'expressly taken away' " from the president in the Constitution.[19] Below we will examine the constitutional requirements for both appointments and removal provisions.

2. Appointment

First, let's look at the law regarding appointments. As noted above, the Appointments Clause of the U.S. Constitution describes the permissible methods of appointing "Officers of the United States," a class of government officials that does not include mere employees.[20] The president, with the advice and consent of the Senate appoints *principal* officers, while the president, a court of law, or a head of department can appoint an *inferior* officer.[21] Inferior officers differ from principal officers in that inferior officers have a superior who is below the president.[22]

The line between officer and mere employee is less bright lined. The Supreme Court has established a two-part test for distinguishing between them. Using the first prong of that test, a court examines whether the individual holds a "continuing" position established by law.[23] The position must be "continuing and permanent," rather than "occasional or temporary."[24] This prong of the test is generally easy to resolve.

Using the second prong, a court examines whether the individual exercises "significant authority" pursuant to the laws of the United States.[25] This prong of the test is more difficult to resolve because the Court has not clearly explained what "significant authority" means.[26] The Court has merely decided the issue in individual cases.

Executive, it is the power of appointing, overseeing, and controlling those who execute the laws." 1 ANNALS OF CONG. 463 (1789).

[18] The Constitution contains only one removal provision, which provides that "all civil officers of the United States [may] be removed from office on impeachment for, and conviction of, treason, bribery, or other high crimes and misdemeanors." U.S. CONST. art. II, § 4.

[19] Free Enter. Fund v. Public Co. Account. Oversight Bd., 561 U.S. 477, 492 (2010) (quoting Letter from James Madison to Thomas Jefferson (June 30, 1789), 16 Documentary History of the First Federal Congress 893 (2004)).

[20] Art. II, § 2, cl. 2.

[21] *Id.*

[22] United States v. Arthrex, Inc., 594 U.S. 1, 13 (quoting Edmond v. United States, 520 U.S. 651, 662 (1997)).

[23] United States v. Germaine, 99 U.S. 508, 511–12 (1879).

[24] *Id.*

[25] Buckley v. Valeo, 424 U.S. 1, 126 (1976).

[26] Lucia v. SEC, 585 U.S. 237 (2018).

For example, the Court has granted inferior officer status to many a lesser functionary, including a district court clerk,[27] a federal marshal,[28] and, special trial judges (STJs) of the United States Tax Court.[29] In the latter case, the Court reasoned that STJs "take testimony, conduct trials, rule on the admissibility of evidence, and have the power to enforce compliance with discovery orders."[30] Moreover, "[i]n the course of carrying out these important functions, [they] exercise significant discretion;"[31] hence, the STJs were officers.[32]

In *Freytag v. Commissioner*, the Supreme Court explicitly rejected the government's argument that officials who "lack authority to enter into a final decision" must be employees and not inferior officers because that argument "ignore[d] the significance of the duties and discretion that special trial judges possess."[33] More recently, the Court held that Securities and Exchange Commission's (SEC) administrative law judges were officers and not employees because they exercised powers identical to those of the STJs.[34]

3. Removal

Removal is the flipside of appointment. As noted, the U.S. Constitution does not specifically address removal; however, the courts presume the president has such power because removal ensures obedience and the president's ability to faithfully execute the laws.[35] For example, in *Myers v. United States*,[36] the Supreme Court struck down a statute that required the president to obtain the advice and consent of the Senate prior to removing the postmaster general, a principal officer.

But the president's removal power is not unlimited. Thus, in *Humphrey's Executor v. United States*,[37] the Court upheld a provision in the Federal Trade Commission Act that permitted the president to

---

[27] In re Hennen, 38 U.S. (13 Pet.) 230, 258 (1839).

[28] Ex parte Siebold, 100 U.S. 371, 397 (1879).

[29] Freytag v. Comm'r, 501 U.S. 868 (1991).

[30] *Id.* at 881–82.

[31] *Id.* at 882.

[32] *Id.*

[33] *Id.* at 881.

[34] *Lucia*, 585 U.S. at 247–49.

[35] Seila Law, LLC v. Consumer Fin. Prot. Bureau, 591 U.S. 197, 215 (2020) ("The President's removal power has long been confirmed by history and precedent. It 'was discussed extensively in Congress when the first executive departments were created' in 1789 (known as the Decision of 1789).") (quoting Free Enter. Fund v. Pub. Co. Acct. Oversight Bd., 561 U.S. 477, 492 (2010)).

[36] 272 U.S. 52, 106–18, 176 (1926).

[37] 295 U.S. 602, 620 (1935) (quoting Federal Trade Commission Act, ch. 311, 38 Stat. 717 (1914); 15 U.S.C. § 1).

dismiss a commissioner of the Federal Trade Commission (FTC), also a principal officer, only for "inefficiency, neglect of duty, or malfeasance in office." The FTC is headed by a multimember board.

The Court distinguished its holding in *Myers* by noting that the postmaster general performed purely executive functions and had to be responsible to the president while the FTC member performed quasi-legislative or quasi-judicial powers and had to be independent of the president.[38] Thus, the Court limited *Myers*'s holding to "all purely executive officers."[39]

This distinction did not last long, however. In *Morrison v. Olson*,[40] the Court rejected the *Myers/Humphrey*'s distinction as determinative. In *Morrison*, the Court upheld a for-cause removal limitation on a "purely executive" *inferior* officer, an independent counsel. The Court said, "the determination of whether the constitution allows Congress to impose a 'good cause'-type restriction on the [p]resident's power to remove an official cannot be made to turn on whether or not that official is classified as 'purely executive.' "[41] The Court reasoned that the most important question was whether the removal restriction "impedes the [p]resident's ability to perform his Constitutional duty" to ensure that the laws are faithfully executed.[42] The Court then reasoned that because the independent counsel (1) was an inferior officer, (2) had limited jurisdiction, (3) did not have tenure, (4) lacked policymaking power, and (5) did not have significant administrative authority, the for-cause removal provision was a reasonable restriction on the president's removal authority. However, *Morrison*'s rejection of the *Myers/Humphrey*'s distinction was similarly short-lived.

In *Free Enterprise Fund v. Public Co. Accounting Oversight Board*,[43] the Court resurrected the *Myers/Humphrey*'s distinction to hold that dual for-cause removal provisions are unconstitutional because the president cannot " 'take care the Laws be faithfully executed' if he cannot oversee the faithfulness of the officers who execute them."[44] In a later case, the Court noted that it had recognized only two exceptions to the president's need to remove

---

[38] *Id.* at 627–28. *See also* Weiner v. United States, 357 U.S. 349, 350 (1958) (limiting the president's ability to remove a Commissioner of the War Claims Commission, which had only a three-year existence, even though the relevant statute was silent regarding removal because Congress intended to insulate the Commission from presidential interference).

[39] *Humphrey's Executor*, 295 U.S. at 628.

[40] 487 U.S. 654, 689 (1988).

[41] *Id.*

[42] *Id.*

[43] 561 U.S. 477, 484 (2010).

[44] *Id.*

officers without limitation: first, for principal officers who serve on multimember boards, which head up independent agencies and do not wield substantial executive power (*Humphrey's Executer*), and second, for inferior officers who have limited duties (*Morrison*).[45] Applying this reasoning, the Fifth Circuit held that the dual removal provisions protecting SEC's ALJs are unconstitutional.[46] Likely, this reasoning applies to all ALJs, but the Supreme Court has yet to rule on this issue.[47]

In sum, whether an appointment or removal provision is constitutional depends on [1] whether the officer involved is a principal officer, an inferior officer, or an employee, [2] whether the officer exercises core executive power or quasi-judicial or quasi-legislative power, and [3] whether the officer serves on a multimember board. In short, removal limitations cannot impede a president's ability to ensure the laws are faithfully executed.

C. Constitutional Constraints on an Agency's Power to Act

1. Introduction to Formalism & Functionalism

In determining the legitimacy of constitutional constraints, you may be expected to know the difference between formalism and functionalism. The Supreme Court has approached questions involving separation of powers issues in two different ways, one of which is more accepting of overlap, the other which is not. Legal scholars have identified these two approaches as *formalism* and *functionalism*.

a. Formalism

The *formalist* approach to separation of powers emphasizes the necessity of maintaining three distinct branches of government, each with delegated powers: one branch legislates, one branch executes, and one branch adjudicates. These powers come from the vesting clauses of the U.S. Constitution. Article I vests in Congress "[a]ll legislative Powers herein granted."[48] Legislative power is the power "to promulgate generalized standards and requirements of citizen behavior or to dispense benefits—to achieve, maintain, or avoid

---

45 *Seila Law, LLC*, 519 U.S. at 218 (holding that a single director independent agency structure was unconstitutional and severing the for-cause removal provision); *see also* Collins v. Yellen, 594 U.S. 220, 251 (2021) (same).

46 Jarkesy v. SEC, 34 F.4th 446, 464 (2022) (*aff'd on other grounds*, 144 S. Ct. 2117 (2024)).

47 *Cf. Free Enter. Fund*, 561 U.S. at 507 n.10 ("[O]ur holding also does not address that subset of independent agency employees who serve as administrative law judges.").

48 U.S. CONST. art. 1, § 1.

particular social policy results."[49] Congress alters legal rights through enacting, amending, and repealing statutes.

Article II of the Constitution vests "[t]he executive Power . . . in a President of the United States of America."[50] Executive acts are those in which an executive official exercises judgment about how to apply law to a given situation.[51] For the executive to execute the law there must be existing law to execute. In other words, while the legislature enacts laws, the executive enforces those laws.

Article III of the Constitution vests "[t]he judicial Power of the United States, . . . in one supreme Court, and in such inferior Courts as the Congress may from time to time ordain and establish."[52] Judicial power is the power to interpret laws and resolve legal disputes. "[T]o declare what the law is, or has been, is a judicial power, to declare what the law shall be is legislative."[53] The judiciary interprets laws by adjudicating cases and rendering dispositive judgments based on findings of law and fact; indeed, this is a court's primary power.

When confronting an issue raising separation of powers concerns, a formalist uses a two-step, rule-based approach. First, the formalist will identify the power being exercised: legislative, judicial, or executive. Second, the formalist will determine whether the appropriate branch is exercising that power in accordance with the U.S. Constitution. A formalist will, therefore, categorize the activity as legislative, executive, or judicial, and then analyze whether the appropriate branch is performing the activity. The chart below illustrates formalism in a very simplified way.

---

[49] Martin H. Redish & Elizabeth J. Cisar, *"If Angels Were to Govern": The Need for Pragmatic Formalism in Separation of Powers Theory*, 41 DUKE L.J. 449, 479 (1991); *accord* INS v. Chadha, 462 U.S. 919, 952 (1983).

[50] U.S. CONST. art. II, § 1, cl. 1.

[51] Bowsher v. Synar, 478 U.S. 714, 732–33 (1986).

[52] U.S. CONST. art. III, § 1.

[53] Koshkonong v. Burton, 104 U.S. 668, 678 (1881) (quoting Ogden v. Blackledge, 6 U.S. 272, 277 (1804)).

FORMALISM

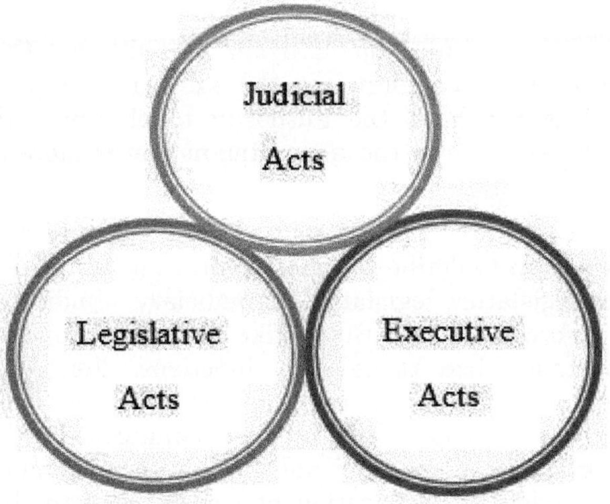

Each branch may constitutionally perform any function that falls within its corresponding "Acts Circle," but may not constitutionally perform any function that falls within another branch's "Acts Circle." Under formalism, a branch violates separation of powers when it attempts to exercise a power that is not constitutionally delegated to it (or not within its Acts Circle). Overlap is permitted only when constitutionally prescribed. So, for example, the president and Senate both play a role in appointing principal officers without violating separation of powers, because the U.S. Constitution delegates this power to both the executive and legislative branches.[54]

b. Functionalism

Functionalism's focus differs from formalism's focus. While formalists focus on strict separation, functionalists focus on balancing the inevitable overlap of powers to preserve the core *functions* the U.S. Constitution assigns to each branch. To maintain a relatively balanced power distribution, functionalists believe that a complete bar against any encroachment between the branches is unnecessary. Instead, functionalists focus on limiting encroachments into the core, constitutionally appointed functions of each branch.

For example, the executive's power of appointment is a core function.[55] However, the appointment power is not absolute, as the power applies only to the appointment of *principal* not *inferior*

---

[54] U.S. CONST. art. II, § 2, cl. 2.

[55] *Id.*

officers and is subject to senate approval. Similarly, the U.S. Constitution implicitly gives the executive the power to remove officers subject to conditions Congress imposes. This power, therefore, is not absolute. Note, however, that although Congress has the authority to place limits on the executive's removal power, Congress does not have the authority to eliminate that power altogether.[56] We covered the appointment power more specifically above.

Like formalists, functionalists turn to the vesting clauses of the U.S. Constitution to define the most central, core functions of each branch: the legislature legislates, the judiciary adjudicates, and the executive enforces the law. But unlike formalists, functionalists do not compartmentalize these core functions. For example, the legislature's power to make law is a core function. The judiciary, however, also makes law, both by developing common law and by interpreting statutes. Under formalism, this encroachment might be sufficient to trigger a separation of powers concern. In contrast, under functionalism, the judiciary's encroachment into a core function of the legislature does not raise concerns. To trigger a separation of powers concern under functionalism, one branch would have to *unduly* encroach and aggrandize a core function of another branch.

Functionalists believe that overlap between the branches is practically necessary and even desirable. Functionalists emphasize the need to maintain pragmatic flexibility to respond to the needs of modern government. Indeed, the existence of the administrative system is an example of functionalism.[57]

While both formalism and functionalism share a common goal—to ensure that no one branch acquires too much unilateral power—these approaches go about meeting this goal in different ways. Recall that formalists use a two-step, brightline rule approach to categorize acts as legislative, judicial, or executive. In contrast, functionalists use a factors approach, which balances the competing power interests with the pragmatic need for innovation. Functionalists recognize the government's need for flexibility to create new power-sharing arrangements to address the evolving needs of the modern century.

---

[56] Bowsher v. Synar, 478 U.S. 714, 725–26 (1986); Myers v. United States, 272 U.S. 52, 126–27 (1926).

[57] *See* Peter B. McCutchen, *Mistakes, Precedent, and The Rise of the Administrative State: Toward a Constitutional Theory of the Second Best*, 80 CORNELL L. REV. 1, 11 (1994) (arguing that "[u]nder a pure formalist approach, most, if not all, of the administrative state is unconstitutional.").

Functionalists do not want to "unduly constrict Congress's ability to take needed and innovative action . . . ."[58]

To foster flexibility, functionalists focus less on maintaining the separateness of each branch and instead favor the independence of each branch, with oversight from the other branches. This independence is achieved when each branch can perform its core functions while also being able to limit the accretion of power by the other branches.

Justice Jackson's tripartite framework from his concurrence in *Youngstown Sheet & Tube Co. v. Sawyer*[59] is informative. Justice Jackson suggested that the Court review separation of powers issues differently, based upon the level of cooperation among the branches. Because the case involved President Truman's seizure of the steel mills, the framework specifically addressed executive power, but the analysis applies to legislative and judicial power by analogy:

> First, "[w]hen the President acts pursuant to an express or implied authorization of Congress, his authority is at its maximum, for it includes all that he possesses in his own right plus all that Congress can delegate." Second, "[w]hen the President acts in absence of either a congressional grant or denial of authority, he can only rely upon his own independent powers, but there is a zone of twilight in which he and Congress may have concurrent authority, or in which its distribution is uncertain." In such a circumstance, Presidential authority can derive support from "congressional inertia, indifference or quiescence." Finally, "[w]hen the President takes measures incompatible with the expressed or implied will of Congress, his power is at its lowest ebb," and the Court can sustain his actions "only by disabling the Congress from acting upon the subject."[60]

Functionalism can be pictured as a set of interlocking circles, as in the chart below. It contrasts with formalism, which was depicted above as a series of separate circles with no overlap.

[58] CFTC v. Schor, 478 U.S. 833, 851 (1986).

[59] 343 U.S. 579 (1952).

[60] Medellin v. Texas, 552 U.S. 491, 494 (2008) (quoting Youngstown Sheet & Tube Co. v. Sawyer, 343 U.S. at 635–38 (Jackson, J., concurring)).

FUNCTIONALISM

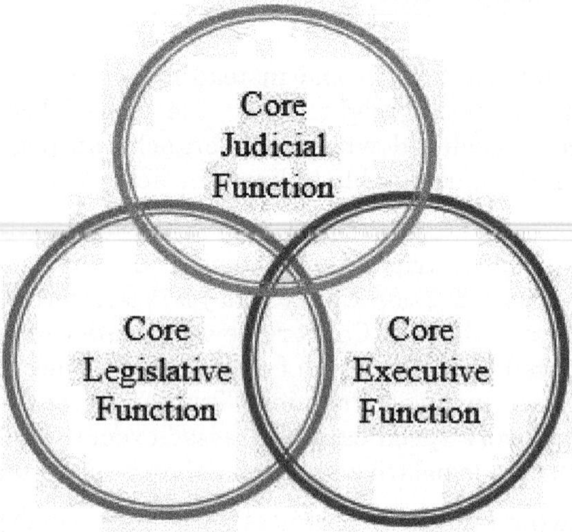

From this chart, it becomes clear that each branch possesses separate, constitutionally assigned, core functions. At the same time, each branch also has a penumbra of overlap (the zone of twilight) that shades gradually into the core functions of the other two branches. So long as the branches steer relatively clear of the other branches' core functions, and so long as the branches do not enlarge the size of their own circle at the expense of another branch's circle, functionalist separation of powers is maintained.

Finally, while the Founders were indeed concerned about the concentration of governmental power in any one of the three branches, they were primarily concerned with congressional self-aggrandizement. In keeping with this concern, the Court more closely scrutinizes legislation that expands Congress's authority rather than the authority of the other branches. The Court has been more accepting of judicial and executive aggrandizement. Indeed, at least one commentator has suggested that the Court uses formalism when Congress overreaches and functionalism when the judiciary or executive overreach.[61]

In summary, functionalists take a pragmatic view of separation of powers and seek to avoid the aggrandizement of one branch at the expense of another branch. Formalists ask what power is being wielded and who is wielding that power. In contrast, functionalists

---

[61] Ronald J. Krotoszynski, *On the Danger of Wearing Two Hats: Mistretta and Morrison Revisited*, 38 WM. & MARY L. REV. 417, 460 (1997).

ask whether one branch has encroached into the core functions of another branch to aggrandize power.

Almost exclusively, when the Court approaches a separation of powers issue under a functionalist approach, the Court approves the exercise of that branch's power.[62] Contrariwise, when the Court approaches a separation of powers issue under a formalist approach, the Court rejects the exercise of that branch's power.[63]

2. *Delegating Legislative & Judicial Power*

a. Delegating Legislative Power

The federal government is a government of limited and enumerated powers; no entity of our government can exercise a power unless the U.S. Constitution expressly grants that power to that entity. Article I, § 1 of the U.S. Constitution provides that "All legislative powers herein granted shall be vested in a Congress of the United States . . . ." And Article III, § 1 provides that "all judicial power of the United States shall be vested in one Supreme Court and such inferior courts as the Congress may from time to time ordain and establish." Yet we know that agencies exercise legislative-like power when they make general rules. Where do agencies get this power? Certainly not from the U.S. Constitution. Instead we say that Congress delegates power to the agencies.

Is delegation allowed under the U.S. Constitution? The U.S. Constitution does not expressly prohibit or allow delegation. Instead, we need to consider a doctrine from agency law, known as the nondelegation doctrine. That doctrine provides that an agent may not subdelegate its power to an assistant. Thus, because a legislature is the agent of the people who elected it, that legislature may not subdelegate its policymaking power to an administrative agency. However, the nondelegation doctrine does permit an agent to tell its assistants how to carry out tasks to accomplish the legislature's policies, so long as the agent itself remains in control of the decisions. Thus, under the nondelegation doctrine, Congress can delegate quasi-legislative power to agencies so long as Congress remains in control of the important policy-making decisions. In other words, so long as Congress ultimately decides policy, agencies can "fill up the details."[64]

---

62 *See, e.g.*, King v. Burwell, 576 U.S. 473, 498 (2015); Mistretta v. United States, 488 U.S. 361, 368 (1989); *CFTC*, 478 U.S. at 852–56.

63 *See, e.g.*, Stern v. Marshall, 564 U.S. 462, 484 (2011); Free Enter. Fund v. Public Co. Acct. Oversight Bd., 561 U.S. 477, 508 (2010); Plaut v. Spendthrift Farm, Inc., 514 U.S. 211, 240 (1995); *Bowsher*, 478 U.S. at 722–23 (1986); United States v. Klein, 80 U.S. 128, 146 (1871).

64 Wayman v. Southard, 23 U.S. 1, 43 (1825).

To determine whether Congress has made the basic policy decision, a court will look to see whether Congress provided an "intelligible principle" in the statute authorizing the agency to act.[65] So long as Congress placed some boundaries on agency authority, delegation is legitimate. If Congress sufficiently and explicitly constrains an agency's policy-making choices, then the agency is not deciding policy; rather, the agency is helping Congress implement the policy it chose. If, however, the delegation is too broad and ambiguous, then the delegation may be unconstitutional. The intelligible principle standard provides a measure for a court to use to determine whether the agency acted within the "limited" authority Congress delegated to it.

At least the above description is the abstract concept behind the delegation doctrine; however, today, the intelligible principle standard lacks teeth. The Supreme Court has only struck down three statutes for violating this standard, and all three cases occurred in the 1930s during a time of great turmoil for the United States. During this time, President Franklin Delano Roosevelt had come into office promising to turn things around for the American people. Just five days after his election, Congress was called into session and enacted five major pieces of legislation after only forty hours of debate. This rate of speed was unprecedented, and the judiciary's reaction to the power grab was hostile, to say the least. The Supreme Court heard three delegation cases and struck down all of them. Two, the Hot Oil Case[66] and the Sick Chicken Case,[67] involved delegation to agencies; the other involved delegation to third parties.

---

[65] J.W. Hampton, Jr., & Co. v. United States, 276 U.S. 394, 409 (1928).

[66] In the first, *Panama Refining Co. v. Ryan,* 293 U.S. 388 (1935), (known as the "Hot Oil Case"), the Court struck down a provision of the National Industrial Recovery Act ("NIRA") that allowed the president to prohibit the interstate transportation of oil in excess of that allowed by state law. *Id.* at 420–21. Under the NIRA, Congress wanted to prevent the evasion of strict state laws limiting the amount of oil that oil producers could sell. Striking down the statute, the Court held that Congress did not provide intelligible principles and stated: "As to the transportation of oil production in excess of state permission, the Congress has declared no policy, has established no standard, has laid down no rule. There is no requirement, no definition of circumstances and conditions in which the transportation is to be allowed or prohibited." *Id.* at 430.

[67] In the second case, *A.L.A. Schechter Poultry Corp. v. United States,* 295 U.S. 495 (1935) (known as the "Sick Chicken Case"), the Court struck down another provision in the NIRA that allowed the president to approve codes for "fair competition" that were established jointly with the chicken industry so long as the following conditions were met: (1) the code was written by a representative group of business, (2) the code did not promote monopolies, and (3) the code served goals identified in another section of the NIRA. *Id.* at 538–39. The Court struck down the provision, stating that the president's authority was "virtually unfettered." *Id.* at 541–42.

The delegation to agencies prong of the intelligible principle standard is the piece that lacks teeth today. Since those cases were decided and the President threatened to pack the Supreme Court with his own appointees, the Court adopted a broader view of federal legislative power and never again struck down a statute on delegation grounds. For example, in *Whitman v. American Trucking Ass'n*,[68] the Supreme Court reviewed the constitutionality of a section of the Clean Air Act that directed the EPA "to set primary ambient air quality standards 'the attainment and maintenance of which . . . are requisite *to protect the public health*.' "[69] The issue for the Court was whether the language "to protect the public health" sufficiently constrained the delegation; the Court held that it did.[70] Similarly, the Court has held many other broad, vague, and standardless statutes to contain intelligible principles.[71]

Challenges to nondelegation reappeared in the last few years. In 2019, Justice Gorsuch dissented in *Gundy v. United States*[72] and thoroughly analyzed the nondelegation doctrine. He built on views from former Justice Rehnquist. Rehnquist believed that Congress and the president must make major national policy decisions via the legislative process; Congress cannot delegate policy decisions to the executive branch.[73] The other justices have not yet followed. Instead, the Supreme Court has enlivened the major questions doctrine rather than reinvigorating the nondelegation doctrine. See Chapter 7 for more on the major questions doctrine.

---

68 531 U.S. 457 (2001).

69 *Id.* at 465 (quoting 42 U.S.C. § 7409(b)(1)) (emphasis added).

70 *Id.* at 472–73.

71 *See, e.g.*, Gundy v. United States, 588 U.S. 128, 132 (2019) (finding constitutional a law directing the attorney general "to specify the applicability" of the sex offender registration requirements to those convicted before the law took effect); Touby v. United States, 500 U.S. 160, 167–68 (1991) (upholding as constitutional a law that directed the attorney general to designate certain drugs as controlled substances for purposes of criminal enforcement if doing so was "necessary to avoid an imminent hazard to the public safety") (quoting 21 U.S.C. § 811(h)); Indus. Union Dep't, ALF-CIO v. Am. Petroleum Inst., 448 U.S. 607, 639 (1980) (upholding as constitutional a provision in the Occupational Safety and Health Act requiring the agency to "set the standard which most adequately assures to the extent feasible, on the basis of the best available evidence, that no employee will suffer any impairment of health") (quoting 29 U.S.C. § 655(b)(6)); Am. Power & Light Co. v. SEC, 329 U.S. 90, 104 (1946) (upholding as constitutional a statute that allowed the agency to modify the structure of holding company systems to ensure that they are not "unduly or unnecessarily complicate[d]" and do not "unfairly or inequitably distribute voting power among security holders.") (quoting Pub. Util Act of 1935, 49 Stat. 803). For a general listing of such holdings, see generally, *Whitman v. Am. Trucking Ass'n, Inc.*, 531 U.S. 457, 474–76 (2001).

72 Gundy v. United States, 588 U.S. 128, 169–73 (2019) (Gorsuch, J., dissenting).

73 Indus. Union Dep't, AFL-CIO v. Am. Petroleum Inst., 448 U.S. 607, 685–86 (1980) (Rehnquist, J., concurring in judgment).

In contrast to nondelegation to agencies, the third case, *Carter v. Carter Coal Co.*,[74] involved delegation to third parties, namely certain mine owners, to set maximum labor hours. The Court struck down the third-party delegation as "legislative delegation in its most obnoxious form; for it is not even delegation to an official or an official body, presumptively disinterested, but to private persons whose interests may be and often are adverse to the interests of others in the same business."[75] This principle—that delegations to third parties are unconstitutional—remains vibrant.

b. Delegating Judicial Power

The doctrine relating to the delegation of judicial power is much more complicated and uncertain than the delegation of legislative power. Moreover, the former doctrine has changed over time. Early in this area of jurisprudence, the Supreme Court distinguished between claims involving *public* and *private* rights. Public rights involve the liability of the government to its citizens, whereas private rights involve the liability of one individual to another. The Court later defined public rights loosely as those "so closely integrated into a public regulatory scheme as to be a matter appropriate for agency resolution with limited involvement by the Article III judiciary."[76]

In allowing public rights cases to be adjudicated before non-Article III courts, the Court reasoned that these courts could adjudicate these claims because the government does not have to agree to be sued at all under the doctrine of sovereign immunity. Therefore, if the government does agree to be sued, the government can set the parameters on being sued, including that such adjudication occur before a non-Article III tribunal.[77] "[T]he whole point of the 'public rights' analysis was that no judicial involvement at all was required—executive determination alone would suffice."[78]

---

[74] 298 U.S. 238 (1936). The statute in the case allowed certain mine owners and miners the authority to set maximum labor hours, which would be binding on other mine owners and miners. *Id.* at 279 (citing 15 U.S.C. §§ 801–827 (1935) (repealed in 1937)).

[75] *Id.* at 311.

[76] Thomas v. Union Carbide Agric. Prods. Co., 473 U.S. 568, 593–94 (1985) (holding that as long as Congress acts within its Article I powers, it can constitutionally "create a seemingly 'private' right that is so closely integrated into a public regulatory scheme as to be a matter appropriate for agency resolution with limited involvement by the Article III judiciary.").

[77] Murray's Lessee v. Hoboken Land & Improvement Co., 59 U.S. (18 How.) 272 (1855) (upholding a statute that authorized the Treasury Department to issue and execute warrants on private property to satisfy tax deficiencies); *accord* Crowell v. Benson, 285 U.S. 22, 50–51 (1932) (upholding a statute that allowed an agency to adjudicate workers' compensation claims).

[78] Peter L. Strauss, *The Place of Agencies in Government: Separation of Powers and The Fourth Branch*, 84 COLUM L. REV. 573, 632 (1984).

In contrast, the Court reasoned that claims involving private rights must be heard by an Article III court or at least be subject to Article III judicial review.[79]

But in 1986, the Supreme Court appeared to retreat from this private-public rights brightline distinction in *Commodity Futures Trading Comm'n v. Schor*.[80] Using a sliding scale approach, the Court allowed the CFTC to hear a counterclaim that involved purely private rights.[81] The government was not a party.

Invoking functionalism, the Court explained that the inquiry regarding "the constitutionality of a given congressional delegation of adjudicative functions to a non-Article III body . . . is guided by the principle that practical attention to substance rather than doctrinaire reliance on formal categories should inform application of Article III."[82] The Court created a three-factor test. The factors include:

> [T]he extent to which the 'essential attributes of judicial power' are reserved to Article III courts, and, conversely, the extent to which the non-Article III forum exercises the range of jurisdiction and powers normally vested only in Article III courts[;] the origins and importance of the right to be adjudicated[;] and the concerns that drove Congress to depart from the requirements of Article III.[83]

Applying its new test, the Court determined that the CFTC's adjudicative process was quasi-judicial enough to survive the delegation challenge. The requirement that the matter involve public rights was no longer determinative.[84]

Schor's new functionalist test appeared short-lived. In *Stern v. Marshall*,[85] the Supreme Court revitalized the public-private rights distinction, finding the claim in that case to be purely private and, thus, outside of the bankruptcy court's authority. "The claim is . . .

---

79 Northern Pipeline Constr. Co. v. Marathon Pipe Line Co., 458 U.S. 50, 77 (1982) (holding that an Article I court could not hear a purely private claim in bankruptcy); *see Crowell*, 285 U.S. at 62–63 (holding that an agency could constitutionally adjudicate a case involving purely private rights because the agency made only factual findings, which were subject to judicial review by an Article III court).

80 478 U.S. 833 (1986).

81 *Id.* at 847.

82 *Id.* at 847–48 (internal quotations omitted).

83 *Commodity Futures Trading Comm'n*, 478 U.S. at 856.

84 *But see* Granfinanciera, S.A. v. Nordberg, 492 U.S. 33 (1989) (noting the "crucial question" is whether the right, though "seemingly private," is nevertheless "so closely integrated into a public regulatory scheme" that agency adjudication is permissible, provided there is some Article III supervision).

85 564 U.S. 462 (2011).

one under state common law between two private parties. It does not 'depend[ ] on the will of congress,' Congress has nothing to do with it . . . ."[86] Justice Scalia put the distinction more clearly:—"a matter of public rights . . . must at a minimum arise between the government and others."[87] And in its most recent case in this area, the Court held that the SEC's enforcement actions seeking civil penalties for alleged securities fraud did not involve public rights, although the Court refused to clarify the distinction further.[88]

The appropriate test to apply to congressional delegations of judicial power thus remains uncertain. The public-private rights doctrine may serve as a brightline starting point: public rights can always be litigated in non-Article III courts, while private rights can be litigated in non-Article III courts if the *Schor* factors support that conclusion. Unfortunately, the Court has not provided clear guidance in this area. On an exam, you may want to address both tests.

Another issue the Supreme Court recently decided regarding the constitutionality of agency adjudication is whether it violates the Seventh Amendment's right to a jury trial for all "[s]uits at common law."[89] Suits at common law include all lawsuits not based in equity, maritime, or admiralty.[90] Civil penalties in the form of monetary relief are the prototypical common law remedy because they are designed to punish and deter, not to compensate.[91] Hence, when agencies seek civil penalties, they may need to pursue their claims in an Article III court. This area of the law is evolving.

AUTHORITY TO ACT CHECKLIST

A. ***Statutory Authority***—Does the agency have *statutory* authority to act?

---

[86] *Id.* at 493 (internal quotations omitted).

[87] *Id.* at 503 (Scalia, J., concurring) (internal quotations omitted). Then, in 2015 in *Wellness Int'l Network, Ltd. v. Sharif*, 575 U.S. 665, 678 (2015), the Court returned to *Schor*'s factor analysis, rejecting the public rights doctrine's "formalistic and unbending rules."

[88] SEC v. Jarkesy, 144 S. Ct. 2117, 2133 (2024) ("The Court 'has not 'definitively explained' the distinction between public and private rights,' and we do not claim to do so today.") (quoting Oil States Energy Servs., LLC v. Greene's Energy Grp., LLC, 584 U.S. 325, 334 (2018)).

[89] U.S. CONST. amend. XII ("In Suits at common law, where the value in controversy shall exceed twenty dollars, the right of trial by jury shall be preserved, and no fact tried by a jury, shall be otherwise re-examined in any Court of the United States, than according to the rules of the common law.").

[90] Parsons v. Bedford, 28 U.S. (3 Pet.) 433, 447 (1830).

[91] *Jarkesy*, 144 S. Ct. at 2129.

1. Does the enabling or another act authorize the agency to conduct rulemaking, adjudication, or investigation, as applicable?

   a. **No**—If no, then the agency has no legal authority to act. Stop here. *Caveat*: Note that an agency does not need statutory authority to announce what its policy is or how it interprets a statute or regulation because such actions do not make law.

   b. **Yes**—If yes, then to see if the agency complied with hybrid procedures, proceed to A.2. below.

2. Did the agency comply with all additional requirements in the enabling act, other relevant acts, and relevant executive orders (*e.g.*, the Regulatory Flexibility Act and E.O. 12,866)?

   a. **No**—If no, then the agency must go back and follow these procedures. Stop here.

   b. **Yes**—If yes, then to see whether the agency has constitutional authority to act, proceed to B. below.

B. ***Constitutional Authority***—Is the agency's structure constitutional? (Warning, the law in this area is far from settled and does not lend itself to a simple checklist answer).

1. **Appointment**—Is the relevant actor a principal officer (typically heads of agencies), an inferior officer (those working closely with the heads of agencies), or an employee? Officers hold *continuing* positions established by law and exercise *significant authority*. Inferior officers have supervisors.

   a. **Principal Officer**—If the officer is a principal officer, does the enabling act provide that the president will appoint the officer and the Senate must confirm him or her?

      i. **No**—If no, then the structure is unconstitutional under U.S. CONST. art. II, § 2, cl. 2, and the agency has no authority to act. Stop here.

      ii. **Yes**—If yes, then the structure is constitutional under U.S. CONST. art. II, § 2, cl. 2. Proceed to B.2. below.

   b. **Inferior Officer**—If the officer is an inferior officer, does the enabling act vest the appointment power in the president, the courts of law, or in the head of a department?

i. **No**—If no, then the structure is unconstitutional under U.S. CONST. art. II, § 2, cl. 2, and the agency has no authority to act. Stop here.

ii. **Yes**—If yes, then the structure is constitutional under U.S. CONST. art. II, § 2, cl. 2. Proceed to B.2. below.

c. **Employee**—If the officer is an employee, there are no constitutional requirements relating to appointment. Congress can limit the appointment and removal of employees as it wishes. Proceed to B.2. below.

2. **Removal**—Is there any limit on the president's power to remove the relevant actor, such as a for-cause restriction?

a. **No**—If no, then the structure is constitutional because there are no limits on the president's power to remove. Proceed to C. below.

b. **Yes**—If yes, then ask whether the relevant actor is a principal officer, an inferior officer, or an employee? (See above for definitions).

i. **Principal Officer**—If the actor is a principal officer, ask whether the officer is a single director of an independent agency and whether the officer performs purely executive acts.

(a). **Single Director**—If the officer is a single director of an independent agency, then any removal restriction is likely unconstitutional under *Seila Law*. Stop here.

(b). **Not a Single Director**—If the officer is not a single director of an independent agency, then the constitutionality of any restriction turns on the types of acts that the officer performs. Proceed to 2.b.i.(c). below.

(c). **Purely Executive Acts**—If the officer performs purely executive acts, then any removal restriction is likely unconstitutional under *Myers*. Stop here.

(d). **Quasi-Legislative/Adjudicatory Acts**—If the officer performs quasi-legislative/ adjudicatory acts, then the removal restriction may be constitutional under *Humphrey's Executor*. This area is unclear so you should argue in the alternative that it is unconstitutional. Then, proceed to C. below.

ii. **Inferior Officer**—If the actor is an inferior officer, then ask whether the president can perform his or her constitutional duty to ensure that the laws are faithfully executed with the removal restriction in place. (Generally, single for-cause removal restrictions are constitutional, while dual for-cause removal restrictions are unconstitutional.).

(a). **No**—If no, then any restriction is likely unconstitutional under *Free Enterprise*. Stop here.

(b). **Yes**—If yes, then any restriction is likely constitutional under *Free Enterprise*. Proceed to C. below.

iii. **Employee**—If the actor is an employee, then the individual is constitutionally removable under the Constitution. Congress can limit the appointment and removal of employees as it wishes. Proceed to C. below.

C. ***Constitutional Authority***—Does the agency have *constitutional* authority to act?

1. **For Rulemaking**—Did Congress provide an *intelligible principle* to guide the agency's decision making? Examples of intelligible principles include "requisite to protect the public health," "necessary to avoid an imminent hazard to the public safety," "adequately assures . . . that no employee will suffer any impairment of health," and "[not] unduly or unnecessarily complicate[d]."

a. **No**—If no, which is highly unlikely, then the statute is unconstitutional, and the agency has no legal authority to act. Stop here.

b. **Maybe**—If maybe, then consider whether the court should apply the constitutional avoidance doctrine to avoid interpreting the statutory language in a way that would raise the constitutional question. If so, proceed to Chapter 3.

c. **Yes**—If yes, then the statute is constitutional. Proceed to Chapter 3.

2. **For Adjudication**—Determine whether you think the court will apply the public rights doctrine or *Schor* factors, being sure to apply the other test in the alternative.

   a. **Apply the Public Rights Doctrine**—Does the issue involve public rights—meaning an issue arising between the government and another, or private rights—meaning an issue arising between individuals and entities other than the government?

      i. **Private Rights**—If the issue involves only private rights, then the delegation is likely unconstitutional. To argue *Schor*'s factors test in the alternative, proceed to C.2.b. below.

      ii. **Public Rights**—If the issue involves public rights—defined as rights so closely integrated into a public regulatory scheme as to be a matter appropriate for agency resolution with limited involvement by the Article III judiciary—then the delegation is likely constitutional. To argue the *Schor* factors in the alternative, proceed to C.2.b. below.

   b. **Apply the *Schor* Factors**—Does the balance of the factors suggest that Article III courts should hear the controversy? The factors are: [1] the extent to which the essential attributes of judicial power are reserved to Article III courts, and, conversely, the extent to which the non-Article III forum exercises the range of jurisdiction and powers normally vested only in Article III courts; [2] the origins and importance of the right to be adjudicated; and [3] the concerns that drove Congress to depart from the requirements of Article III.

      i. **Yes**—If yes, then the delegation is likely unconstitutional. Proceed to C.2.a. above if you have not analyzed the public/private rights doctrine already, otherwise stop here.

      ii. **No**—If no, then the delegation is likely constitutional. If so, proceed to C.2.a. above if you have not analyzed the public/private rights doctrine already, otherwise proceed to Chapter 4.

3. **For Investigation and Disclosure**—The agency likely has constitutional authority. Proceed to Chapter 5.

ILLUSTRATIVE PROBLEMS

■ PROBLEM 2.1 ■

A federal statute authorizes the Secretary of the Food and Drug Administration (FDA) to engage in rulemaking and adjudication to determine which ingredients are "safe for ingestion by children under age five for use in the production of infant formula." The FDA promulgated a regulation using notice-and-comment rulemaking prohibiting a particular ingredient from being included in infant formulas, deeming it unsafe. You are general counsel for the manufacturer of that ingredient. The manufacturer wishes to sue the FDA to stop the regulation from taking effect. The manufacturer asks you whether the FDA's action is constitutional. What do you advise?

Analysis

This issue here is whether Congress's delegation to the FDA to engage in rulemaking to regulate infant formulas is constitutional. Using the checklist above (C.1.), you should ask whether Congress provided an *intelligible principle* to guide the agency's decision making. Examples of intelligible principles that have been upheld include "requisite to protect the public health," "necessary to avoid an imminent hazard to the public safety," "adequately assures . . . that no employee will suffer any impairment of health," and "[not] unduly or unnecessarily complicate[d]." Here, the language in the statute is "safe for ingestion by children under age five for use in the production of infant formula." This intelligible principle would be sufficient under the Supreme Court's current nondelegation doctrine to support the agency's rulemaking.

■ PROBLEM 2.2 ■

Your client is the Secretary of the Department of Veterans Affairs (VA) (an executive agency). Recently, the VA was involved in a scandal involving patient care. Your client has been getting pressure from the President to resign because he is angry at your client's handling of the publicity from the event. She would like advice from you regarding whether the President can fire her if she refuses to step down. Assume the relevant statute allows for-cause removal only. What would you advise?

Analysis

This issue here is whether the President has unfettered power to remove the Secretary of the VA. It is unclear whether the removal limitation is constitutional. Using the checklist above (B.2.), you must determine whether the Secretary is a principal officer or an inferior officer. Secretaries of agencies are typically principal officers because they have no superiors between themselves and the president. She is not a single director of a multimember agency head, so that concern does not apply. Next you ask what type of functions the Secretary performs. Here, the Secretary performs purely executive functions and heads an executive agency; she does not adjudicate or promulgate rules directly. Hence, any restriction is likely unconstitutional under *Myers v. United States*, 272 U.S. 52, 239 (1926).

POINTS TO REMEMBER

- The act that creates an agency, authorizes the agency to act, and identifies the agency's agenda is known as the enabling, or organic, act. It is the first law to search when trying to determine whether an agency has the power to act.
- Other acts may augment or limit agency powers, such as the Congressional Review Act. Under that Act, agencies must send all new rules to the Comptroller General for review. Rules with economic impacts greater than $100 million are stayed for sixty days.
- Executive orders may also place limits on agencies. For example, E.O. 12,866 provides that agencies may promulgate regulations only when they are "required by law," "necessary to interpret the law," or "are made necessary by compelling public need, such as material failures of private markets to protect or improve the health and safety of the public, the environment, or the well-being of the American people."
- The U.S. Constitution places limits on the appointment and removal of agency officials. Principal officers, like agency heads, must be appointed by the president with the advice and consent of the Senate. Inferior officers, like other higher level agency officials, must be appointed by the president, the courts of law, or the head of the department.
- The *formalist* approach to separation of powers emphasizes the necessity of maintaining three distinct branches of government, each with delegated powers: one branch legislates, one branch adjudicates, and one branch executes. These powers come from the vesting clauses of the U.S. Constitution.
- To maintain a relatively balanced power distribution, *functionalists* believe that a complete bar against any encroachment between the branches is unnecessary. Instead, functionalists focus on limiting encroachments into the core,

constitutionally appointed functions of each branch. Functionalists turn to the vesting clauses of the U.S. Constitution to define the most central, core functions of each branch: the legislature legislates, the judiciary adjudicates, and the executive enforces the law.

- The U.S. Constitution limits agency power. Pursuant to the nondelegation doctrine Congress must provide the agency with an *intelligible principle* in the act authorizing the agency to exercise quasi-legislative power. The Court has only struck down three acts for violating this standard, and all three cases occurred during the Great Depression, a time of great turmoil in the United States.
- The standard for the proper delegation of quasi-judicial power is less clear. If the delegated power involves resolving public rights, then the delegation is likely constitutional. If the delegated power involves resolving private rights, then courts apply a factors test to determine whether the delegation is constitutional.

CHAPTER 3

What Procedures Are Required for Rulemaking?

From Chapter 1, you learned first to identify the type of agency action. From Chapter 2, you learned next to evaluate the enabling act, other acts, executive orders, and the U.S. Constitution to be sure that the agency structure is constitutional and that the agency has the power to act. In the next three chapters, you will learn the appropriate procedures for each of the three types of agency action: rulemaking, adjudication, and investigation. In this chapter, you will learn what procedures the APA requires for rulemaking. In Chapters 4 and 5, you will learn the procedures required for adjudication and investigation respectively.

REVIEW

Assuming an agency has statutory and constitutional authority to promulgate rules, the agency must issue those rules pursuant to the applicable procedures provided in the enabling act and the APA. Always check the enabling act first because the APA rules are default rules, which can be overridden by the enabling act.

A. Initiating a Rulemaking

While an agency may choose to begin the rulemaking process, anyone may petition an agency to issue, amend, or repeal a rule.[1] In response, the agency will (1) grant the petition and begin a rulemaking proceeding, (2) deny the petition, or (3) delay ruling on the petition.

If the agency denies the petition, the agency must provide a prompt explanation for its denial.[2] Denial of a petition is subject to

---

[1] APA § 555(e).

[2] *Id.* In addition, the agency's own rules may affect the manner or timing of an agency's response to a citizen's petition, such as requiring the agency to ask for

judicial review.[3] Typically, courts sustain an agency's denial unless the court finds that decision to be arbitrary and capricious.[4] Chapter 7 more fully explains this standard of review; in short, an agency's decision to deny a petition is considered to be arbitrary and capricious when the agency either fails to adequately explain the facts and policy concerns leading to its decision or when the facts the agency relied on have no basis in the record.[5] Sometimes Congress requires an agency to issue a rule. If Congress does so, judicial review of the denial may be more demanding.[6]

If, instead of denying the petition for rulemaking, the agency delays ruling on the petition, that delay may violate the enabling act or the APA. Check whether there is a timetable in the enabling act. If not, then turn to the APA. The APA requires the agency to respond within a reasonable time: "Prompt notice shall be given of the denial in whole or in part of a written . . . petition."[7] Despite this language, courts are very deferential to agency delay. Delays of five years have survived judicial review.

Courts apply what is commonly referred to as the TRAC rule of reason test[8] to determine whether a delay is unreasonable. TRAC's four factors are (1) whether Congress provided a timetable for the agency action in the enabling act; (2) whether the agency's delay would negatively affect human health and welfare; (3) whether expediting a response would lead to negative effects on issues of higher priority for the agency; and (4) whether the nature and extent of other interests would be unduly prejudiced by the delay.[9] The court need not find that the agency acted inappropriately to find that it delayed unreasonably.[10] When a court finds that the agency unreasonably delayed acting on a petition, the court will typically provide the agency with a timeframe within which to respond to the petition rather than ordering the agency to respond immediately.[11]

---

public comment before denying a petition or requiring the agency publish the reasons for denial.

3 APA §§ 551(13), 704.

4 APA § 706(1)(A).

5 Arkansas Power & Light Co. v. ICC, 725 F.2d 716, 723 (1984).

6 *See, e.g.*, Massachusetts v. EPA, 549 U.S. 497, 497 (2007) (reversing the EPA's decision to refuse to act in light of the statutory direction to the agency to act).

7 APA § 555(e).

8 Telecomms. Rsch. & Action Ctr. v. FCC, 750 F.2d 70 (D.C. Cir. 1984) ("*TRAC*").

9 *Id* at 80.

10 *Id.*

11 *See* Norton v. South Utah Wilderness All., 542 U.S. 55, 65 (2004).

B. Types of Rules & Rulemaking Procedures

Once an agency decides to issue a rule, the agency must decide how to do so. Check the agency's enabling act first to see if specific procedures are required. In addition to the procedures the enabling act may require, the APA provides default procedures for those areas the enabling act does not address. For the rest of this analysis, we will assume the enabling act does not specify any specific procedures the agency must follow.

Under the APA, agencies may issue rules in one of three ways: formal rulemaking, notice-and-comment rulemaking (also known as informal rulemaking), and publication rulemaking. The sections below explain the different types of rules (legislative and non-legislative) and the corresponding rulemaking procedures required for each type of rule.

1. Types of Rules

The APA defines a rule as "the whole or a part of an agency statement of general or particular applicability and future effect designed to implement, interpret, or prescribe law or policy or describing the organization, procedure, or practice requirements of an agency . . . ."[12] This broad definition covers two kinds of rules: (1) legislative rules, and (2) non-legislative rules. Legislative rules have legal (or binding) effect. If a regulated entity violates a legislative rule, the entity will be subject to some form of penalty. Legislative rules are typically contained in regulations.

Non-legislative rules do not have independent, binding legal effect. Rather, any legal effect they have comes from preexisting legislative rules (whether from Congress or the agency). Non-legislative rules are often collectively called *guidance documents.* There are two kinds of guidance documents identified in the APA: (1) interpretive rules,[13] and (2) general statements of policy.[14] Interpretive rules are rules interpreting language in an existing statute or regulation. In contrast, policy statements are communications that prospectively advise the public and agency personnel on the way in which the agency plans to exercise discretionary power in the future.

---

12 APA § 551(4).

13 While the APA uses the term *interpretative,* the term *interpretive* is more commonly used in Administrative Law.

14 APA § 553(b)(3)(A).

2. *Types of Rulemaking*

The APA sets forth three kinds of rulemaking *procedures*: (1) formal rulemaking, (2) notice-and-comment rulemaking (also called informal rulemaking), and (3) publication rulemaking. A fourth form of rulemaking also exists: hybrid rulemaking. The procedures for each are explained below.

a. Formal Rulemaking

Formal rulemaking is relatively rare, in part because the procedures used in this type of rulemaking are better suited for resolving adjudicative facts (*e.g.*, who is telling the truth), rather than for resolving legislative facts (*e.g.*, what degree of arsenic in the soil is safe). Under the APA, formal rulemaking requires the agency hold a hearing with civil, trial-like procedures. Entities and individuals whom the rule might impact have a right to notice of the hearing and a right to participate in it in some fashion.[15] The rules of evidence do not apply.[16] A hearing officer, known as an ALJ, compiles the record and makes either an initial decision or recommendation to the agency head.[17] The agency head then either adopts the ALJ's decision or issues a final decision. That decision is subject to judicial review.[18] These procedures are identical to those the APA requires for formal adjudication.[19] Hence, these procedures are covered in more detail in Chapter 4.

b. Notice-and-Comment Rulemaking Procedures

Notice-and-comment (informal) rulemaking is significantly more common. This form of rulemaking is known as notice-and-comment rulemaking because the APA requires an agency to publish *notice* of its proposed rule in the Federal Register (notice) and to solicit and respond to *comments* from the public and others about the proposed rule (comment).[20] Let's look at each requirement more carefully.

The APA requires agencies to give adequate notice of the substance of a new rule to provide members of the public an opportunity to comment on the proposed rule. The notice must be "sufficient to fairly apprise interested persons of the issues involved,

---

15 APA § 554(b)–(c).

16 *See* APA § 556(c)(3) (instructing ALJs to receive relevant evidence).

17 APA § 554(d).

18 APA § 706(2).

19 *See* APA §§ 554, 556.

20 APA § 553(b)–(c).

so that they may present responsive data or argument."[21] The agency must include the time, place, and nature of any public proceedings; the legal authority for the rule; and either the substance of the proposed rule or a description of the subjects and issues involved.[22] Additionally, the D.C. Circuit Court has held that the notice of proposed rulemaking ("NPRM") must include all the scientific data and methodology on which the agency relied.[23] Most agencies today include a final draft of their proposed rule and statements showing their compliance with the requirements other statutes and executive orders impose even though the additional information is not always required to be included.

Any *interested person* can submit "written data, views, or arguments" on a proposed rule.[24] The APA does not require oral commenting, and it is generally not allowed. No fixed time period for commenting is required. Typically, the rulemaking record will include all the rulemaking notices, copies of all written factual material the agency substantially relied upon or seriously considered, and all written comments submitted.[25]

The APA does not prohibit *ex parte* communications for notice-and-comment rulemaking; however, the Due Process Clause limits *ex parte* communications when those proceedings involved "conflicting private claims to a valuable privilege."[26] This limitation applies only when the parties are essentially arguing about agency action that results in a property-like award, such as a license. It is very rare that rulemaking involves property-like awards. In addition to the U.S. Constitution, an agency's own rule or the agency's enabling act may prohibit *ex parte* communications.[27]

After the comment period, the agency must *consider* the submitted comments and draft its final rule.[28] With the final rule, the agency must prepare and publish a "concise general statement of [the

---

[21] H.R. Rep. No. 79–1980, at 2 (1946), *as reprinted in* Legislative History of the Administrative Procedure Act, S. Doc. No. 79–248, at 200 (1946).

[22] APA § 553(b)(1)–(3).

[23] Portland Cement Ass'n v. Ruckelshaus, 486 F.2d 375, 394 (D.C. Cir. 1973). Yet this requirement is contrary to the actual language of § 553 and may be invalid under a later Supreme Court case: *Vermont Yankee Nuclear Power Corp. v. Nat. Res. Def. Council, Inc.*, 435 U.S. 519, 524 (1978).

[24] APA § 553(c).

[25] *See* Citizens to Preserve Overton Park v. Volpe, 401 U.S. 402, 420 (1971); Home Box Office, Inc. v. FCC, 567 F.2d 9, 54 (D.C. Cir. 1977).

[26] Sangamon Valley v. United States, 269 F.2d 221, 224 (D.C. Cir. 1959).

[27] *See* Home Box Office Inc. v. FCC, 567 F.2d 9, 56–57 (D.C. Cir. 1977) (analyzing an enabling act that included a restriction on agency *ex parte* communications).

[28] APA § 553(c).

rule's] basis and purpose."[29] The statement is rarely concise these days.

The final rule need not be identical to the proposed rule to satisfy the APA's notice requirement, which makes sense. If agencies could not change course at all then why have public comment? However, if there is too much change, then the notice may be insufficient to *fairly apprise interested persons* of the substance of the proposed rule. Courts have sought to ensure that the final rule is close enough to the rule as proposed so that the opportunity to comment is meaningful. Notice is insufficient if it does not give fair notice of the rule as finally promulgated. If the final rule can be characterized as a *logical outgrowth* of the proposed rule—meaning that the final rule does not materially alter the issues involved in the rulemaking and does not substantially depart from the substance of the proposed rule, then notice was adequate.[30] "Notice [is] inadequate when the interested parties could not reasonably have anticipated the final rulemaking from the draft."[31] Or as one court put it, the agency must avoid the "surprise switcheroo."[32] The goal of the logical outgrowth test is to balance the inconvenience to the agency of having to redo the notice and comment process with the rights of regulated entities to be put on notice that their interests are at stake. In other words, regulated entities should know the issue is on the table and be able to comment.

c. Publication Procedures

Publication rulemaking is becoming increasingly common as agencies find notice-and-comment rulemaking more cumbersome. The APA allows agencies to avoid both formal rulemaking and notice-and-comment rulemaking altogether when promulgating specific kinds of rules.[33] The specific kinds of rules were detailed above. To issue these kinds of rules, agencies must use publication procedures. These procedures are explained here.

Publication rulemaking is significantly easier than notice-and-comment rulemaking. Indeed, all an agency need do is publish the rule in the Federal Register (as opposed to the Code of Federal Regulations, where agencies publish legislative rules) or provide the

---

[29] *Id.* Although the language in the APA requires a concise statement, under pressure from the lower courts setting aside rules the courts considered inadequately explained, agencies have acted in preemptive self-defense by crafting lengthy and detailed explanations called preambles.

[30] Chocolate Mfrs., Ass'n v. Block, 755 F.2d 1098, 1105 (4th Cir. 1985).

[31] Nat'l Mining Ass'n v. MSHA, 116 F.3d 520, 531 (D.C. Cir. 1997).

[32] Env't Integrity Project v. EPA, 425 F.3d 992, 997 (D.C. Cir. 2005).

[33] APA § 553(b).

entity to be regulated with actual notice.[34] Then, these rules typically take effect no sooner than thirty days after they are promulgated.[35] That is it.

d. Hybrid Procedures

As noted in Chapter 2, Congress may add additional procedures in either the enabling act or in another act.[36] And the president may do so in an executive order.[37] Further, agencies may require additional procedures of themselves.[38] Congress, the president, and even agencies can impose additional rulemaking procedures to those the APA requires. Rulemaking involving additional procedures is typically known as hybrid rulemaking. Importantly, however, the Supreme Court has held that courts cannot require more procedure than that required by the APA, the Constitution, or an act.[39] Thus, the APA is just one point to check for procedural requirements, but it is not the ending point.

3. *Summary of Types of Rules & Rulemaking*

The flowchart below shows the types of rules and rulemaking available to agencies.

---

[34] APA § 552(1). Alternatively, the agency may provide actual notice to anyone against whom the agency wishes to enforce a rule. *See e.g.*, United States v. F/V Alice Amanda, 987 F.2d 1078, 1084 (4th Cir. 1993) (holding that lack of publication was harmless error when person had actual notice of the rule).

[35] APA § 553(d).

[36] For example, the Regulatory Flexibility Act requires agencies to create a Regulatory Flexibility Analysis for any proposed rule that will significantly impact a substantial number of small businesses, organizations, or governments. 5 U.S.C. § 601 *et seq.* And the Unfunded Mandates Reform Act requires agencies to prepare a statement assessing the effect of any proposed regulation that will cause state, local, or tribal governments to incur more than $100 million annually. 2 U.S.C. § 1501 *et seq.*

[37] *See, e.g.*, E.O. 12,866, 58 Fed. Reg. 51735 (1993) (requiring agencies to conduct a cost-benefit analysis on all proposed rules that are "significant.").

[38] *Cf.* APA § 553(b)(3)(A) (exempting agency procedural rules from notice-and-comment requirements).

[39] Vermont Yankee Nuclear Power Corp. v. Nat. Res. Def. Council, Inc., 435 U.S. 519, 524 (1978).

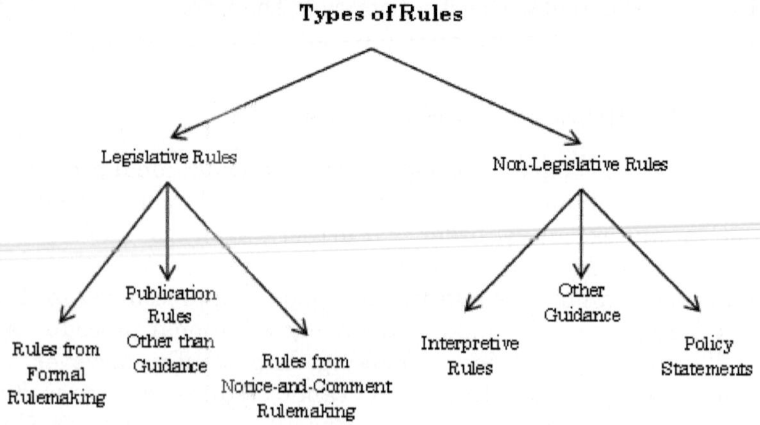

C. Choosing the Appropriate Rulemaking Procedure

Which form of rulemaking must an agency use? It depends on the enabling act and the APA. If the enabling act does not clearly require one or the other, then the APA provides default rules to help agencies interpret the ambiguous direction in the enabling act. Check the enabling act first. If the appropriate process is not clear, then the APA applies. The APA's requirements are explained next.

1. *Formal Rulemaking v. Notice-and-Comment Rulemaking*

The APA requires agencies to use formal rulemaking, rather than notice-and-comment rulemaking, only when the enabling act require the rules " to be made on the record after opportunity for an agency hearing . . . ."[40] Interpreting this language, the Supreme Court held that agencies must use formal rulemaking only when the enabling act requires both a hearing *and* that the hearing be on the record.[41] When an agency's enabling act merely requires rules to be made "after hearing," formal rulemaking is not required. It is a rare enabling act that requires both a hearing and that it be on the record. In the absence of such *magic language*, an agency may use notice-and-comment rulemaking, as augmented by any hybrid requirements from sources other than the APA.

---

[40] APA § 553(c).

[41] United States v. Florida E. Coast R.R., 410 U.S. 224, 238 (1973) (holding that a statute that required the agency to issue a rule "after a hearing" did not trigger formal rulemaking); United States v. Allegheny-Ludlum Steel Corp., 406 U.S. 742, 757 (1972) (same).

2. Notice-and-Comment Rulemaking v. Publication Rulemaking

The APA requires agencies to use notice-and-comment rulemaking, rather than publication rulemaking, for most rules. However, the APA allows an agency to use publication procedures for some kinds of rules. For example, an agency may use publication procedures for the following types of rules: (1) rules relating to military and foreign affairs; (2) rules relating to agency management and personnel; (3) rules relating to public property, loans, grants, benefits, and contracts; (4) rules for which the agency has a "good cause" reason to avoid notice-and-comment rulemaking; and (5) rules of agency organization and practice.[42] An agency's choice to use publication procedures for these types of rules is rarely challenged. You are unlikely to be tested on this topic.

In addition, an agency may use publication procedures to issue procedural rules, good cause rules, interpretive rules, and policy statements.[43] You are more likely to get tested on these exceptions to notice-and-comment rulemaking, so let's explore each and when the agency's choice to use them is valid.

First, procedural rules: the APA allows agencies to use publication procedures for "rules of agency organization, procedure, or practice."[44] Rules of agency organization and practice are generally not challenged. In contrast, rules of agency procedure are more commonly challenged. The APA does not define rules of agency procedure. Most courts distinguish between procedural rules and substantive rules based on whether the rule has a substantial, or substantive, impact on the rights of people affected.[45] Rules that have a substantial impact on the parties must be promulgated via notice-and-comment rulemaking.

However, the D.C. Circuit rejected the substantive impact test, claiming that even rules that are clearly procedural affect substantive rights. Instead, this circuit examines whether the rule encodes a substantive value judgment and substantially alters the rights of the parties; if so, notice-and-comment rulemaking is required.[46]

Second, good cause rules: the APA allows agencies to use publication procedures when the agency has good cause to believe that notice would be impracticable, unnecessary, or contrary to the

42 APA § 553(a), (b)(4)(A)–(b)(4)(B).

43 APA § 553(b)(4)(A).

44 *Id.*

45 Am. Hosp. v. Bowen, 834 F.2d 1037, 1061–62 (D.C. Cir. 1987).

46 JEM Broad. Co., Inc. v. FCC, 22 F.3d 320, 328 (D.C. Cir. 1994).

public interest.[47] The agency must include the basis for the good cause exception in its final rule.[48] Although this exception was meant to be a narrow one, agencies often find good cause when none exists.

Third, interpretive rules: the APA allows agencies to use publication procedures when issuing non-legislative interpretive (interpretative) rules. Interpretive rules are self-describing; they are rules interpreting language in an existing statute or regulation. An agency may issue an interpretive rule using formal rulemaking, notice-and-comment rulemaking, or publication rulemaking. However, an agency's choice of publication rulemaking is valid only if the interpretive rule is non-legislative in nature, meaning the requirement can be found in the existing statute or regulation.

In *American Mining Congress v. MSHA*,[49] the D.C. Circuit explained that whether a rule is a legislative or non-legislative interpretive rule depends on whether the agency intended to exercise its legislative rulemaking powers (the intent to exercise test).

The intent to exercise test has four factors, any one of which is determinative. First, if the basis for agency enforcement of the rule would be inadequate without an existing legislative rule, then the agency likely intended to use its legislative rulemaking authority. Second, if the agency published the rule in the Code of Federal Regulations rather than the Federal Register, then the agency likely intended to use its legislative rulemaking authority. Third, if the agency explicitly invoked its legislative rulemaking authority when it issued the rule, then the agency likely intended to use its legislative rulemaking authority. Fourth, if the rule repudiates, is irreconcilable with, or otherwise effectively amends a prior legislative rule, the agency likely intended to use its legislative rulemaking authority. If any of these four factors are present, then the rule is legislative not non-legislative, and the agency cannot use publication procedures.

Fourth, policy statements: the APA allows agencies to use publication procedures when issuing a policy statement. Policy statements are statements from an agency that advise the public and agency personnel prospectively on the way in which the agency plans to exercise *discretionary* power in the future. Agencies may issue policy statements to announce new duties the agency plans to adopt by future adjudication or rulemaking. To determine whether a rule is a valid policy statement for which an agency may use publication procedures, courts apply the *binding effects test*. Under this test, a rule is a legislative rule rather than a non-legislative policy

---

47 APA § 553(b)(4)(B).

48 *Id.*

49 512 F.3d 696, 700 (D.C. Cir. 2008).

statement if the rule imposes rights and obligations or restricts an agency's ability to exercise its discretion. Additionally, courts consider whether the agency characterized the rule as legislative or non-legislative; however, this latter factor is not determinative. If these factors are present, then the rule is legislative not non-legislative, and the agency cannot use publication procedures.

PROCEDURES REQUIRED FOR RULEMAKING: CHECKLIST

A. **Initiating Rulemaking**—Who initiated the rulemaking?

1. Did a citizen petition to issue, amend, or repeal a rule?

   a. **No**—If no, then the agency initiated the rulemaking, and you will need to evaluate the agency's choice of rulemaking procedure. <u>Proceed to B. below</u>.

   b. **Yes**—If yes, then to determine what the agency did with the petition, <u>proceed to A.2. below</u>.

2. Did the agency grant the petition and initiate rulemaking?

   a. **No**—If no, then the agency either denied or delayed acting on the petition. <u>Proceed to A.3. below</u>.

   b. **Yes**—If yes, then you will need to evaluate the agency's choice of rulemaking procedure. <u>Proceed to B. below</u>.

3. Did the agency delay acting on the petition?

   a. **No**—If no, then the agency must have denied the petition. <u>Proceed to A.4. below</u>.

   b. **Yes**—If yes, then the agency's delay is subject to judicial review under TRAC's rule of reason test. Evaluate (1) whether Congress provided a timetable for the agency action; (2) whether the delay would negatively affect human health and welfare; (3) whether expediting the delay would lead to negative effects on issues of higher priority for the agency; and (4) whether the nature and extent of other interests would be unduly prejudiced by the delay. Courts are very deferential of agency decisions to delay. <u>Stop here</u>.

4. Did the agency deny the petition?

   a. **No**—If no, then the agency must have either granted the petition or delayed acting on it. <u>Return to A.2. and A.3. above</u>.

b. **Yes**—If yes, then the denial is agency action subject to judicial review. To determine whether judicial review is available and whether the agency's decision was valid, proceed to the checklists in Chapters 6 and 7.

B. Choice of Rulemaking Procedure—Did the agency use the appropriate procedure: formal rulemaking, notice-and-comment rulemaking, or publication rulemaking?

1. Was the agency required to use formal rulemaking? Did the enabling act include the phrase "on the record after a hearing" or similar words?

   a. **No**—If no, then the agency could choose to use formal rulemaking procedures but was not required to do so under the APA. To see whether the agency was required to use notice-and-comment rulemaking, proceed to B.2.below.

   b. **Yes**—If yes, then the agency was required to use formal rulemaking procedures. If the agency used formal rulemaking procedures, then to see whether the procedures were proper, proceed to C.3.below. And if the agency did not do so its decision is invalid. Stop here.

2. Was the agency required to use notice-and-comment rulemaking procedures?

   a. Does the rule relate to (1) to military and foreign affairs; (2) to agency management and personnel, or (3) to public property, loans, grants, benefits, and contracts?

      i. **No**—If no, then the rule may still be exempt from notice-and-comment rulemaking procedures. To see whether the agency has good cause to avoid notice-and-comment procedures, proceed to B.2.b. below.

      ii. **Yes**—If yes, then the agency was not required to use notice-and-comment rulemaking procedures, including publication. The choice to use publication procedures is valid. Stop here.

   b. Did the agency have *good cause* to believe that notice would be impracticable, unnecessary, or contrary to the public interest?

      i. **No**—If no, then the rule may still be exempt from notice-and-comment rulemaking procedures. To determine whether the rule is a valid procedural rule exempt from notice-and-comment rulemaking, proceed to B.2.c. below.

ii. **Yes**—If yes, then the agency was not required to use notice-and-comment rulemaking procedures because it has *good cause* to skip those procedures. The choice to use publication procedures is valid. To see whether the procedures were proper, proceed to C.1. below.

c. Does the rule relate only to procedure?

i. **No**—If no, then the rule may still be exempt from notice-and-comment rulemaking procedures. To determine whether the rule is a valid policy statement exempt from notice-and-comment rulemaking, proceed to B.2.d. below.

ii. **Yes**—If yes, then ask whether the rule has a substantial impact on the rights of the people affected by it (or, if in D.C., whether it encodes a substantial value judgment).[50]

(a) **No**—If no, then the agency was not required to use notice-and-comment rulemaking procedures. The choice to use publication procedures is valid. To see whether the procedures were proper, proceed to C.1. below.

(b) **Yes**—If yes, then the agency's choice to use publication procedures is invalid. Stop here.

d. Does the rule *prospectively* advise the public and agency personnel on the way in which the agency plans to exercise *discretionary* power in the future?

i. **No**—If no, then the rule is not a policy statement but may still be exempt from notice-and-comment rulemaking procedures. To see whether the rule is a valid interpretive rule exempt from notice-and-comment procedures, proceed to B.2.e. below.

ii. **Yes**—If yes, then the rule is a non-legislative rule, specifically a policy statement, for which the agency was not required to use notice-and-

50 Remember, the D.C. Circuit applies a different test. It examines whether the rule encodes a substantive value judgment and substantially alters the rights of the parties; if so, notice-and-comment procedures are necessary. JEM Broad. Co., Inc. v. FCC, 22 F.3d 320, 328 (D.C. Cir. 1994).

comment rulemaking so long as the rule does not impose rights and obligations or restrict the agency's ability to exercise its discretion (the binding effects test). The choice to use publication procedures is valid. To see whether the procedures were proper, proceed to C.1. below.

e. Does the rule interpret language in an existing statute or regulation?

i. **No**—If no, then either you made a mistake or the rule is a legislative rule, and the agency was required to use notice-and-comment rulemaking procedures. The choice to use publication procedures is invalid. Stop here.

ii. **Yes**—If yes, then determine whether the agency intended to exercise legislative rulemaking authority. Determine whether any one of the *intent to exercise* factors are present: (1) must the agency refer to an existing legislative rule to enforce the new rule; (2) is the new rule published in the Code of Federal Regulations; (3) did the agency invoke its legislative rulemaking authority to issue the new rule; or (4) is the new rule inconsistent with a prior legislative rule. Are any of the four *intent to exercise* factors present?

(a). No—If no, then the rule is a non-legislative, interpretive rule, for which the agency was not required to use notice-and-comment rulemaking. The choice to use publication procedures is valid. To see whether the procedures were proper, proceed to C.1. below.

(b). Yes—If yes, then the agency likely intended to use its legislative rulemaking authority and should not have used publication procedures. The choice to use publication procedures is invalid. Stop here.

C. **Rulemaking Procedures**—Did the agency follow the appropriate procedures?

1. Did the agency use publication procedures?

a. **No**—If no, then the agency used either notice-and-comment rulemaking or formal rulemaking procedures. Proceed to C.2. below.

b. **Yes**—If yes, and the agency published the rule or provided personal notice to the relevant entity, the rule is valid under the APA. Stop here.

2. Did the agency use notice-and-comment rulemaking procedures?

   a. **No**—If no, then the agency likely used formal rulemaking procedures. Proceed to C.3. below.

   b. **Yes**—If yes, did the *notice* include the time, place, and nature of any public proceedings; the legal authority for the rule; and either the substance of the proposed rule or a description of the subjects and issues involved? Was the notice "sufficient to fairly apprise interested persons of the issues involved, so that they may present responsive data or argument"?[51]

      i. **No**—If no, then the notice was insufficient, and the rule is invalid. Stop here.

      ii. **Yes**—If yes, then the notice was sufficient, and the rule may be valid. To determine whether the agency engaged in improper *ex parte* communications, proceed to C.2.c. below.

   c. Did the agency engage in improper *ex parte* communications during the rulemaking process? Generally, *ex parte* communications are not prohibited for notice-and-comment rulemaking.

      i. **No**—If no, then then the rule may be valid. To determine whether the comment process was sufficient, proceed to C.2.d. below.

      ii. **Yes**—If yes, then ask whether the rulemaking proceeding involved "conflicting private claims to a valuable privilege," like a license.

         (a) Yes—If yes, then the *ex parte* communications violated the Due Process Clause of the Fifth Amendment, and the rule is invalid. Stop here

         (b) No—If no, then the rule may be valid. To determine whether the comment process was sufficient, proceed to C.2.d. below.

---

[51] The D.C. Circuit also requires the notice contain all the scientific data and methodology on which the agency relied. Portland Cement Ass'n v. Ruckelshaus, 486 F.2d 375, 394 (D.C. Cir. 1973).

d. Did the agency allow interested parties to submit *written data, views, or arguments* on the proposed rule?

i. **No**—If no, then the commenting process was insufficient, and the rule is invalid. Stop here.

ii. **Yes**—If yes, then the commenting opportunity was sufficient, and then the rulemaking process may be valid. To determine whether the agency properly followed any required hybrid procedures, proceed to C.2.e. below.

e. Did the agency follow any hybrid procedures as required by the enabling act, the agency's regulations, or other acts? Note that a court cannot require additional procedures under *Vermont Yankee*.

i. **No**—If no, then the rulemaking process was insufficient, and the rule is invalid. Stop here.

ii. **Yes**—If yes, then the rule may be valid. To determine whether the notice was sufficient, proceed to C.2.f. below.

f. Can the final rule be characterized as a *logical outgrowth* of the proposed rule, meaning that the final rule did not materially alter the issues involved in the rulemaking and the final rule did not substantially depart from the substance of the proposed rule (there were no surprise switcheroos)?

i. **No**—If no, then the notice was insufficient, and the rule is invalid. Stop here.

ii. **Yes**—If yes, then the notice was sufficient, and the final rule was validly promulgated (meaning the rule is valid). To see if the substance of the rule is valid and can be challenged in court, proceed to the checklists in Chapters 6 and 7.

3. Did the agency use formal rulemaking procedures?

a. **No**—If no, then you have reached a wrong answer at some point in your analysis. Start over.

b. **Yes**—If yes, then to determine whether the agency correctly followed the formal rulemaking procedures, proceed to the checklist in Chapter 4.

ILLUSTRATIVE PROBLEMS

■ PROBLEM 3.1 ■

Assume that the National Park Service (NPS) promulgated a regulation banning the use of off-road vehicles in national parks. The enabling act requires the NPS to promulgate rules "after hearing." The NPS promulgates its regulation using notice-and-comment rulemaking procedures. The NPS's final rule, along with a general statement of basis and purpose, was just published. You work for an association that promotes the interests of snowmobilers and off-road recreation vehicle owners. You have been asked whether the NPS used proper procedures in promulgating its new regulation. What do you advise?

Analysis

This issue here is whether the NPS must use formal rulemaking procedures or may use notice-and-comment procedures. Using the checklist above (B.1.), you should ask whether the agency was required to use formal rulemaking procedures. To answer this question, you would look to see whether the enabling act includes the phrase "on the record after a hearing" or similar language. *United States v. Florida E. Coast R.R. Co.*, 410 U.S. 224, 234–35 (1973).

The NPS's enabling act requires only that the NPS promulgate rules "after hearing." This language is insufficient to trigger formal rulemaking. Thus, the NPS could choose to use formal rulemaking procedures but was not required to do so. The rulemaking process was valid.

■ PROBLEM 3.2 ■

Marijuana is becoming a big business in the United States. To help promote the marijuana producing industry, coordinate state laws, and protect consumers, Congress enacted the Marijuana Trade Commission Act ("MTCA"). The MTCA created the Marijuana Trade Commission (the Commission), an independent agency. The Commission is authorized to proceed by adjudication and rulemaking to further the purposes of the Act. The Act directs the Commission to "promulgate rules as necessary to further the public interest."

You are general counsel to the Commission, which wants to promulgate a rule limiting the volume of marijuana retailers can sell to one consumer. The enabling act does not have relevant language. The Chair of the Commission, who is not a lawyer, would like to issue the rule without using publication procedures. He has asked you whether this type of rulemaking fits within any of the APA § 553(b) exceptions. What do you advise?

Analysis

This issue here is whether the Commission can choose not to use notice-and-comment (and formal) rulemaking under APA § 553 and instead use publication procedures. Because the enabling act contains no relevant language, the APA default rules control. Using the checklist above (B.2.), you should conclude first that the rule does not relate to (1) to military and foreign affairs; (2) to agency management and personnel, or (3) to public property, loans, grants, benefits, and contracts. Therefore, this exception does not apply.

Second, you should conclude that the Commission does not have cause to believe that notice would be impracticable, unnecessary, or contrary to the public interest, so the good cause exception does not apply.

Third, you should conclude that this rule is not procedural; it would have a substantial impact on the rights of those affected (or, if in D.C., it encodes a substantive value judgment that too much marijuana is bad). Hence, the procedural exception does not apply.

Fourth, you should conclude that the rule does not prospectively advise the public and Commission personnel on the way the Commission plans to exercise discretionary power in the future. Rather, the rule is meant to bind the industry immediately; it would impose rights and obligations and restrict the Commission's ability to exercise its discretion. It does not *prospectively* advise the public and agency personnel on the way in which the agency plans to exercise *discretionary* power in the future. Hence, it is not a valid policy statement, exempt from notice-and-comment rulemaking.

Fifth, and finally, you should conclude that the rule does not appear to interpret language in an existing statute or regulation, although it would be helpful to have more of the enabling act to confirm this point. Assuming the rule does not interpret any such language, the rule is a legislative rule and not an interpretive rule, and the Commission must use notice-and-comment rulemaking procedures to promulgate it.

POINTS TO REMEMBER

- There are three types of rulemaking procedures: formal, informal, and hybrid. Formal rulemaking is rare and resembles formal adjudication under sections 556 & 557. Hence, it is addressed in Chapter 5.

- Most rulemaking is informal rulemaking under section 553. This section contains the most common rulemaking procedures required, known as notice-and-comment procedures.
- Unless the enabling act requires the agency to issue the rule only after holding a hearing on the record, the agency may use notice-and-comment rulemaking rather than formal rulemaking.
- Congress has added additional procedures to those required by section 553 in other acts. These additional procedures require rulemaking that is less procedural than formal rulemaking but more procedural than notice-and-comment rulemaking. We call rulemaking with additional procedures hybrid rulemaking.
- Rules regarding (1) to military and foreign affairs; (2) to agency management and personnel, and (3) to public property, loans, grants, benefits, and contracts are exempt from all the section 553 requirements, including publication.
- Interpretive rules, policy statements, rules of procedure, and good cause rules are exempt from the notice-and-comment requirements of section 553 but remain subject to the publication requirements.
- While agencies may initiate rulemaking on their own, citizens may also petition an agency to promulgate a rule. If the agency denies the petition or unreasonably delays making a decision on the petition, the citizen may file suit.
- *Ex parte* communications are not prohibited during informal rulemaking because agency officials are acting more like legislators than like judges. The exception is when the proceeding involves conflicting claims to a valuable privilege, like a license.
- Executive orders, other statutes, and an agency's own procedural rules may augment the minimal rulemaking procedures in the APA. Under *Vermont Yankee*, courts may not add procedures beyond those that come from these sources.

CHAPTER 4

What Procedures Are Required for Adjudication (and Formal Rulemaking)?

In the last chapter, you learned the procedures the APA requires an agency to follow when it engages in rulemaking. This chapter will explain the procedures the APA requires an agency to follow when it engages in adjudication. While some of these procedures are similar to those for rulemaking, especially formal rulemaking, many more are different. Chapter 5 will address the procedural requirements for investigations.

REVIEW

Assuming an agency has statutory and constitutional authority to adjudicate, the agency must do so pursuant to the applicable procedures provided in its enabling act, in the APA, and in the Due Process Clause of the U.S. Constitution.

A. Types of Orders & Adjudicatory Procedures

While there are two types of rules (legislative and non-legislative), there is only one type of order. And while there are three types of rulemakings (formal, notice-and-comment, and publication), there are only two types of adjudications (formal and informal).

In the last chapter, you learned that the Supreme Court interpreted § 553(c) of the APA to require the equivalent of "on the record after opportunity for an agency hearing" to appear in the enabling act for formal rulemaking to be required.[1] This decision makes some sense because the formal procedures are better suited to finding adjudicative facts (who said what) rather than legislative facts (should the public wear masks to avoid COVID). As we move to adjudication, be aware that the Supreme Court has not yet decided

[1] United States v. Florida E. Coast R.R., 410 U.S. 224 (1973).

whether the same approach should apply despite identical language in the APA. The APA requires agencies to use formal adjudication, rather than informal, only when the enabling act requires the case "to be determined on the record after opportunity for an agency hearing . . . ."[2] Whether an agency must use formal instead of informal procedures is question of statutory interpretation. Possibly, the Court will apply the same approach it applied to formal rulemaking: formal adjudication is required only when the enabling act requires both a hearing and that the hearing be on the record.[3]

The APA provides a number of procedures for formal adjudication, which are explained next.

B. Formal Adjudication & Rulemaking Procedures

Recall that the APA requires the same procedures for formal rulemaking and formal adjudication. Because formal procedures are more typically used during adjudication, we delayed learning about them until now.

1. Notice

First, agencies must notify "[p]ersons entitled to notice of an agency hearing" of where and when the hearing will occur.[4] The APA does not define *who* is entitled to notice; rather, other statutes and the Due Process Clause of the U.S. Constitution identify these persons. The APA requires the agency to give all *interested parties* the opportunity to submit facts, arguments, and offers of settlement so long as time and the public interest permit it.[5]

Assuming notice is required, the notice must be timely and identify the matters of fact alleged, the relevant law and legal authority, and the agency's jurisdiction to hold the hearing.[6] Notice is adequate when it is complete enough, or sufficient, to fairly apprise interested parties of an agency action that will affect their interests.[7] In other words, notice is sufficient when the regulated entity knows what it did wrong and can respond to the allegations.[8]

---

2 APA § 554(a).

3 See Chapter 2.

4 APA § 554(b).

5 APA § 554(c).

6 APA § 554(b).

7 NLRB v. Local Union No. 25, 586 F.2d 959, 961 (2d Cir. 1978); Southwest Sunsites, Inc. v. FTC, 785 F.2d 1431, 1435 (9th Cir. 1986).

8 *See, e.g.*, John D. Copanos & Sons, Inc. v. FDA, 854 F.2d 510, 521 (D.C. Cir. 1988) (holding that notice was sufficient despite coming "perilously close to . . . denying the applicant a meaningful opportunity to respond" to the agency's allegations).

The APA grants *parties* the right to appear in person in an agency proceeding by or with counsel or another duly qualified representative.[9] Also, any person who is compelled to appear in person before an agency, as a witness for example, is also entitled to counsel.[10]

2. *The Hearing*

The proponent of a rule or order, usually the agency, has the burden of proof.[11] For an administrative hearing, the burden of proof includes both the burden of production and the burden of persuasion.[12]

The federal rules of evidence do not apply in administrative hearings. Hearsay is admissible; however, the agency's factual findings must be supported by *substantial evidence*.[13] Hearsay evidence alone can be substantial evidence within the meaning of the APA judicial review provisions, but it likely has to be the kind of hearsay that is reliable, such as medical records and police reports.[14] Parties in formal adjudications have a right to present their cases personally, to present rebuttal evidence, and to conduct cross-examination *if necessary*.[15] There is no absolute right to cross-examination.[16]

For claims seeking benefits, for applications for initial licenses, and for formal rulemakings, an agency may limit oral testimony, requiring the parties submit relevant information in writing only.[17]

3. *The Presiding Officer*

One of three individuals must preside at the hearing: (1) the agency, (2) one or more members of the body that comprises the

---

[9] APA § 555(b).

[10] *Id.*

[11] APA § 556(d).

[12] Dir., OWCP v. Greenwich Collieries, 512 U.S. 267, 279 (1994).

[13] APA §§ 556(d), 706(2)(E).

[14] *Compare* Consolidated Edison v. NLRB, 305 U.S. 197, 229–30 (1938) (holding that there must be at least a residuum of "competent," non-hearsay evidence in the record to support an order), *with* Richardson v. Perales, 402 U.S. 389, 410 (1971) (upholding an order based entirely on uncorroborated hearsay in the form of a written report from standard and routine medical examinations made by a trained professional).

[15] APA § 556(d).

[16] Citizens Awareness Network, Inc. v. United States, 391 F.3d 338, 351 (1st Cir. 2004) (holding that a party seeking cross-examination had the burden to show that cross was required for a "full and true disclosure of the facts.").

[17] APA § 556(d).

agency, or (3) one or more ALJs.[18] Most commonly ALJs preside, and they have powers similar to that of a judge.[19]

The ALJ is an employee of the agency he or she serves, but ALJs have some independence from the agency. ALJs can be removed only for cause or due to a reduction in workforce.[20] Additionally, ALJ compensation is determined based on length of service, rather than on performance evaluations.[21]

ALJs are not neutral in the way that an Article III judge is neutral; ALJs are agency employees and must further the agency's substantive mission.[22] However, ALJs are supposed to be impartial.[23] Hence, a litigant may seek to disqualify a biased ALJ by filing an affidavit with the agency.

4. *Separation of Functions*

The U.S. Constitution does not prohibit agencies from being investigator, prosecutor, and factfinder all in one.[24] However, the APA requires agencies to separate employees based on function, meaning that agency officials who perform investigative or prosecutorial functions cannot supervise or oversee an ALJ.[25] Further, agency prosecutors and investigators cannot participate or advise an ALJ in deciding the case or in internally reviewing the case except as witnesses or counsel in the actual hearing.[26]

One caveat: when the agency or a member or members of the body comprising the agency is deciding the case rather than an ALJ, the separation of functions provision does not apply because investigating and prosecuting are functions agency officials are conducting in the administrator's name and with the administrator's delegated authority.[27]

---

18 APA § 556(b).

19 APA § 556(c).

20 5 U.S.C. § 7521.

21 *See generally* 5 U.S.C. § 5372; 5 U.S.C. § 4301(2)(D).

22 *See, e.g.*, FTC v. Cement Inst., 333 U.S. 683, 726–27 (1948) (noting a court's comparative lack of familiarity and experience with an agency's mission).

23 APA § 556(b).

24 Withrow v. Larkin, 421 U.S. 35, 49–50 (1975).

25 APA § 554(d)(2).

26 *Id.* This restriction applies not only to the specific case but also to any "factually related" cases, meaning different cases arising out of the same set of facts.

27 APA § 554(d)(2)(C). Also, the separation of functions prohibition does not apply in two situations: (1) proceedings involving applications for initial licenses, and (2) proceedings involving the validity or application of rates, facilities, or practices of public utilities or carriers. APA § 554(d)(2)(B)–(C). Proceedings for initial licensing often turn on general, policy considerations (do we need another nuclear reactor?) rather than on contested facts (is this applicant for a license qualified?). For this

5. *Ex Parte Communications*

Ex parte communications are communications not on the public record and to which notice to all parties was not given.[28] Status reports are not *ex parte* communications.[29]

There is a difference between *ex parte* communications and *prohibited ex parte* communications. The APA prohibits some forms of *ex parte* communications in formal adjudications and rulemakings but allows *ex parte* communications in informal adjudications and rulemakings. Because the APA does not limit *ex parte* communications in either informal adjudication or informal rulemaking, any limits that do exist come from another statute, an agency procedural rule, or the Due Process Clause.[30]

For formal hearings, an ALJ cannot discuss *facts in dispute* in a case with *anyone* inside or outside the agency, except in the presence of all other parties.[31] There are three exceptions to this prohibition: (1) proceedings involving applications for initial licenses; (2) proceedings involving the validity or application of rates, facilities, or practices of public utilities or carriers; and (3) proceedings involving the agency or a member or members of the body comprising the agency as the decision maker.[32] Thus, the agency head may communicate with agency staff when making a decision in a case.

Additionally, the decision maker (including the agency and agency head) cannot discuss *the merits of the case* with *interested persons* outside the agency.[33] *Interested persons* includes not only the parties to the case but also anyone who has an interest in the proceeding that is greater than the interest a general member of the public would have.[34] The three exceptions that apply to *ex parte fact* communications do not apply to *ex parte merits* communications.

If an improper *ex parte* communication occurs and is discovered while the action is still pending before the agency, the APA allows

---

reason, the separation of functions limits are unnecessary. The second exception applies to proceedings involving the validity or application of rates, facilities, or practices of public utilities and carriers. Because the APA includes ratemaking as a form of rulemaking, section 554(d)'s quintessentially adjudicative protections are unnecessary.

28 APA § 551(14).

29 *Id.*

30 Sangamon Valley v. United States, 269 F.2d 221, 224 (D.C. Cir. 1959) (holding that *ex parte* communications violate Due Process when the case involves "conflicting private claims to a valuable privilege.").

31 APA § 554(d)(1).

32 APA § 554(d)(2)(A)–(C).

33 APA § 557(d)(1).

34 Pro. Air Traffic Controllers Org. v. FLRA, 685 F.2d 547, 570 (D.C. Cir. 1982) (holding that members of Congress and the White House are interested parties).

the agency to both cure the violation and sanction the violator. To cure the improper *ex parte* communication, the decision maker "shall place on the public record" all written *ex parte* communications and a memoranda describing the substance of any oral communications.[35] Cure can be effective only if the prohibited communication is discovered before the agency reaches a final decision. In addition to curing the *ex parte* violation, the agency may sanction the violator by ruling against a party on the merits of a case where the party made or caused to be made a prohibited *ex parte* communication.[36] Note that ruling against the party must be consistent with the public interest and with the policy of the underlying agency statute.

If an improper *ex parte* communication occurs and is not discovered until after the agency renders a final decision, then the appellate court must determine whether the violation was grave enough to void the agency's decision. Courts will consider the following factors to decide whether the decision should be voided:

(1) the gravity of the *ex parte* communication;

(2) whether the *ex parte* communications may have influenced the agency's decision;

(3) whether the party making the *ex parte* communications ultimately benefited from making them;

(4) whether the contents of the *ex parte* communications were known to the other side, who would thus have had an opportunity to respond; and

(5) whether vacating the agency's decision would serve a useful purpose.[37]

6. *The Initial Decision*

As a result of a formal proceeding, a record is compiled. The *exclusive record* includes "[t]he transcript of testimony and exhibits, together with all papers and requests filed in the proceeding."[38]

Assuming an ALJ presided at the hearing, the ALJ will make an *initial decision* after the hearing ends.[39] The ALJ must rule "on each finding, conclusion, or exception presented."[40] All decisions must

---

[35] APA §§ 557(d)(1)(C)(i) & (ii).

[36] APA § 557(d)(1)(D).

[37] *Pro. Air Traffic Controllers Org.*, 685 F.2d at 565 (refusing to void an agency decision despite improper *ex parte* communications).

[38] APA § 556(e).

[39] APA §§ 554(d) & 557(b). If the agency prefers to retain the power to make the initial decision, it can elect to have an ALJ preside at the hearing and make a "recommended" decision. APA § 557(b).

[40] APA § 557(c)(3).

include a statement of the "findings and conclusions, and the reasons or basis therefor, on all the material issues of fact, law, or discretion presented on the record; and the appropriate rule, order, sanction, relief, or denial thereof."[41] The initial decision "becomes the decision of the agency" if there is no appeal.[42]

7. *Appealing the Initial Decision to the Agency*

If either the regulated entity or agency[43] appeals the initial decision, then the agency head or an internal body acting for the agency head will resolve the appeal. On appeal in the agency, the agency reviews the ALJ's findings on both questions of law and fact *de novo*.[44]

If the agency's final decision is then appealed to a court, the reviewing court will evaluate the agency's factual findings to see if there is *substantial evidence* in the record to support those findings.[45] We will address this topic in Chapter 7. For now, know that the ALJ's initial decision is part of the record that the reviewing court will examine.[46] In those cases where the demeanor of the witnesses was critical to the decision, the reviewing court will consider the ALJ's demeanor findings, known as testimonial findings, because the ALJ actually observed the witnesses. Courts expect agencies to defer to the ALJ testimonial findings—findings regarding the credibility of witnesses based on how they appeared. In contrast, agencies heads are free to reject ALJ derivative findings—findings not based on demeanor—because agencies have expertise.

Thus, although the agency head applies a *de novo* standard to review an ALJ's findings of fact, the agency should keep in mind that a reviewing court will be less likely to reverse the agency's final decision if it carefully considers the ALJ's findings regarding demeanor.[47]

C. Informal Adjudication Procedures

1. *APA Procedures*

The procedures above apply only to formal adjudications, not informal adjudications. Administrative judges (AJs), who lack the

---

[41] APA §§ 557(c)(3)(A)–(B).

[42] APA § 557(b).

[43] Either party can appeal at this stage; however, the agency cannot appeal if the agency head rules against it. APA § 702 (providing that any "person," not including agencies, suffering legal wrong may appeal).

[44] APA § 557(b).

[45] APA § 706(2)(E).

[46] Universal Camera v. NLRB, 340 U.S. 474, 493 (1951).

[47] *See, e.g.*, Jackson v. VA, 768 F.2d 1325, 1330 (Fed. Cir. 1985).

status and independence of the ALJs, preside over informal adjudications.

While formal adjudication resembles civil trials, informal adjudication is altogether different. Often, no hearing is offered. Indeed, under the APA, few procedures are required at all; an agency need only promptly decide an issue and notify the affected party.[48] Informal adjudications can be as simple as an agency administrator approving an individual's application for a license or permit.

2. *Due Process Procedures*

Although the APA requires very few procedures for informal adjudication, the U.S. Constitution or the agency's enabling act may require additional procedures. In cases involving the deprivation of property or liberty rights, the Due Process Clause of the U.S. Constitution requires some form of a pre-deprivation hearing.[49] Absent exigent circumstances,[50] the agency must offer some form hearing before acting, although an abbreviated form is sufficient if the agency offers a post-deprivation hearing that comports with the three *Mathews*'s requirements below.[51]

To have a constitutionally protected *property* interest, a plaintiff must show that he or she has "more than an abstract need or desire for [the interest and] more than a unilateral expectation of it."[52] The plaintiff must have a "legitimate claim of entitlement" to that interest.[53] Legitimate claims of entitlement are created and their dimensions are defined by existing rules or understandings that stem from an independent source of law, such as state law.[54]

To have a constitutionally protected *liberty* interest, a plaintiff must show not only that the agency will or has harmed his or her reputation but also that the plaintiff will suffer a future harm stemming from that reputational harm.[55] This test is known as *the stigma plus test*. Reputational injury is the stigma; future harm is the plus. Additionally, the plaintiff must actually dispute the validity of the stigma, or there is no reason for a hearing.[56]

---

[48] APA § 552(e).

[49] U.S. CONST. amend. V.

[50] *See, e.g.*, Ewing v. Mytinger & Casselberry, Inc., 339 U.S. 594, 601 (1950) (misbranded drugs); N. Am. Cold Storage Co. v. Chicago, 211 U.S. 306, 320 (1908) (spoiled poultry).

[51] Cleveland Bd. of Ed. v. Loudermill, 470 U.S. 532, 542 (1985).

[52] Bd. of Regents v. Roth, 408 U.S. 564, 577 (1972).

[53] *Id.*

[54] *Id.*

[55] Paul v. Davis, 424 U.S. 693, 702 (1976).

[56] Codd v. Velger, 429 U.S. 627 (1977).

Assuming the plaintiff has demonstrated that an agency has or will harm a property or liberty interest, the court will determine what hearing procedures are required by balancing three competing interests identified in *Mathews*.[57] Those three interests are (1) the seriousness of the harm to the individual (the individual's interest), (2) the risk of erroneous deprivation if the requested procedures are not used (the court's interest), and (3) the administrative and fiscal burden of requiring the additional procedures (the government's interest).[58] Additionally, while "a fair tribunal is a basic requirement of due process"[59] including a neutral decision maker, the fact that an agency combines investigative and adjudicative functions does not alone create an unconstitutional risk of bias because administrative officials are presumed to be honest and have integrity.[60] The plaintiff must show actual bias.

In sum, informal adjudication procedures are generally minimal under the APA, may also be governed by Due Process, and are quicker in comparison to formal adjudication procedures.

PROCEDURES REQUIRED FOR ADJUDICATION: CHECKLIST

A. **Choice of Adjudication Procedure**—Was the agency required to use formal adjudication procedures? Does the enabling act includes the phrase "on the record after a hearing" or similar words?

   1. **No**—If no, then the agency was allowed to proceed using informal procedures. To determine whether the agency used the proper informal procedures, proceed to C. below.

   2. **Yes**—If yes, then did the agency use formal procedures?

      a. **Yes**—If yes, then the agency's choice of procedure was valid. To determine whether the agency correctly used formal procedures, proceed to B. below.

      b. **No**—If no, then the agency's choice of procedure was unlawful, and the adjudication is invalid. Stop here.

B. **Formal Adjudication Procedures**—Did the agency use appropriate procedures?

---

57 Mathews v. Eldridge, 424 U.S. 319, 335 (1976).

58 *Id.*

59 Withrow v. Larkin, 421 U.S. 35, 47 (1975).

60 *Id.*

1. Did the agency notify "persons entitled to notice of an agency hearing" regarding when and where the hearing would occur, the matters of fact alleged, the relevant law, and the agency's legal authority to hold the hearing? Was the notice sufficient to inform the regulated entity of what it did wrong?

   a. **No**—If no, then notice was insufficient, and any ensuing order or rule would be invalid under APA § 554(b). Stop here.

   b. **Yes**—If yes, then notice was sufficient to fairly apprise the interested parties of the allegations. To determine whether the APA's separation of functions provision was violated, proceed to B.2. below.

2. Did the agency allow officials who performed investigative or prosecutorial functions to supervise or oversee the ALJ who presided over the hearing?

   a. **No**—If no or if the agency head presided over the hearing, then there was no violation of the APA's separation of functions provision. To determine whether the allocation of the burden of proof was proper, proceed to B.3. below.

   b. **Yes**—If yes, then any ensuing order or rule would be invalid under APA § 554(d)(2) (the APA's separation of functions provision). Stop here.

3. Did the proponent of the order or rule, usually the agency, have the burden of proof?

   a. **No**—If no, then any ensuing order or rule would be invalid under APA § 556(d). Stop here.

   b. **Yes**—If yes, then the burden was correct. To determine whether the hearing procedures were sufficient, proceed to B.4. below.

4. Did the parties have the ability to present their cases personally or through counsel, to present rebuttal evidence, and to conduct cross-examination *if necessary*?

   a. **No**—

      i. If no and the proceeding was not one seeking benefits, one seeking an initial license, or a formal rulemaking, then any ensuing order or rule would be invalid. Stop here.

ii. If no and the proceeding was one seeking benefits, one seeking an initial license, or a formal rulemaking, then the agency may limit oral testimony and require all relevant information be submitted in writing under APA § 556(d). To determine whether improper *ex parte* communications occurred, proceed to B.5. below.

b. **Yes**—If yes, then to determine whether improper *ex parte* communications occurred, proceed to B.5. below.

5. Did any communications occur that were not on the public record and to which notice to all parties was not given, other than status reports?

a. **No**—If no, then no improper *ex parte* communications occurred as defined in APA § 551(14). To determine whether the agency applied the appropriate standard of review when the issue was appealed to the agency, proceed to B.8. below.

b. **Yes**—If yes, then prohibited *ex parte* communications may have occurred. To determine whether the *ex parte* communications were prohibited, proceed to B.6. below.

6. Did the ALJ (but not the agency or agency head) discuss a *fact in dispute* with anyone while not in the presence of all the parties in a proceeding other than one involving an application for an initial license or one challenging the validity or application of rates for public utilities and carriers? (Note that the agency and agency head are allowed to make such communications under APA § 554(d)(2)(A)–(C)).

a. **No**— If no, then to determine whether other prohibited *ex parte* communications took place, proceed to B.7. below.

b. **Yes**—If yes, then the ALJ engaged in prohibited *ex parte* communications under APA § 554(d)(1). To determine the remedy, ask whether the prohibited communication was discovered while the action was pending before the agency.

i. **No**—If no, then the reviewing court will consider whether to void the order by considering the following factors: (1) the gravity of the *ex parte* communications; (2) whether the *ex parte* communications may have influenced the agency's decision; (3) whether the party making the *ex parte* communications ultimately benefited from making them; (4) whether the contents of the *ex parte* communications were known to the other side, who would thus have had an opportunity to respond; and (5) whether vacating the agency's decision would serve a useful purpose. If the order or rule must be voided, stop here. If the order or rule is not voided for this reason, then to consider whether other prohibited *ex parte* communications took place, proceed to B.7. below.

ii. **Yes**—If yes, then the agency must cure the violation by placing the communication on the public record and must consider whether to sanction the violator under APA § 557(d)(1)(C)(i)–(ii). To consider whether other prohibited *ex parte* communications took place, proceed to B.7. below.

7. Did the decision maker (the ALJ, agency, or agency head) discuss *the merits of the case* with *interested persons outside the agency* while not in the presence of all the parties?

a. **No**—If no, then no prohibited *ex parte* communications occurred. To determine whether the agency applied the appropriate standard when the case was appealed to the agency, proceed to B.8. below.

b. **Yes**—If yes, then the decision maker engaged in prohibited *ex parte* communications APA § 557(d)(1). To determine the remedy, ask whether the prohibited communication was discovered while the action was pending before the agency?

i. **No**—If no, then the reviewing court will consider whether to void the order or rule by considering the following factors: (1) the gravity of the *ex parte* communications; (2) whether the *ex parte* communications may have influenced the agency's decision; (3) whether the party making the *ex parte* communications ultimately benefited from making them; (4) whether the contents of the *ex parte* communications were known to the other side, who would thus have had an opportunity to respond; and (5) whether vacating the agency's decision would serve a useful purpose. If the order or rule must be voided, stop here. If the order or rule is not voided for this reason, then to determine whether the agency applied the appropriate standard when the case was appealed to the agency, proceed to B.8. below.

ii. **Yes**—If yes, then the agency must cure the violation by placing the communication on the public record and must consider whether to sanction the violator under APA § 557(d)(1)(C)(i)–(ii). To determine whether the agency applied the appropriate standard when the case was appealed to the agency, proceed to B.8. below.

8. On appeal to the agency, in applying *de novo* review, did the agency defer to the ALJ's testimonial findings but not the derivative findings?

   a. **No**—If no, then a reviewing court may reverse the agency's decision as not supported by substantial evidence unless the agency had a good reason for rejecting the testimonial findings. To determine whether the substance of the order is valid and whether the plaintiff can sue, proceed to the checklists in Chapters 6 and 7.

   b. **Yes**—If yes, then a reviewing court is less likely to reverse the agency's findings as not supported by substantial evidence. To determine whether the substance of the order is valid and whether the plaintiff can sue, proceed to the checklists in Chapters 6 and 7.

C. **Informal Adjudication Procedures**—To determine whether the agency followed the appropriate procedures for informal adjudication, ask the following questions.

1. Did the agency promptly decide the issue and notify the affected party?

   a. **No**—If no, then the agency violated the APA § 552(e), and the order is invalid. Stop here.

   b. **Yes**—If yes, then the agency complied with all procedures required by the APA but may also have to follow additional procedures to comply with the U.S. Constitution or the enabling act. Proceed to C.2. below.

2. To determine whether Due Process applies, ask whether the regulated entity has a constitutionally protected interest at stake.

a. Does the regulated entity have more than a *unilateral expectation* or abstract need for the interest being deprived?

i. **No**—If no, then the regulated entity does not have a protected property interest. To determine whether the regulated entity has a protected liberty interest, proceed to C.2.b. below.

ii. **Yes**—If yes, then the regulated entity has a protected property interest, and the agency must provide some form of a hearing. To determine what hearing procedures are necessary, proceed to C.3. below.

b. Will the regulated entity suffer both reputational harm (stigma) and future harm as a result of the deprivation (plus)?

i. **No**—If no, then the regulated entity does not have a protected liberty interest and, assuming the regulated entity did not have a protected property interest, has no right to any procedures other than that required by the APA (prompt notice of the decision). The agency's order is procedurally valid. To determine whether the substance of the order is valid and whether the plaintiff can sue, proceed to the checklists in Chapters 6 and 7.

ii. **Yes**—If yes, then the regulated entity has a protected liberty interest. To determine whether the regulated entity has a right to a hearing, ask whether the regulated entity disputes the underlying facts leading to the reputational injury.

(a). **No**—If no, then under *Codd v. Velger*[61] the regulated entity has no right to a hearing. Stop here.

(b). **Yes**—If yes, then the agency must provide some form of a hearing. To determine what type of hearing is necessary, proceed to C.3. below.

3. To determine what hearing procedures are required when Due Process applies, ask the following questions.

---

[61] 429 U.S. 627 (1977).

a. Do exigent circumstances prevent the agency from providing some form of a pre-deprivation hearing?

i. **No**—If no, then the agency must provide some form of a pre-deprivation hearing.

(a). If the agency failed to do so, the order is invalid. Stop here.

(b). If the agency did so, then to determine whether the procedures provided were constitutionally sufficient, proceed to C.3.b. below.

ii. **Yes**—If yes, then the agency may provide a post-deprivation hearing rather than a pre-deprivation hearing. To determine whether the procedures provided were constitutionally sufficient, proceed to C.3.b. below.

b. Ask the following question for each specific procedure the regulated entity wants, such as the right to the assistance of counsel or the ability to conduct cross-examination: Does the seriousness of the harm to the individual and the risk of erroneous deprivation if the procedure is not used outweigh the administrative and fiscal burden on the agency if it is?

i. **No**—If no, then the agency need not provide that procedure under *Mathews v. Eldridge*,[62] and the order is procedurally valid. To determine whether the substance of the order is valid and whether the plaintiff can sue, proceed to the checklists in Chapters 6 and 7.

ii. **Yes**—If yes, then the agency must provide the relevant procedure and any order resulting from a hearing that did not include the procedure would be invalid. Stop here.

ILLUSTRATIVE PROBLEMS

■ PROBLEM 4.1 ■

Assume that State University hired a professor to fill a *visiting professor* position. The position was for a fixed term of one academic year. At the end of the term, the professor was not rehired. Further, the University did not provide any reason for the non-retention.

[62] 424 U.S. 319, 335 (1976).

Finally, the University indicated only when asked that the professor was not rehired because the position was only needed for the one year. The professor has challenged the decision, claiming the University violated her due process rights because she was not afforded notice and an opportunity to challenge the University's decision. You are general counsel for the University and have been asked whether the professor's claim has any merit. How would you respond?

Analysis

This issue here is whether the University violated the Due Process Clause by not providing notice or a hearing before the termination. Using the checklist above (C.2.), you should first ask whether the professor has a protected property interest in her job. Because the term of the position was fixed at one academic year, the professor had no more than a unilateral expectation in keeping her position beyond that one year; hence, she does not have a protected property interest. Moreover, the professor will not suffer reputational harm; she was not rehired because the position was for only one year either in the present or future., Thus, she does not have a protected liberty interest either. So, the Due Process Clause of the U.S. Constitution does not require the University to provide notice or a hearing.

■ PROBLEM 4.2 ■

The Environmental Protection Agency (EPA) is involved in a formal adjudication under the APA to revoke a manufacturer's permit to market a specific pesticide because the EPA believes the pesticide is unsafe. A key *factual* issue in the adjudication is the health hazards caused by use of the pesticide. You are counsel to the EPA. You have been asked whether any of the conversations below would violate the APA?

I. An *ex parte* discussion concerning the health hazards caused by use of the pesticide between the administrative law judge hearing the case and an agency scientist who is not involved in the case.

II. An *ex parte* discussion concerning the health hazards caused by use of the pesticide between the administrative law judge hearing the case and a non-agency scientist, who has written widely about pesticide risks and who is not connected to either the agency or the manufacturer.

III. An *ex parte* discussion concerning the health hazards caused by use of the pesticide between the agency decision maker and an agency lawyer who is involved in prosecuting the permit revocation case. The conversation took place when the agency head was reviewing the ALJ's decision.

IV. An *ex parte* discussion concerning the health hazards caused by use of the pesticide between the agency decision maker and another manufacturer of pesticides who is interested in this adjudication. The conversation took place when the agency head was reviewing the ALJ's decision.

Analysis

This issue here is whether any of the communications violate the APA's prohibitions against *ex parte* communications and separation of functions. Using the checklist above (B.2.), you should first determine whether the agency officials who performed investigative or prosecutorial functions were supervised or overseen by the ALJ who presided over the hearing? The answer is no, so there was no violation of the APA's separation of functions provision. Note that the separation of functions provision does not apply to the agency decision maker, only to the ALJ.

Second, you determine that *ex parte* communications occurred (according to the problem) and proceed to B.6. to determine whether the communications were prohibited. Under the APA, it is not enough that the communications are *ex parte*; they must also be prohibited under either APA §§ 554(d)(1) or 557(d)(1).

To determine whether any of the communications were prohibited, you should ask whether either of the communications with the ALJ were improper; these communications are in I and II above. Did the ALJ discuss a *fact in dispute* with anyone, inside or outside of the agency, while not in the presence of all parties? The answer in both cases is "yes;" the ALJ discussed the health hazards of the pesticide (a disputed issue of fact) with an agency scientist and a non-agency scientist. Thus, the ALJ engaged in prohibited *ex parte* communications under APA § 554(d)(1) in both cases.

Next, you should ask whether any of the communications with the agency decision maker were improper; these communications are in III & IV above. The decision maker is prohibited from discussing *the merits of the case* with *interested persons outside the agency* while not in the presence of all the parties. APA § 557(d)(1). *Interested persons* includes not only the parties to the case but also anyone who has an interest in the proceeding that is greater than the interest a general member of the public would have. In III, the agency decision maker spoke to someone *inside* the agency about the merits of the case; this communication is not prohibited by the APA. In IV, however, the agency decision maker spoke to someone *outside* the agency about the health hazards of the pesticide, which relates to the merits of the case. Even though the non-party manufacturer is not a party to the case, it is likely an *interested person*. As such, the *ex parte* communication was prohibited by APA § 557(d)(1).

Finally, to determine the remedy for the violations above, you should ask whether the prohibited communication was discovered while the action was pending before the agency (B.6.b. & B.7.b.). If yes, then the agency must cure the violation by placing the communication on the public record and must consider whether to sanction the violator under APA §§ 557(d)(1)(C)(i) & (ii). If no, then the reviewing court will consider whether to void the order (or rule if formal rulemaking) by considering the following factors: (1) the gravity of the *ex parte* communications; (2) whether the *ex parte* communications may have influenced the agency's decision; (3) whether the party making the *ex parte* communications ultimately benefited from making them; (4) whether the contents of the *ex parte* communications were known to the other side, who would thus have had an opportunity to respond; and (5) whether vacating the agency's decision would serve a useful purpose.

POINTS TO REMEMBER

- The Supreme Court has not yet decided how a court should review an agency's decision to use informal procedures. If the Court applies the same approach it took to formal rulemaking, then unless the language of the enabling act is very clear that Congress wanted the agency to use formal procedures (includes a phrase similar to "on the record after an opportunity for an agency hearing"), an agency's decision to use informal procedures will likely be upheld.
- The same procedures apply both to formal rulemaking and formal adjudication; however, formal rulemaking is less common.
- When an agency conducts formal adjudication or rulemaking, it must essentially provide a trial-like hearing, with notice, the right to counsel, and the ability to cross-examine witnesses. However, the rules of evidence do not apply.
- Pursuant to the separation of functions prohibition in the APA, an investigator or prosecutor cannot supervise an ALJ.
- There are two *ex parte* prohibitions in the APA: First, an ALJ cannot discuss *facts is dispute* in a case with *anyone* inside or outside the agency, except in the presence of all other parties.

Second, any agency decision maker cannot discuss *the merits of the case* with *interested persons outside* the agency.

- If prohibited *ex parte* communications occur, the agency must cure and may sanction the violating party.
- Courts may void any agency action if improper *ex parte* communications occurred and was not cured at the agency level.

CHAPTER 5

What Procedures Are Required for Investigation & Disclosure?

In the last two chapters, you learned the procedures the APA requires an agency to follow when it engages in rulemaking and adjudication. This chapter addresses the procedures an agency must follow when it wishes to obtain information either through an investigation or disclose information via disclosure. As with rulemaking and adjudication, the agency acts pursuant to the applicable procedures provided in its enabling act, the APA, and the U.S. Constitution. Additionally, however, an agency must follow a number of other acts when it discloses information to the public or holds meetings.

REVIEW

It is unlikely that your professor will test you on this subject matter. It is often the last subject covered in Administrative Law courses, if it is covered at all. However, this chapter addresses a large part of what agencies do; hence, a law professor's oversight of this important area may seem odd to a practitioner. In case you are tested on this information or encounter an issue in practice, here is what you need to know.

A. Agency Power to Investigate

Agencies obtain information from citizens and businesses in two ways. First, an agency may require that citizens produce information in documentary or testimonial form, either *voluntarily* through reports (such as your annual income tax return) or by compulsion in the form of a subpoena. Second, an agency may conduct a physical inspection of a residence or place of business to gather information relevant to some regulatory or enforcement standard. Again, compliance may be voluntary or forced through a warrant.

1. *Documents and Testimony*

The primary way agencies collect information is by obtaining documents (records and reports). Regulated entities may be required by statute or subpoena to provide written reports or to complete forms. Because agencies' demand for such information has mushroomed in recent years, Congress has required agencies to maintain minimal standards of necessity, efficiency, non-duplication, and interagency coordination.[1]

a. Voluntary Production

Most individuals and businesses voluntarily provide information to the government either because they feel obligated to do so or because they want something in return, for example a tax refund, a license to practice law, financial aid, or a global entry pass. Additionally, the government can compel disclosure by issuing a subpoena.

b. Involuntary Production

Agencies can compel regulated entities to provide information by way of a subpoena or a subpoena *duces tecum*. A subpoena seeks testimony, while a subpoena *duces tecum* seeks documents. Federal agencies do not have the power to enforce a subpoena. If someone refuses to comply, the agency must go to federal court to obtain an order of compliance.

A court will *quash*, or refuse to enforce, a subpoena in three situations. First, a court will quash a subpoena if the agency does not have statutory authority to issue the subpoena; it is rare for an agency to not have such authority.

Second, a court will quash a subpoena if it violates the Fourth Amendment of the U.S. Constitution. This Amendment protects "[t]he right of the people to be secure in their persons, houses, papers, and effects, against unreasonable searches and seizures."[2] To prevail on its action to enforce a subpoena, an agency must prove that (1) the subpoena was issued for a congressionally authorized purpose, (2) the information sought is relevant to an authorized purpose, and (3) the information sought is adequately described.[3] Because courts interpret these elements liberally, the Fourth Amendment provides little protection to those trying to quash a subpoena.

---

[1] *See, e.g.*, Paperwork Reduction Act, 44 U.S.C. § 3501; Information Quality Act, 44 U.S.C. § 3516.

[2] U.S. CONST. amend IV.

[3] United States v. Sturm, Ruger & Co., Inc., 84 F.3d 1, 4 (1st Cir. 1996).

Third, a court will quash a subpoena if it violates the Fifth Amendment of the U.S. Constitution. This Amendment protects people from "be[ing] compelled in any criminal case to be a witness against himself."[4] While administrative agencies are not normally engaged in criminal law enforcement, administrative action may lead to criminal prosecution. Generally, the scope of the Fifth Amendment is explored in Constitutional Law and Criminal Procedure courses, not Administrative Law courses.

For our purposes, here is the law in a nutshell: the Supreme Court has interpreted the Fifth Amendment principally to restrict the government's power to compel natural persons to testify orally against themselves if testifying would lead to criminal prosecution. With one very limited exception,[5] the Fifth Amendment does not apply to the production of records that were voluntarily[6] or involuntarily created.[7] To be clear, the Fifth Amendment does not protect artificial entities from producing incriminating business records; it does not protect the custodian of business records from producing incriminating records, even when the custodian would be implicated personally by the production; it does not protect the owners of sole proprietorships from producing involuntarily created public records; and it does not protect the owners of sole proprietorships from producing voluntarily created documents unless the act of production itself would be incriminating.

2. *Inspections*

a. Voluntary Compliance

Most individuals and businesses voluntarily comply with inspection requests, because non-compliance has costs, including negative publicity and a lack of good will in the future from the agency both short and long term.

b. Involuntary Compliance

If the regulated entity refuses to allow an inspection, the agency may go to court to obtain a search warrant. To comply with the Fourth Amendment, the agency seeking the search warrant must

---

4 U.S. CONST. amend. V.

5 The act of production exception provides that while the contents of a document may not be privileged because it was voluntarily created, the very act of producing the document may be privileged if would serve as testimony that a crime occurred. United States v. Hubbell, 530 U.S. 27, 36–37 (2000); Braswell v. United States, 487 U.S. 99, 117–18 (1988).

6 Fisher v. United States, 425 U.S. 391, 407–09 (1976).

7 Shapiro v. United States, 335 U.S. 1, 34 (1948) (holding that various records a wholesaler of fruit and produce was obliged to keep under the Emergency Price Control Act were not protected from disclosure by the Fifth Amendment).

demonstrate *administrative probable cause*, meaning either that the agency has specific evidence that the regulated entity is violating the law or that a statute or regulation allows periodic inspections and this inspection falls within the statutory or regulatory parameters.[8]

Importantly, a warrant is not required for every search. There are several well-recognized exceptions to the warrant requirement, including (1) searches of locations in plain view,[9] (2) searches in emergency situations,[10] (3) searches subject to informed consent,[11] and (4) searches of "closely," or "pervasively," regulated businesses.[12] The closely regulated business exception to the warrant requirement is essentially an outgrowth of the implied consent doctrine: by voluntarily engaging in a heavily regulated business, business owners give up their expectations of privacy. To date, the following businesses have been found to be closely regulated: liquor dealers;[13] weapon dealers;[14] stone quarries;[15] and junkyards engaging in vehicle dismantling.[16]

Because administrative proceedings are civil in nature, the exclusionary rule generally does not apply.[17] However, in some cases

---

[8] *See* Marshall v. Barlow's, Inc., 436 U.S. 307, 320 (1978) (explaining that the "[p]robable cause justifying the issuance of a warrant [in the administrative context] may be based not only on specific evidence of an existing violation but also on a showing that reasonable legislative or administrative standards for conducting an . . . inspection are satisfied.").

[9] *See, e.g.*, Air Pollution Variance Bd. v. Western Alfalfa Corp., 416 U.S. 861, 864–65 (1974) (upholding an inspection of factory emissions from smokestacks when those emissions were visible from outside the factory).

[10] *See, e.g.*, N. Am. Cold Storage Co. v. Chicago, 211 U.S. 306 (1908) (allowing seizure of unwholesome food); Jacobson v. Massachusetts, 197 U.S. 11, 37 (1905) (allowing compulsory smallpox vaccination); Campagnie Francaise De Navigation A Vapeur v. Louisiana State Bd. of Health, 186 U.S. 380, 397 (1902) (allowing health quarantine).

[11] *See, e.g.*, Vernonia School District 47J v. Acton, 515 U.S. 646, 664–65 (1995) (holding that public school student athletes could be subject to urinalysis testing because they elected to participate in school activities); Board of Ed. v. Earls, 536 U.S. 822, 837–38 (2002) (extending *Vernonia School District*'s holding to all public school students who wished to participate in after school activities); *but see* Safford Unified School Dist. #1 v. Redding, 557 U.S. 364, 376 (2009) (holding that the strip search of a thirteen-year-old girl by public school officials who were searching for drugs violated the Fourth Amendment).

[12] Colonnade Catering Corp. v. United States, 397 U.S. 72, 77 (1970) (allowing warrantless search of liquor licensee); United States v. Biswell, 406 U.S. 311, 315 (1972) (allowing warrantless search of gun dealer).

[13] *Colonnade Catering Corp.*, 397 U.S. at 77.

[14] *Biswell*, 406 U.S. at 315.

[15] Donovan v. Dewey, 452 U.S. 594, 602–03 (1981).

[16] New York v. Burger, 482 U.S. 691, 707 (1987).

[17] United States v. Janis, 428 U.S. 433, 459–60 (1976); *see* INS v. Lopez-Mendoza, 468 U.S. 1032, 1033 (1984); Pa. Bd. of Probation & Parole v. Scott, 524 U.S. 357, 363 (1998).

in which a civil penalty was involved, lower courts have applied the exclusionary rule.[18]

B. Agency Duty to Disclose

1. The Freedom of Information Act

If your professor decides to test information in this chapter, it is likely this topic will be addressed. The Freedom of Information Act (FOIA)[19] is critically important to both agencies and the public.

FOIA requires that agencies provide information to the public in three ways. First, FOIA requires that agencies publish certain information in the Federal Register.[20] Such information includes agency descriptions, addresses, rules of procedure, and forms for all reports and examinations. Further, agencies must publish "substantive rules of general applicability . . . and statements of general policy or interpretations."[21] In other words, agencies must publish non-legislative rules in the Federal Register.

Second, FOIA requires that agencies make certain information available for inspection and copying, including all final opinions and orders in adjudicated cases.[22] Full indexing is required for ease of access. And FOIA provides that matters not properly published or indexed are not binding on a regulated entity unless the regulated entity had actual notice of them.[23]

Third, the best known, and most likely tested, requirement in FOIA is that agencies must make some records available upon request. FOIA provides: "[E]ach agency, upon request for records which . . . reasonably describe such records . . . shall make such records promptly available to any person."[24] FOIA's definition of "agency" is broader than the definition in APA § 551(1). FOIA's definition includes both executive branch and independent agencies, government-owned and government-controlled corporations, and the executive office; however, FOIA does not apply to the president, the president's personal staff, nor entities that exist solely to advise the

---

18 *See, e.g.*, Trinity Indus., Inc. v. OSHRC, 16 F.3d 1455, 1461–62 (6th Cir. 1994); Lakeland Enters. of Rhinelander, Inc. v. Chao, 402 F.3d 739, 744–45 (7th Cir. 2005).

19 FOIA is part of the APA and is codified in section 552.

20 APA § 552(a)(1).

21 APA § 552(a)(1)(D).

22 APA § 552(a)(2).

23 *Id.*

24 APA § 552(a)(3)(A).

president.[25] Further, FOIA does not apply to Congress or the federal courts.

"Any person" may make a FOIA request, including any "individual, partnership, corporation, association, or public or private organization other than an agency."[26] Subject to only a couple of narrow exceptions, the purpose of the requester is not relevant to the agency's obligation to disclose.[27] A requester need only "reasonably describe the record."[28] Then, the agency must make a good faith search of its files for the requested record.[29] In some situations, agencies may impose reasonable charges for their costs in searching for and copying records.[30] For example, agencies may charge reasonable fees for document search, duplication, and review, when records are requested for commercial use.[31]

Not all information must be disclosed. FOIA contains nine types of information that are exempted from disclosure: (1) classified information; (2) internal agency personnel rules and practices; (3) matters that another statute specifically exempts from disclosure; (4) trade secrets and commercial or financial information that the agency obtained from someone other than the requester; (5) inter-agency or intra-agency memoranda and letters, not otherwise available through discovery in a civil action against the agency; (6) personnel files, medical files, and similar files, the disclosure of which would constitute a clearly unwarranted invasion of personal privacy; (7) records and information compiled for law enforcement purposes; (8) matters related to the regulation of banks and other financial institutions; and (9) geological and geophysical information.[32] Notably, a regulated entity that wants to prevent an agency from disclosing material the regulated entity believes should be exempt cannot sue to prevent the disclosure. Such reverse FOIA claims are not allowed.[33]

---

[25] *See* Kissinger v. Reporters Comm. for Freedom of the Press, 445 U.S. 136, 156 (1980) (holding that FOIA did not apply to the National Security Council and the Council of Economic Advisors).

[26] APA § 551(2). The phrase includes foreign governments and aliens, although since 9/11, Congress has placed some limits on the ability of foreign governments to obtain records. APA § 552(a)(3)(E)(i).

[27] *See, e.g.*, Durns v. Bureau of Prisons, 804 F.2d 701, 706 (D.C. Cir. 1986) (saying, "Congress granted the scholar and the scoundrel equal rights of access to federal records under the FOIA.").

[28] APA § 552(a)(3)(A).

[29] *See* APA § 552(a)(3)(C)–(D).

[30] APA § 552(a)(4)(A)(ii).

[31] APA § 552(a)(4)(A)(ii)(I).

[32] APA § 552(b)(1)–(9).

[33] Chrysler Corp. v. Brown, 441 U.S. 281, 285 (1979).

When a request for documents is made to an agency, the agency has twenty days to determine whether one of the above exceptions applies and to notify the requester whether the agency plans to comply with the request.[34] If the agency denies the request in part or whole, the agency must provide an explanation and information about how to appeal its decision internally.[35] Internal agency appeals are subject to a similarly short time frame. After any internal appeal, and assuming the agency denied the internal appeal, the requester may seek judicial review immediately in a federal district court.[36]

On appeal, the court will decide *de novo* whether the agency's decision to withhold the information was valid.[37] It is the agency's burden to prove that its failure to disclose was legal.[38] Moreover, the court may award a requester who *substantially prevails* attorneys' fees and costs.[39]

Despite these tight deadlines, agencies often do not respond promptly. Agencies' heavy workload has frustrated Congress's clear desire for *prompt* agency response. No one anticipated the tremendous volume of requests FOIA would generate. And courts have been understandably sympathetic to the agencies' cries of request overload.

2. The Government in Sunshine Act

Congress enacted the Government in the Sunshine Act, or the Sunshine Act, in 1976, during a time when Congress believed that government functions should be open to public inspection.[40] The Sunshine Act requires that "every portion of every meeting of an agency . . . be open to public observation."[41] It provides further that agencies must provide advance notice of meetings to ensure the public is aware of them.[42] Note that the public has no right to participate, only to observe.

Although the language quoted above appears broad, the Sunshine Act narrowly defines both *agency* and *meeting*. First, the Sunshine Act defines *agency* as one "headed by a collegial body composed of two or more individual members, a majority of whom are

---

34 APA § 552(a)(6); APA § 552(a)(6)(A)(i).

35 APA § 552(a)(6).

36 APA § 552(a)(4)(B).

37 *Id.*

38 *Id.*

39 APA § 552(a)(E).

40 Pub. L. No. 94–409, 90 Stat. 1241(1976)(codified at 5 U.S.C. § 552b). It is codified directly after FOIA at APA § 552b.

41 APA § 552b(b).

42 APA § 552b(b)(e).

appointed to such position by the President and with the advice of the Senate."[43] Thus, the Sunshine Act applies only to the so-called independent agencies, such as the Federal Communications Commission, the Securities and Exchange Commission, and the Federal Trade Commission, because multi-member bodies typically head independent agencies. In contrast, individuals typically head executive agencies. Because these agency heads have no one with whom to deliberate, their deliberations need not be public.

Second, the Sunshine Act defines *meeting* as "the deliberations of at least the number of individual agency members required to take action on behalf of the agency where such deliberations determine or result in the joint conduct or disposition of official agency business."[44] There is no requirement that the members meet in person; a telephone or video call counts. The definition of *meeting* includes three requirements for a gathering of agency members to be covered: (1) the number of agency members must constitute a quorum of the agency or a subpart that has power to act on behalf of the agency; (2) the agency members must deliberate, but not necessarily decide anything;[45] and (3) the deliberations must "determine or result in the joint conduct or disposition of official agency business."[46]

Like FOIA, the Sunshine Act allows an agency to hold a closed meeting when the discussion involves one of ten exempt matters and when the public interest does not require otherwise. Seven of those ten track FOIA's exemptions,[47] while three are unique to the Sunshine Act. The unique ones allow for closed meeting when the meeting "[1] involve[s] accusing any person of a crime, or formally censuring any person; [2] [involves] disclos[ing] information the

---

[43] APA § 552b(b).

[44] APA § 552b(a)(2).

[45] *See, e.g.*, FCC v. ITT World Commc'ns, Inc., 466 U.S. 463, 471 (1984) (stating that the Sunshine Act applies if the discussions are "sufficiently focused . . . as to cause or be likely to cause the individual participating members to form reasonably firm positions regarding matters pending or likely to arise before the agency.").

[46] APA § 552b(a)(2).

[47] APA § 552b(c)(1)–(4), (6)–(8), which provide as follows:

(1) disclose matters that are . . . to be kept secret in the interests of national defense or foreign policy. . .;

(2) relate solely to the internal personnel rules and practices of an agency;

(3) disclose matters specifically exempted from disclosure by [another] statute;

(4) disclose trade secrets and commercial or financial information obtained from a person and privileged or confidential;

(6) disclose information of a personal nature where disclosure would constitute a clearly unwarranted invasion of personal privacy;

(7) disclose investigatory records compiled for law enforcement purposes . . .;

(8) disclose information contained in or related to . . . financial institutions.

premature disclosure of which would . . . be likely to significantly frustrate implementation of a proposed agency action . . .; or [3] specifically concern[s] the agency's issuance of a subpoena, or the agency's participation in a civil action or proceeding . . . ."[48]

Judicial enforcement of the Sunshine Act is similar to judicial enforcement of FOIA. "Any person" can bring suit in federal district court against an agency that violates the Act.[49] The agency carries the burden to prove that its decision not to open its meeting was legal.[50] Attorney fees and costs are also available.[51]

Importantly, a court cannot invalidate an agency action solely on the ground that the agency failed to abide by the Sunshine Act.[52] Thus, a litigant should sue before the meeting; otherwise, the litigant's only remedy may be to obtain a transcript of the illegally closed meeting.[53]

3. *The Federal Advisory Committee Act*

The Federal Advisory Committee Act (FACA)[54] applies to federal advisory committees, which are composed of private individuals and are established to help Congress and the executive branch make law and policy and award grants. These committees have offered advice on various topics from organ transplant practices to improving operations at the Department of Homeland Security. FACA enhances public scrutiny of and participation in advisory committees in several ways. Specifically, meetings must be announced in advance and be open to the public.[55] "Interested persons" must be given a chance "to attend, appear before, or file statements with any advisory committee."[56] Relevant documents and minutes must be publicly available.[57] Also, the exemptions that apply under the Sunshine Act and FOIA also apply.[58]

FACA defines a federal advisory committee broadly as "any committee, board, commission, council, conference, panel, task force, or other similar group, or any subcommittee . . . established by

---

[48] APA § 552b(c)(5), (9)–(10).

[49] APA § 552b(h).

[50] *Id.*

[51] APA § 552b(j).

[52] *See* APA § 552b(h)(2).

[53] *Cf.* Common Cause v. NRC, 674 F.2d 921, 923 (D.C. Cir. 1982).

[54] *See* Pub. L. No. 92–463, § 1, 86 Stat. 770 (1972) (codified at 5 U.S.C. app. § 2) [hereinafter FACA].

[55] FACA § 10(a)(1), (2).

[56] FACA § 10(a)(3).

[57] FACA § 10(b), (c).

[58] FACA § 10(b), (d).

statute or reorganization plan, . . . established or utilized by the President, or . . . established or utilized by one or more agencies" to obtain advice or recommendations.[59]

Unlike the other open-government laws, which exempt the president, FACA expressly applies to the president. But the Supreme Court has, in the past, expressed separation of powers concerns when Congress has interfered with the president's constitutionally assigned functions.[60]

Finally, unlike FOIA and the Sunshine Act, FACA does not provide for judicial review.[61]

PROCEDURES REQUIRED FOR INVESTIGATION: CHECKLIST

A. **Information Gathering**—Did the agency seek or disclose information?

   1. **No**—If no, then return to the checklist in Chapter 1. You have made a mistake in identifying the type of agency action at issue.

   2. **Yes**—If yes, then ask whether the agency sought or disclosed information.

      a. If the agency sought information, proceed to B.1. below.

      b. If the agency disclosed information, proceed to C.1. below.

B. **Information Flowing to the Agency**—

   1. Did the agency seek information in documentary or testimonial form?

      a. **No**—If no, then the agency likely inspected a regulated entity. Proceed to B.2. below.

      b. **Yes**—If yes, then ask whether the regulated entity voluntarily provided the information.

---

59 FACA § 3(2).

60 *See, e.g.*, Public Citizen v. DOJ, 491 U.S. 440, 455 (1989) (holding that the American Bar Association's Standing Committee on the Federal Judiciary was not an advisory committee under FACA).

61 However, the courts have allowed plaintiffs who were personally injured to file an action for violations of some of the act's provisions. *See, e.g.*, Alabama-Tombigee Rivers Coal. v. DOI, 26 F.3d 1103, 1107 (11th Cir. 1994) (finding injunctive relief an appropriate remedy when an agency failed to satisfy the requirements for committee meetings proscribed in FACA).

i. **Yes**—If yes, then stop here. The agency can ask for information and the regulated entity can voluntarily provide that information. There is no constitutional violation.

ii. **No**—If no, then to determine whether the agency constitutionally obtained the information, proceed to B.1.c. below.

c. **Involuntary Production**—Did the agency go to court to compel compliance with an agency subpoena (for testimony) or subpoena *duces tecum* (for documents)?

i. **No**—If no, stop here. The agency has no independent power to enforce its subpoena and must go to federal court to seek the information.

ii. **Yes**—If yes, then to determine whether the regulated entity can quash the subpoena, proceed to B.1.d. below.

d. **Quashing a Subpoena**—Check to see if the agency has both statutory and constitutional authority to issue the subpoena.

i. Did the agency prove that it has statutory authority to issue the subpoena?

(a). **No**—If no, then stop here. The court should quash the subpoena because the agency does not have statutory authority to issue it.

(b). **Yes**—If yes, then to determine whether the agency has constitutional authority to issue the subpoena, proceed to B.1.d.ii. below.

ii. **Fourth Amendment**—Did the agency prove that (1) the subpoena was issued for a congressionally authorized purpose, (2) the information sought was relevant to an authorized purpose, and (3) the information sought was adequately described?

(a). **No**—If no, then stop here. The court should quash the subpoena because enforcing it would violate the Fourth Amendment of the U.S. Constitution.

(b). **Yes**—If yes, then to determine whether enforcing the subpoena would violate the Fifth Amendment to the U.S. Constitution, proceed to B.1.e.iii. below.

iii. **Fifth Amendment**—Did the person moving to quash the subpoena prove that complying with it would compel an individual, not a business, to testify *orally* against himself or herself and that testifying would lead to criminal prosecution?

(a). **No**—If no, then to determine whether the subpoena would require an individual to produce voluntarily created documents, proceed to B.1.e.iv. below.

(b). **Yes**—If yes, then stop here. The court should quash the subpoena because it violates the Fifth Amendment of the U.S. Constitution.

iv. **Fifth Amendment**—Did the person moving to quash the subpoena prove that complying with it would compel an individual, not a business, to produce voluntarily created documents, not involuntarily created documents, and that the very act of production could serve as proof that a crime occurred?

(a). **No**—If no, then the court should not quash the subpoena, and the regulated entity must comply. Stop here.

(b). **Yes**—If yes, then stop here. The court should quash the subpoena because it violates the Fifth Amendment of the U.S. Constitution. But this is likely the wrong answer because the act of production doctrine is so narrow you have likely missed one of the elements.

2. Did the agency seek to inspect a regulated entity?

a. **No**—If no, then you have made a mistake. Return to A.1.

b. **Yes**—If yes, then ask whether the regulated entity voluntarily allowed the inspection.

i. **Yes**—If yes, then stop here. The agency can ask to inspect without a warrant and the regulated entity can voluntarily allow the inspection.

ii. **No**—If no, then to determine whether a warrant was required, proceed to B.2.c. below.

c. **Involuntary Production**—Does the agency need a warrant to conduct the inspection?

i. Is the location to be searched in plain view?

(a). No—If no, then to determine whether an emergency justifies the search without a warrant, <u>proceed to B.2.c.ii. below</u>.

(b). Yes—If yes, then <u>stop here</u>. A warrant is not needed under the Fourth Amendment to the U.S. Constitution. The search is valid.

ii. Is there an emergency that justifies a search without a warrant?

(a). No—If no, then to determine whether the search was conducted pursuant to informed consent, <u>proceed to B.2.c.iii. below</u>.

(b). Yes—If yes, then <u>stop here</u>. A warrant is not needed under the Fourth Amendment to the U.S. Constitution. The search is valid.

iii. Is the search conducted pursuant to informed consent?

(a). No—If no, then to determine whether the search is of a closely regulated business, <u>proceed to B.2.c.iv. below</u>.

(b). Yes—If yes, then <u>stop here</u>. A warrant is not needed under the Fourth Amendment to the U.S. Constitution. The search is valid.

iv. Is the search of a closely regulated business, such as a liquor dealer, weapon dealer, stone quarries, or dismantling junkyard?

(a). No—If no, then <u>stop here</u>. A warrant is required under the Fourth Amendment to the U.S. Constitution. However, the agency need only show administrative probable cause, meaning the statute or regulation allows periodic inspections and this inspection falls within the statutory parameters.

(b). Yes—If yes, then <u>stop here</u>. A warrant is not needed under the Fourth Amendment to the U.S. Constitution. The search is valid.

C. Information Flowing from the Agency—

1. Did a requester seek information from the agency?

   a. **No**—If no, then FOIA does not apply. To see if the Sunshine Act applies, proceed to C.2. below.

   b. **Yes**—If yes, then FOIA applies. To see if an exception allows the agency to withhold the information, proceed to C.1.c. below.

   c. Does one of the nine exceptions in APA § 552(b)(1)–(9) apply?

      i. **No**—If no, then stop here. FOIA applies, and the information must be disclosed. The requester can sue in federal court; if the requester substantially prevails, the court may award costs and attorneys' fees.

      ii. **Yes**—If yes, then stop here. The agency is allowed to withhold the information.

2. Did an independent agency hold a meeting with a quorum of its members, to deliberate, which resulted in the disposition of official agency business that was not open to the public?

   a. **No**—If no, then the Sunshine Act does not apply, and the meeting did not need to be open to the public. To see whether FACA applies, proceed to C.3. below.

   b. **Yes**—If yes, then the Sunshine Act applies. To see if an exception allows the agency to keep the meeting closed, proceed to C.2.c. below.

   c. Does one of the ten exceptions in APA § 552b(c)(1)–(10) apply?

      i. **No**—If no, then stop here. The Sunshine Act applies, and the meeting should have been open to the public. If the meeting has not yet occurred, anyone can sue to have the meeting opened. If the meeting already occurred, the only judicial remedy is likely to be a transcript of the illegally closed meeting, costs, and attorneys' fees.

      ii. **Yes**—If yes, then stop here. The agency is allowed to conduct a closed meeting.

3. Did the agency hold a meeting with "any committee, board, commission, council, conference, panel, task force, or other similar group, or any subcommittee . . . established by

statute or reorganization plan, . . . established or utilized by the President, or . . . established or utilized by one or more agencies" that was not open to the public?

a. **No**—If no, then FACA does not apply, and the meeting did not need to be open to the public. Stop here .

b. **Yes**—If yes, then the FACA applies. To see if an exception allows the agency to keep the meeting closed, proceed to C.3.c. below.

c. Does one of the exceptions in FACA § 10(b) & (d) apply?

   i. **No**—If no, then stop here. FACA applies, and the meeting should have been open to the public. However, FACA does not provide for judicial review, so there is no remedy.

   ii. **Yes**—If yes, then stop here. The agency is allowed to conduct a closed meeting.

ILLUSTRATIVE PROBLEMS

■ PROBLEM 5.1 ■

Assume that you represent the owner of a junk yard that dismantles vehicles. An agency inspector has appeared at your client's door asking for permission to inspect the premises. Assuming your client does not wish to agree to the inspection, may the inspector inspect the plant without a warrant?

Analysis

This issue here is whether the agency must first obtain a warrant before conducting an involuntary inspection. Using the checklist above (B.2.c.), you should ask whether any of the exceptions apply: plain view, emergency, informed consent, or closely regulated business.

Here, the problem notes that the client operates a dismantling junkyard, which is a closely regulated business. According to *New York v. Burger*, 482 U.S. 691, 702–03 (1987), the Fourth Amendment applies, but it does not require either a warrant or probable cause. Rather the standard for a valid warrantless search is threefold: (1) the regulatory scheme has to be justified by a substantial governmental interest, (2) warrantless inspections must be necessary to further the regulatory scheme, and (3) the terms of the inspection must provide a constitutionally adequate substitute for a warrant. This third requirement requires that the scheme be detailed enough to put regulated entities on notice that they are subject to periodic inspections and that the scheme limit the inspector's discretion, requiring the inspector to act reasonably.

■ PROBLEM 5.2 ■

Assume that you are a staff attorney for the Occupational Safety and Health Administration (OSHA). The enabling act specifically authorizes OSHA to conduct inspections "when it receives a complaint that a workplace safety violation exists." According to the act, "the purpose of any inspection is for the agency to determine whether a violation of safety laws occurred."

An employee of Manufacturer, Inc. complained to OSHA that Manufacturer, Inc. was violating specific safety regulations; the violations do not present an emergency that needs immediate attention. Manufacturer, Inc. is not a liquor dealer, weapons' dealer, stone quarry, or dismantling junkyard. The OSHA Administrator asks you whether it must obtain a warrant prior to inspecting Manufacturer, Inc. and whether the inspection may be comprehensive (a wall-to-wall search) or must be limited to the allegations in the employee's complaint. How do you respond?

Analysis

This issue here is whether OSHA must obtain a search warrant and, if so, what the limits are on the search. Using the checklist above (B.1.), you should note that the agency is not seeking information in either documentary or testimonial form and proceed to B.2. Pursuant to B.2., OSHA is seeking to inspect a regulated entity. Assuming that Manufacturer's, Inc. is not willing to allow the inspection voluntarily, then a warrant is needed unless an exception applies. No exception seems to apply: (1) the locations to be searched do not appear to be within plain view; (2) the violations do not rise to the level of an emergency; (3) the search would not be conducted pursuant to informed consent; (4) the search is not of a closely regulated business. Absent an exception to the warrant requirement, agencies must obtain a warrant prior to a search, even when a statute provides authority to the agency to search. Hence, a warrant is necessary in this case.

Under the terms of the enabling act, the employee complaints would serve as administrative probable cause for a warrant to issue. The ensuing inspection must be within the statutory parameters. In this case, the statute grants OSHA authority to conduct an inspection that is limited to "determin[ing] whether a violation of safety laws occurred" when OSHA receives a complaint. OSHA cannot conduct a "wall-to-wall" search.

POINTS TO REMEMBER

- Citizens and business overwhelmingly provide information to agencies voluntarily.
- Agencies must have a statutory grant of authority to request information if a regulated entity is unwilling to provide the information voluntarily.
- Pursuant to the Fourth Amendment, an agency can subpoena records if it has statutory authority, the records are relevant, and the request is not oppressively broad.
- If necessary, agencies must seek to enforce their subpoenas in court.
- Regarding oral *testimony*, the Fifth Amendment protects individuals from being compelled to testify against themselves.
- Regarding the production of *documents*, the Fifth Amendment provides very little protection.
- Agencies must have a statutory grant of authority to conduct an inspection.
- Most regulated entities voluntarily comply with inspection requests.
- Pursuant to the Fourth Amendment, an agency needs a warrant to conduct an inspection if the regulated entity does not agree to the inspection; however, the agency need only show that the inspection complies with "reasonable legislative or administrative standards."
- Agencies do not need a warrant to inspect closely regulated businesses.
- The Freedom of Information Act requires that agencies provide information to the public (1) by publishing certain information in the Federal Register, (2) by making certain information available for inspection and copying, and (3) by responding to requestor's requests.
- FOIA contains nine types of information that are exempt from disclosure.
- The Government in the Sunshine Act requires that meetings involving the deliberations of independent agencies must be open to the public, subject to ten exemptions.
- The Federal Advisory Committee Act enhances public involvement in advisory committees and their meetings but is not judicially enforceable.

CHAPTER 6

Is Judicial Review of the Agency's Action Available?

In Chapter 1, you learned to identify the type of agency action. In Chapter 2, you learned to evaluate whether the agency had statutory and constitutional power to act. In Chapters 3, 4, and 5, you learned what procedures the APA requires for the various types of actions an agency can take. In the next two chapters, we look at what happens when an agency acts and someone or some entity is unhappy with that action. In this chapter, you will learn about the doctrines limiting the unhappy person's ability to obtain judicial review of the agency's action. Then, in Chapter 7, you will learn what standard of review a court will apply when evaluating the agency's action, assuming the unhappy person or entity is able to get into court.

REVIEW

This chapter addresses the *availability* of judicial review. To determine whether judicial review is available, you must answer three questions. First, you must ask whether the court can hear the specific claim, meaning the plaintiff can demonstrate that the court has jurisdiction and that the plaintiff has a cause of action. Second, you must ask whether this particular plaintiff can sue, meaning the plaintiff can demonstrate that he or she has constitutional, prudential, and statutory standing. Third, you must ask whether the plaintiff can sue now or must wait for something further to occur, meaning the plaintiff must demonstrate finality, exhaustion, and ripeness. Each of these doctrines are explained below.

A. The Court & the Claim

1. Jurisdiction

The first question in every case filed in federal court is whether that court has jurisdiction to hear the particular claim. Jurisdiction focuses on the courts' power to hear the *claim*, each claim if there is more than one. This power must come from an act other than the APA, because the APA contains no jurisdiction-granting language.

Often, Congress explicitly grants jurisdiction to federal courts in the agency's enabling act. However, even when Congress fails to grant jurisdiction in the enabling act, the general federal question statute provides federal courts with jurisdiction to hear "all civil actions arising under the Constitution, law, or treaties of the United States."[1] Hence, jurisdiction over a claim against agency action is rarely a problem.

2. Cause of Action

In addition to establishing that the court has jurisdiction over the claim, a plaintiff must demonstrate that he or she has a cause of action, meaning that some statute grants this particular plaintiff a right to sue for this claim. Cause of action focuses on the power of this *plaintiff* to bring this claim. When Congress provides a grant of jurisdiction in an enabling act, Congress also typically provides the plaintiff with a cause of action. For example, an enabling act might provide that any person who is adversely affected by the agency's action may file a petition challenging the validity of that action in federal court.[2] Judicial review pursuant to a specific grant like this one is called statutory review and comes with its own procedural requirements. We will not focus on those specific requirements, because they will vary with each enabling act.

For those agency actions where Congress has not provided for judicial review in the enabling act (a fact pattern you are more likely to see on an Administrative Law exam), the APA provides that any "person suffering legal wrong because of agency action, or adversely affected or aggrieved by agency action within the meaning of a relevant statute, is entitled to judicial review thereof."[3] Judicial review pursuant to the APA is often called *non-statutory review*, even though the APA is a statute. Next, we examine the three things the plaintiff must show to have a cause of action.

a. Agency Action

First, for a plaintiff to have a cause of action, the court must find that what the agency did was *agency action*. The APA defines agency action as "includ[ing] the whole or a part of an agency rule, order, license, sanction, relief, or the equivalent or denial thereof, or failure

---

1 28 U.S.C. § 1331.

2 *See, e.g.*, 29 U.S.C. § 655(f).

3 APA § 702.

to act."[4] Generally, a plaintiff can easily meet this requirement, because this definition is so broad.

So let's look at two cases in which the plaintiffs were unable to demonstrate that the challenged decision was agency action. First, the Supreme Court held that the Bureau of Land Management's (BLM) decision to reclassify public lands for mining individually rather than collectively was not agency action subject to judicial review.[5] While each individual BLM decision regarding a specific piece of land would be agency action, the Court held that the BLM's decision to consider lands collectively rather than individually was not agency action.[6]

Second, the Court held that the BLM's decision not to protect wildness areas from off-road vehicle use was not agency action.[7] Although the APA does define *agency action* to include an agency's "failure to act," the Court explained that the "failure to act" language applied only to those situations in which an agency failed to issue a specific "rule, order, license, sanction, [or other] relief" when required.[8] In this case, there was no required action.

b. Statutory Preclusion

Second, for a plaintiff to have a cause of action, judicial review cannot be precluded either explicitly or implicitly. Article III, Section 2 of the U.S. Constitution grants Congress the power to regulate the jurisdiction of the federal courts, including the power to preclude judicial review altogether. Recognizing this fact, the APA provides that judicial review is available "except to the extent that . . . [a] statute preclude[s] judicial review."[9] Preclusion can be express or implied.

As noted above, district courts can generally hear challenges to agency actions pursuant to federal question jurisdiction because such challenges "aris[e] under" federal law.[10] However, sometimes Congress provides an alternative review scheme in the enabling act.

Express preclusion is relatively rare but does occur; implied preclusion is more common. Moreover, implied preclusion is more

---

4 APA § 551(13).

5 Lujan v. Def. of Wildlife, 504 U.S. 555, 562 (1992).

6 *Id.* at 568.

7 Norton v. S. Utah Wilderness All., 542 U.S. 55, 67 (2004).

8 *Compare id.* at 62–63, *with* Massachusetts v. EPA, 549 U.S. 497, 526 (2007) (holding that the EPA's denial of a rulemaking petition was agency action because the statute required the EPA to issue a rule).

9 APA § 701(a)(1).

10 28 U.S.C. § 1331.

likely to arise on an exam because the law is less clear. Hence, we will focus our attention on implied preclusion.

In implied preclusion cases, the relevant act will direct a court of appeals to review the claims immediately following the agency's own review process. The district court is skipped; for these claims, the agency fills in for the district court.

This review scheme thus divests the district court of jurisdiction to hear *some* claims. Not all claims are divested; only those claims that fall within the statutory language. To determine whether the claim falls within the statutory language, the court asks whether the claim is "of the type Congress intended to be reviewed within this statutory structure."[11]

To determine whether the claim is one Congress thought belonged within a statutory scheme, the court must consider the three factors known as the *Thunder Basin* factors: (1) would a finding of preclusion foreclose all meaningful judicial review, (2) is the federal suit wholly collateral to a statute's review provisions, and (3) are the claims outside of the agency's expertise.[12] The first factor recognizes that Congress generally wants claims about agency action to be subject to effective judicial review. The second and third factors recognize that the agency may have a heighted review role in areas related to its expertise.[13] In sum, the answers to these questions help the court determine which reviewing body would be more appropriate: a court or the agency.

The Supreme Court has not been entirely clear regarding the relationship among these three factors.[14] The Supreme Court's most recent case to address implied preclusion in any detail was *Axon Enterprises v. FTC*.[15] There, the Court found all three factors present and concluded judicial review was not precluded.[16] In contrast, in *Elgin v. Department of the Treasury*,[17] the Court examined each

---

[11] Axon Enter. v. FTC, 598 U.S. 175, 186 (2023) (quoting Thunder Basin Coal Co. v. Reich, 510 U.S. 200, 208 (1994)). If the answer to this question is no, then judicial review can proceed. If the answer to this question is yes, then judicial review cannot proceed (at least until the agency has finished its own review process). *See, e.g.*, *Block*, 467 U.S. at 345 (holding that Congress intended to preclude review for consumer litigants in the Agricultural Marketing Agreement Act).

[12] *Thunder Basin*, 510 U.S. at 212–13.

[13] *Axon Enter.*, 598 U.S. at 186.

[14] *See, e.g.*, Free Enter. Fund v. Public Co. Acct. Oversight Bd., 561 U.S. 477, 489–90 (2010) (examining the factors in a conclusory fashion).

[15] 598 U.S. 175 (2023).

[16] *Id.* at 195–96.

[17] 567 U.S. 1 (2012).

factor, concluding that because none were present, judicial review was precluded.[18]

Must a court find all three factors present or would a finding that just one is present be sufficient? Because the purpose of the factors is to ensure that only those cases that truly benefit from agency expertise are precluded, a finding that any one factor is present should prevent the court from finding implied preclusion, meaning the district court can hear the case. But the relationship among the factors is not yet clear.

c. Committed to Agency Discretion

Third, for a plaintiff to have a cause of action, the plaintiff must be able to demonstrate that Congress did not leave the decision entirely to the agency's discretion, because the APA precludes courts from reviewing agency actions that are "committed to agency discretion by law."[19]

What does "committed to agency discretion by law" mean? Occasionally, Congress confers such broad discretion on an agency that the courts would be unable to determine whether the agency abused its discretion when exercising its delegated authority. In such situations, the courts would have no meaningful standard against which to judge the agency's exercise of discretion,"[20] or "no law to apply."[21] Note that if the plaintiff files multiple claims, only the claim that is committed to agency discretion is non-reviewable; the court can review any other claims.[22]

B. The Plaintiff

We now turn from the court and the claim to the plaintiff. To determine who can bring a lawsuit against an agency, courts use the standing doctrine. There are two aspects to standing: constitutional standing and prudential standing. The standing doctrine is an incoherent doctrine because the Supreme Court's holdings are inconsistent in this area. The Court has generously interpreted constitutional standing when it wants to reach the merits of a case and ungenerously interpreted constitutional standing when it does not want to reach the merits. You can anticipate that you will likely be tested on this topic.

---

18 *Id.* at 16.

19 APA § 701(a)(2).

20 Heckler v. Chaney, 470 U.S. 821, 831 (1985).

21 Citizens to Preserve Overton Park v. Volpe, 401 U.S. 402, 410 (1971).

22 Webster v. Doe, 486 U.S. 592, 603–04 (1988) (holding that while a statutory claim was unreviewable, the constitutional claim remained valid).

1. *Constitutional Standing Requirements*

The U.S. Constitution restricts the power of the federal courts to hear only "cases and controversies."[23] The Supreme Court has interpreted this phrase to require plaintiffs to have a personal stake in the outcome of their case.[24] To demonstrate that their stake is personal, plaintiffs must show three things: (1) injury in fact, (2) causation, and (3) redressability.[25] Each element is addressed below.

a. Injury in Fact

First to establish constitutional standing, a plaintiff must show *injury in fact*. When an agency does something directly to a regulated entity—by revoking a license, imposing a fine, or requiring specific labeling—that entity suffers a direct, economic injury. In these cases, injury in fact is easily met.

When an agency acts less directly on a regulated entity—by approving a ski resort in a national park or by defining *organic foods* to allow for some pesticides—the plaintiff will have a harder time demonstrating injury in fact because he or she may not be uniquely affected.

To show injury in fact, the plaintiff must demonstrate that he or she has a *concrete*, *particularized*, and *imminent injury*.[26] The injury can be economic, aesthetic, environmental, recreational, or informational.[27] Importantly, a plaintiff cannot establish injury in fact by complaining that the agency failed to follow a statutorily required procedure, like failing to complete an environmental impact statement.[28] A plaintiff cannot establish injury in fact in such a case because all citizens are affected identically when an agency fails to follow a statutorily required procedure.[29] Thus, the plaintiff would need to show that the agency's failure to follow the required

---

[23] U.S. CONST. art. III, § 2, cl. 1.

[24] *See* Allen v. Wright, 468 U.S. 737, 750 (1984) (holding that parents of a public school student lacked standing to sue to force schools to integrate).

[25] *Lujan*, 504 U.S. at 560–61.

[26] *Id.* at 572–73 (finding that standing was missing when the plaintiffs did not have immediate and concrete plans to observe various animal species in the wild).

[27] *Massachusetts*, 549 U.S. at 521 (2007) (environmental injury); Friends of the Earth, Inc. v. Laidlaw Envtl. Servs., 528 U.S. 167, 183–84 (2000) (fear of physical harm); Bennett v. Spear, 520 U.S. 154, 161–62 (1997) (economic injury); United States v. Students Challenging Regul. Agency Procs., 412 U.S. 669, 699 (1973) (recreational and aesthetic injury); FEC v. Akins, 524 U.S. 11, 19 (1998) (informational injury); *Lujan*, 504 U.S. at 555 (aesthetic injury); Ass'n of Data Processing v. Camp, 397 U.S. 150, 151 (1970) (economic injury).

[28] *Lujan*, 504 U.S. at 573, n.8.

[29] *See, e.g.*, FDA v. All. for Hippocratic Med., 602 U.S. 367, 386 (2024) (noting that "sincere legal, moral, ideological, and policy objections" to an agency's decision did not establish injury).

procedure injured (concrete) or will injure (imminent) the plaintiff in a unique way (particularized). Note also that a threatened injury "must be *certainly impending* to constitute injury in fact, and . . . allegations of *possible* future injury are not sufficient."[30]

In addition to demonstrating injury in fact, plaintiffs must demonstrate two other elements: causation and redressability.

b. Causation

Second, to establish constitutional standing, a plaintiff must demonstrate that the injury in fact was *caused by*, or is *fairly traceable to*, the agency action that the plaintiff is challenging as wrong. Specifically, plaintiffs must establish that the injury alleged is *fairly traceable* to the agency's action. To determine whether the injury is fairly traceable, ask whether the plaintiff's injury resulted from the agency's decision to act or not act or whether the injury resulted from the actions of a third party.

For direct injuries, like a fine or loss of a license, a plaintiff will have no difficulty establishing causation. In contrast, a plaintiff will have difficulty establishing causation when the plaintiff alleges that the agency's action induced a third party to cause the harm.[31]

c. Redressability

Third, to establish constitutional standing a plaintiff must demonstrate not only that the injury in fact was caused by, or is fairly traceable to, the agency action that is being challenged, but also that a favorable court decision will likely *redress* that injury, remedying the plaintiff's harm. In other words, even if the plaintiff gets what he or she wants (*e.g.*, immediate implementation, rather than delay, of a rule), would this result redress the alleged injury? If not, the plaintiff cannot demonstrate redressability.

Courts often address causation and redressability simultaneously, failing to separate the two elements. When an agency action causes injury, a favorable court decision will almost always redress the injury, so, courts have little to discuss. In contrast, a plaintiff will have difficulty demonstrating redressability when the

---

[30] Clapper v. Amnesty Int'l USA, 568 U.S. 398, 409 (2013).

[31] *See, e.g.*, Simon v. E. Ky. Welfare Rights Org., 426 U.S. 26, 42 (1976) (rejecting standing to a welfare rights organization that sued claiming an IRS regulation would cause hospitals to reduce medical care for indigent people); *Allen*, 468 U.S. at 757 (holding that the parents of African-American children could not demonstrate causation regarding the impact of a tax regulation because the schools were an independent third party not before the court); *cf. Bennett*, 520 U.S. at 169–70 (finding that causation was met where one agency was required to follow another agency's recommendation).

plaintiff alleges that the agency's action induced a third party to cause the harm.[32]

2. *Prudential Standing Requirements*

Even if a plaintiff meets the constitutional standing requirements, courts retain the discretion to dismiss a complaint on prudential standing grounds. Because prudential standing requirements are not constitutionally based, Congress can alter them by statute.

There are two prudential standing issues: (1) standing for individualized, not generalized, grievances, and (2) standing for associations. We turn to each of these doctrines.

One prudential concern is that courts prefer *not* to hear lawsuits addressing injuries shared by many citizens in the same way. For example, an illegal public expenditure injures all citizens because the money comes from a treasury to which all citizens contribute. Additionally, all citizens have an interest in the government's obligation to follow the law in general. Yet courts are reluctant to use such wide-spread and generally shared injuries as the basis for finding standing likely because the legislature is a more appropriate forum for addressing generalized grievances.[33] In any event, courts require plaintiffs to have an individualized injury. An individualized injury is one that affects the plaintiff or plaintiffs in a more personal and individual way.[34]

A second prudential concern is that third parties generally cannot sue to enforce the rights of others. Yet, interest groups and associations, like the Sierra Club, often have more resources to mount better legal challenges and are more likely to sue in the public interest than individuals. Thus, the Supreme Court has developed a doctrine to allow these interest groups to sue on behalf of individuals and entities who meet the constitutional standing requirements. Be aware that standing questions on exams commonly address associational standing.

To have associational standing, interest groups must show three things. First, they must show that one or more of their members have

---

32 *Allen*, 468 U.S. at 758–59.

33 Cf. *All. for Hippocratic Med.*, 602 U.S. at 396 ("The 'assumption' that if these plaintiffs lack 'standing to sue, no one would have standing, is not a reason to find standing.' Rather, some issues may be left to the political and democratic processes . . . .' ") (quoting Schlesinger v. Reservists Comm. to Stop the War, 418 U.S. 208, 227 (1974)).

34 *See Massachusetts*, 549 U.S. at 526 (holding that Massachusetts had standing to sue the Environmental Protection Agency to regulate greenhouse gas emissions because its coastline would be uniquely affected).

constitutional standing, meaning the member can demonstrate injury in fact, causation, and redressability (all addressed in the last section).

Second, the interest group must show that the group's purpose relates to the issues in the lawsuit, meaning that an environmental group can sue to enforce the environmental concerns of its members while a labor union cannot.

Third, the interest group must show that the presence of individual members is not needed in the litigation, meaning, simply, that no monetary relief is sought, just injunctive and declaratory relief.[35] Once the interest group has established standing, the group can "argue the public interest to support the claim that the agency failed to comply with its statutory mandate."[36]

3. Statutory Standing Requirements: Zone of Interests

In addition to the constitutional and prudential standing requirements, there is an additional standing requirement that comes from APA § 702 known as the zone of interest test. You should be aware, however, that some courts consider the zone of interest test a part of prudential standing.

Section 702 of the APA provides: "a person . . . adversely affected or aggrieved by agency action *within the meaning of a relevant statute*, is entitled to judicial review thereof."[37] The italicized language limits standing to persons who are "arguably" within the zone of interests the statute protects or regulates. For example, a statute addressing postal routes protects and regulates postal routes, not postal employee jobs.[38] While the courts generously interpreted this requirement in the past, more recently, they have been less generous.[39]

---

[35] Hunt v. Washington Apple Advert. Comm'n, 432 U.S. 333, 342 (1977).

[36] Sierra Club v. Morton, 405 U.S. 727, 737 (1972).

[37] APA § 702 (emphasis added).

[38] Air Courier Conference v. Am. Postal Workers Union, 498 U.S. 517, 530 (1991) (holding that a union representing postal workers did not have statutory standing because the employees' interests were not within the zone of interests that the postal act was designed to protect).

[39] *See e.g., Ass'n of Data Processing*, 397 U.S. at 153 (holding that data-processing services were within the zone of interest of a statute that allowed banks to provide data-process services).

4. *Standing Requirements: Summary*

The following chart summarizes these standing doctrines:

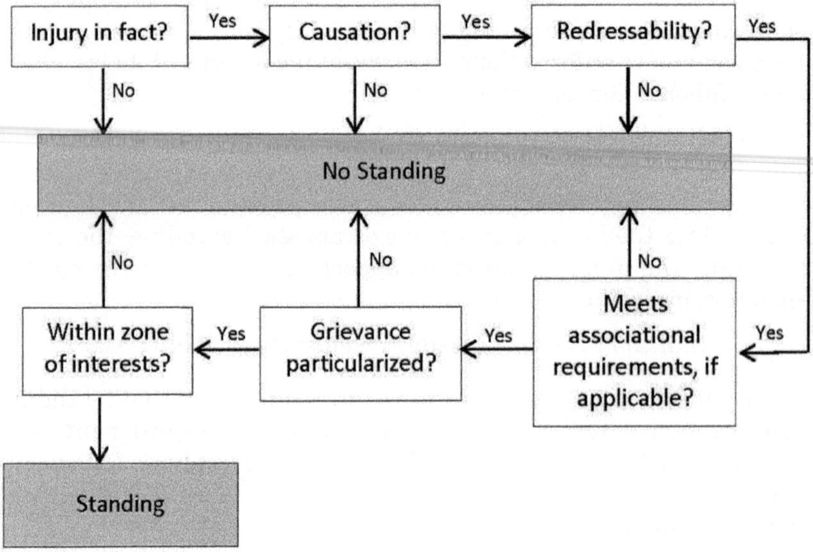

C. The Timing

We now turn from the plaintiff to timing. There are four doctrines regarding the timing of judicial review: statute of limitations, finality, exhaustion, and ripeness. Each of these four doctrines serve different purposes. The statute of limitations bars the assertion of stale claims to protect defendants from never-ending liability. The finality doctrine respects the right of the agency to complete its work before courts intervene and use judicial resources that may be unnecessary. The exhaustion doctrine respects the right of the agency to correct its own mistakes before courts intervene. The ripeness doctrine respects the need of the courts to have the issues in the case sufficiently developed for judicial review. However, these doctrines do not have clear boundaries; there is overlap.

1. *Statute of Limitations*

First, as you know from your other courses, Congress uses statutes of limitations to limit the length of time for a plaintiff to file a lawsuit. The purpose of any statute of limitations is to bar the assertion of stale claims, because of the difficulty involved in asserting, and defending, a legal claim after a substantial lapse of time from the date of accrual.

As always, check the enabling act first. Many acts include statutes of repose, limiting the time to file an action against an agency to sixty days. If the enabling act does not include a limitation, you'll need to find a default. The APA does not include a statute of limitations. But there is a general statute of limitation for non-tort actions against the government. It provides, "[E]very civil action commenced against the United States shall be barred unless the complaint is filed within six years after *the right of action first accrues*."[40] The Supreme Court recently interpreted the italicized language to mean that a right (or cause) of action accrues when the plaintiff has a right to file a lawsuit and obtain relief, not when the agency action is final.[41]

2. Finality

Second, courts only review decisions that are *final* because the function of a reviewing court is to *review* not to *decide* issues.[42] Finality is a common law doctrine derived from Article III's case or controversy requirement. It was codified in section 704 of the APA, which provides that "*final* agency action for which there is no other adequate remedy" is subject to judicial review.[43]

In examining whether an agency action is final, courts focus on two questions: "First, the action must mark the 'consummation' of the agency's decision making process—it must not be of a merely tentative or interlocutory nature. And second, the action must be one by which 'rights or obligations have been determined,' or from which 'legal consequences will flow.' "[44] The first question focuses on the agency's actions to see whether the agency has reached the end of its decision making process. The second question focuses on the impact of that action on the plaintiff; how directly will the complaining plaintiff be affected?

Pursuant to the first question, a court must determine whether the action challenged is the culmination of the agency's process. For adjudication and legislative rulemaking, the question of whether the agency has completed its decision making process is usually clear.

---

[40] 28 U.S.C. § 2401(a).

[41] Corner Post, Inc. v. Bd. of Governors of the Fed. Rsrv. Sys., 144 S. Ct. 2440, 2460 (2024).

[42] *See* Rochester Tel. Corp v. United States, 307 U.S. 125, 131 (1939) (explaining that the finality doctrine is routed in Article III's case or controversy requirement).

[43] APA § 704 (emphasis added).

[44] *Bennett*, 520 U.S. at 177–78 (citations omitted); *accord* Franklin v. Massachusetts, 505 U.S. 788, 797 (1992) (stating that the Court must look to whether the agency has completed its decision making process and whether the result of that process is one that will directly affect the parties).

However, for non-legislative rulemaking, the question of whether the agency has completed its decision making process is more commonly disputed.[45]

Pursuant to the second question, a court must decide whether the agency's action affects the plaintiff in a concrete way. The Supreme Court has provided varying articulations of this question, sometimes requiring that legal consequences flow, more often requiring that the plaintiff suffer some direct effect.[46] Because non-legislative rules generally are not ones from which legal consequences will flow, the Court's articulation may differ depending on the type of action being challenged.

3. *Exhaustion*

The next timing doctrine is exhaustion. For non-APA actions, the common law exhaustion doctrine applies.[47] The common law doctrine provides that courts should not review an agency action unless and until the plaintiff has exhausted any remedies available from the agency itself. There are three exceptions to the common law exhaustion requirement. First, a plaintiff need not exhaust administrative remedies when the administrative remedy would undermine the ability of the courts to provide effective relief.[48] For example, a plaintiff need not exhaust administrative remedies when agency relief will be unreasonably delayed or the injury needs immediate relief if any relief is to be had at all.[49]

---

[45] *Compare*, Nat'l Automatic Laundry & Cleaning Council v. Shultz, 443 F.2d 689, 702 (D.C. Cir. 1971) (holding that an opinion letter was final agency action because the agency head had issued the letter and it applied to an entire industry), *with* Taylor-Callahan-Coleman Cntys. Dist. Adult Prob. Dep't v. Dole, 948 F.2d 953, 960 (5th Cir. 1991) (holding that an opinion letter was not final agency action because the letter was directed only to a particular local government and not to all local governments).

[46] *See, e.g.*, *Bennett*, 520 U.S. at 178 (test whether "rights or obligations have been determined," or from which "legal consequences will flow"); Dalton v. Specter, 511 U.S. 462, 470 (1994) (test whether action "will directly affect the parties"); Darby v. Cisneros, 509 U.S. 137, 144 (1993) (test whether there is "actual, concrete injury"); *Franklin*, 505 U.S. at 797 (test whether agency's action has a "direct effect on" the plaintiff); Abbott Labs v. Gardner, 387 U.S. 136, 149 (1967) (test whether the "effects are felt in a concrete way").

[47] *See, e.g.*, McCarthy v. Madigan, 503 U.S. 140, 145–46 (1992).

[48] *See, e.g.*, Walker v. S. Ry. Co., 385 U.S. 196, 198 (1966) (finding a possible delay of ten years in an administrative proceeding made exhaustion unnecessary).

[49] *See, e.g.*, Bowen v. New York, 476 U.S. 467, 483 (1986) (waiving exhaustion for disability claimants); Moore v. East Cleveland, 431 U.S. 494, 497, n.5 (1977) (determining exhaustion is not required of a criminal defendant when the statute in question did not mandate exhaustion of remedies prior to judicial review).

Second, a plaintiff need not exhaust administrative remedies when the administrative remedy would be inadequate because the agency cannot provide the requested relief.[50]

Third, a plaintiff need not exhaust administrative remedies when the administrative agency is biased or prejudiced against the plaintiff such that exhaustion would be futile.[51]

However, for APA actions, Congress codified the exhaustion doctrine in APA § 704. That section provides:

> Except as otherwise expressly required by statute, agency action otherwise final is final whether or not there has been . . . any form of reconsideration . . . unless the agency otherwise requires by rule and provides that the action meanwhile is inoperative.[52]

Thus, exhaustion is required in two situations only: (1) when a statute expressly requires exhaustion, and (2) when an agency's own rule requires exhaustion *and* the agency stays its action pending the appeal.[53] Note that under § 704, exhaustion is the exception, whereas at common law, exhaustion is required.

Finally, while the Court has not yet said so explicitly, the exceptions to the common law exhaustion doctrine likely do not apply to lawsuits brought under the APA because § 704 does not include any such exceptions.

4. *Ripeness*

The fourth timing doctrine is ripeness, which differs from exhaustion. Exhaustion is the appropriate doctrine to apply when a plaintiff could have tried to address his or her concerns with the agency directly but chose not to. In contrast, ripeness is the appropriate doctrine to apply when there was no way for the plaintiff to address his or her concerns with the agency first, such as when a final regulation is challenged pre-enforcement.

Unlike finality and exhaustion, the ripeness doctrine is not codified in the APA. Hence, its development and application come

---

[50] *McCarthy*, 503 U.S. at 156–58 (Rehnquist, J., concurring) (stating that exhaustion should not be required when the petitioner sought monetary damages that the agency had no authority to grant); *Moore*, 431 U.S. at 497, n.5 (concluding it would be "wholly inappropriate" to require criminal defendants to exhaust administrative remedies).

[51] Houghton v. Shafer, 392 U.S. 639, 640 (1968) (stating that requiring exhaustion would be a futile act).

[52] APA § 704.

[53] *See Darby*, 509 U.S. at 148 (holding that the plaintiff did not need to exhaust administrative remedies because neither the relevant statute nor the regulation required exhaustion).

from case law. Ripeness issues usually arise when a plaintiff challenges an agency rulemaking, rather than adjudication, and seeks pre-enforcement review.

To determine whether a case is ripe, a court must "evaluate both [1] the fitness of the issues for judicial decision and [2] the hardship to the parties of withholding court consideration."[54] The first factor requires the court to determine whether the issues are legal or factual questions; legal questions do not benefit from further factual development. The second factor requires the court to determine whether the plaintiff will actually be harmed if judicial review is delayed.

Applying these factors, courts typically find cases to be ripe when plaintiffs challenge agency regulations that require entities to change their behavior, to comply with new duties, or to abide by new restrictions.[55] In contrast, when agency regulations do not require regulated entities to make immediate changes, courts typically find challenges to them unripe.[56]

5. Timing Requirements: Summary

Finality, exhaustion, and ripeness are related doctrines, resolution of which turns on the consideration of similar factors; hence, courts sometimes carelessly interchange them. However, their focus is different; understanding these differences will help you keep them straight on your exam.

Finality focuses on whether the agency has finished its work so that the records will be complete and the judiciary will not waste its time on moot issues. The beneficiary of finality is the court because finality ensures that the court will have a complete record and a non-mooted case before it.

Exhaustion focuses on whether there are means of review or redress available within the agency. The beneficiary of exhaustion is the agency because exhaustion ensures that the agency's internal review processes will be followed before the courts intrude into the process.

Ripeness focuses on the issues to be decided and the degree to which those issues have reached the state of development and refinement that will permit a court to make a decision about their

[54] *Abbott Labs,* 387 U.S. at 149.

[55] *See, e.g., Id.* at 149; *Nat'l Automatic Laundry*, 443 F.2d at 689 (finding ripe a challenge to an agency opinion letter regarding hour and wage requirements).

[56] *See, e.g.*, Toilet Goods Ass'n v. Gardner, 387 U.S. 158, 160–61 (1967); Florida Power & Light Co. v. EPA, 145 F.3d 1414, 1421 (D.C. Cir. 1998) (finding unripe challenges to an agency's interpretation of its authority, which were contained in a preamble to a proposed rulemaking).

legality. The beneficiary of ripeness is the court, because ripeness protects the court from inserting itself into a speculative or abstract question.

AVAILABILITY CHECKLIST

A. **Jurisdiction—**

1. Does the enabling act give federal courts jurisdiction?

   a. **No**—If no, then jurisdiction must be found based on the federal question statute, 28 U.S.C. § 1331. The APA does not provide jurisdiction. To determine whether the federal question statute applies, proceed to A.1.2. below.

   b. **Yes**—If yes, then the court has jurisdiction. To see if the plaintiff has a cause of action, proceed to B. below.

2. Does the plaintiff allege a claim that "aris[es] under the Constitution, law, or treaties of the United States"?

   a. **No**—If no, then the court does not have jurisdiction. Stop here. But this answer is likely wrong because most challenges to agency action will involve questions about federal law.

   b. **Yes**—If yes, then the court has jurisdiction. To see if the plaintiff has a cause of action proceed to B. below.

B. **Cause of Action—**

1. Does the enabling act provide that "anyone adversely affected by the agency's action may file an action challenging its validity" or otherwise provide a cause of action?

   a. **No**—If no, then the enabling act does not provide a cause of action. To see if the APA provides a cause of action, proceed to B.2. below.

   b. **Yes**—If yes, then the plaintiff has a cause of action. To see if the plaintiff has standing proceed to C. below.

2. Does APA § 702 provide the plaintiff with a cause of action?

   a. **Agency Action**—Did the agency either act in a discrete manner or fail to act when required to act?

      i. **No**—If no, then there is no agency action. The court cannot hear the case. Stop here.

ii. **Yes**—If yes, then there was agency action. To determine whether the statute precludes review implicitly or explicitly, proceed to B.2.b. below.

b. **Statutory Preclusion**—

i. Does the statute explicitly preclude the court from reviewing plaintiff(s)'s claim?

(a). **No**—If no, then Congress did not explicitly preclude review. To determine whether Congress implicitly precluded review, proceed to B.2.b.ii. below.

(b). **Yes**—If yes, then the court cannot hear the case. Stop here. But this answer is likely wrong because Congress rarely precludes review explicitly.

ii. Does the statute implicitly preclude the court from reviewing plaintiff(s)'s claim by providing for appellate review after agency proceedings of some claims?

(a). **No**—If no, then Congress did not implicitly preclude review. To determine whether the issue is committed to agency discretion, proceed to B.2.c. below.

(b). **Yes**—If yes, then ask (1) would a finding of preclusion foreclose all meaningful judicial review, (2) is the federal suit wholly collateral to a statute's review provisions, and (3) are the claims outside of the agency's expertise?

— **Yes**—If you answered yes to any of these questions, then Congress likely did not implicitly preclude review, although whether meeting one factor is sufficient to overcome preclusion is currently unclear. To determine whether the issue is committed to agency discretion, proceed to B.2.c. below.

— **No**—If you answered no to all the questions, then Congress precluded review, and the district court cannot hear the case. Stop here.

c. **Committed to Agency Discretion**—Does the act provide meaningful standards with which to measure the agency's action?

i. **No**—If no, then Congress committed this particular decision to the agency's discretion, and the court cannot hear the case (assuming that is the only challenge). Stop here. But this answer is likely wrong because judicial review is preferred.

ii. **Yes**—If yes, then the plaintiff has a cause of action that the court can hear. To determine whether the plaintiff(s) has standing, proceed to C. below.

C. Standing—

1. **Prudential Standing**—Is the plaintiff an association suing on behalf of the public rather than for its own personal injury?

a. **No**—If no, then plaintiff must be suing directly (whether it is the association suing for its own harm or a plaintiff suing for his/her/its own harm). Associational standing is irrelevant. To determine whether the plaintiff has constitutional standing, proceed to C.2. below.

b. **Yes**—If yes, then the plaintiff must meet the associational standing requirements. Proceed to C.1.c. below.

c. **Associational Standing—**

i. Assuming an association is suing, does the lawsuit relate to the purposes of the association?

(a). **No**—If no, then the association has no prudential standing. Stop here. But this answer is likely wrong because associations generally only sue for issues related to their mission.

(b). **Yes**—If yes, then the association meets one element of associational standing. To see if the association meets the other elements, proceed to C.1.c.ii. below.

ii. Assuming an association is suing, can the lawsuit proceed without an individual's participation, meaning that the lawsuit is for injunctive or declaratory relief only?

(a). **No**—If no, then the association has no standing pursuant to prudential standing. Stop here. But this answer is likely wrong because associations generally only sue for declaratory and injunctive relief.

(b). **Yes**—If yes, then the association meets another element of associational standing. To see if the association meets the remaining element, proceed to C.1.c.iii. below.

iii. Assuming an association is suing, does one member have constitutional standing, meaning injury in fact, causation, and redressability? (You will need to work through C.2. below, then return here).

(a). **No**—If no, then the association has no standing pursuant to prudential standing, and the court cannot hear the case. Stop here.

(b). **Yes**—If yes, then the association meets the prudential standing requirements. To see if the plaintiff meets the statutory standing requirements, proceed to C.3. below.

2. Constitutional Standing—

a. Injury in Fact—Can the plaintiff show a unique injury?

i. Does the plaintiff allege that he or she would be directly injured economically (*e.g.*, by a fine) or physically by the agency?

(a). **No**—If no, then the plaintiff must be alleging an indirect injury. Proceed to C.2.a.ii. below.

(b). **Yes**—If yes, then the plaintiff has an injury in fact that is concrete and particularized, which is one element of constitutional standing. To determine whether plaintiff can show causation, proceed to C.2.b. below.

ii. Does the plaintiff allege only that he or she suffered a procedural injury, meaning the agency failed to follow a legally required procedure?

(a). **No**—If no, then plaintiff must be alleging a different indirect injury. Proceed to C.2.a.iii. below.

(b). **Yes**—If yes, the plaintiff does not have injury in fact, which is one element of constitutional standing, and the court cannot hear the case. Stop here.

iii. Does the plaintiff allege that he or she suffered an informational injury, meaning the agency failed to disclose information *it was required* to disclose to this plaintiff?

(a). **No**—If no, then to see if plaintiff must be alleging a different indirect injury, proceed to C.2.a.iv. below.

(b). **Yes**—If yes, then plaintiff has injury in fact. To determine whether plaintiff can show causation, proceed to C.2.b. below.

iv. Does the plaintiff allege that he or she suffered a recreational, aesthetic, or environmental injury?

(a). **No**—If no, then the plaintiff does not have injury in fact, which is one element of constitutional standing. Stop here. This answer is likely wrong; plaintiff more likely is alleging one of the injuries above.

(b). **Yes**—If yes, then ask whether the plaintiff can show concrete plans to visit the location or see the area to be harmed in the near future?

— **No**—If no, then the plaintiff does not have injury in fact, which is one element of constitutional standing, and the court cannot hear the case. Stop here.

— **Yes**—If yes, then plaintiff has injury in fact. To see if the plaintiff can show causation, proceed to C.2.b. below.

b. **Causation**—Can the plaintiff show that the alleged illegal action by the agency caused the plaintiff's harm?

i. **No**—If no, then the harm was likely caused by a third party, and plaintiff cannot show causation, which is one element of constitutional standing, and the court cannot hear the case. Stop here.

ii. **Yes**—If yes, then the plaintiff can show causation. To determine whether plaintiff can show redressability, proceed to C.2.c. below.

c. **Redressability**—Can the plaintiff show that a favorable decision will remedy the plaintiff's harm?

i. **No**—If no, then the harm cannot be remedied by the agency, and the plaintiff cannot show redressability, which is one element of constitutional standing. The court cannot hear the case. Stop here.

ii. **Yes**—If yes, the plaintiff can show redressability, which is one element of constitutional standing. To determine whether plaintiff meets statutory standing requirements, proceed to C.3. below.

3. **Statutory Standing (Zone of Interests)**—Is plaintiff suing pursuant to APA § 702?

a. **No**—If no, then the plaintiff must be suing pursuant to the enabling act, the zone of interest requirement does not apply because the plaintiff must be within the protection of the relevant act. To determine whether plaintiff's lawsuit meets the timing requirements, proceed to D. below.

b. **Yes**—If yes, then the plaintiff must demonstrate that he/she/it is "arguably" within the zone of interests the specific statute was meant to protect. Can plaintiff meet this burden?

i. **No**—If no, then the plaintiff cannot meet statutory standing requirements. The court cannot hear the case. Stop here.

ii. **Yes**—If yes, the plaintiff can meet the statutory standing requirements. To determine whether plaintiff's lawsuit meets the timing requirements, proceed to D. below.

D. **Timing**—

1. Assuming the enabling act does not include a limitations period, ask whether the plaintiff's action is barred by the six-year statute of limitations in 28 U.S.C. § 2401(a)? (Consider whether the plaintiff was harmed in the preceding six years, not whether the agency's action occurred in the last six years.).

a. **No**—If no, then to determine whether now is the appropriate time for a court to hear the plaintiff's claim, proceed to D.2. below.

b. **Yes**—If yes, then the statute of limitations bars the case from being heard, and the court must dismiss it. Stop here.

2. Is the plaintiff suing pursuant to APA § 704?

   a. **No**—If no, then the *common law* doctrines of finality, exhaustion, and ripeness may apply. Stop here and apply those doctrines. But in an Administrative Law course, it is more likely that you will be tested on these doctrines as codified in APA § 704.

   b. **Yes**—If yes, then to determine whether now is the appropriate time for a court to hear the plaintiff's claim, proceed to D.3. below.

3. **Finality**—Has the agency completed its consideration of the issue?

   a. Is the action the culmination of the agency's decision making process?

      i. **No**—if no, then the agency's action is not final, and the court cannot hear the case at this time. Stop here.

      ii. **Yes**—If yes, then the agency's action meets one of the finality elements. To determine whether the case meets both elements, proceed to D.3.b. below.

   b. Is the agency action one from which "rights or obligations have been determined,' or from which 'legal consequences will flow?' "

      i. **No**—if no, then the agency's action is not final, and the court cannot hear the case at this time. Stop here.

      ii. **Yes**—If yes, then the agency's action is final. To see if the plaintiff meets the exhaustion requirements, proceed to D.4. below.

4. **Exhaustion**—If the plaintiff is suing under the APA, must the plaintiff appeal to the agency before suing?

   a. Does the enabling act expressly require the plaintiff to exhaust administrative remedies?

      i. **No**—If no, then APA § 704 does not require the plaintiff to exhaust administrative remedies. To determine whether a regulation requires the plaintiff to exhaust administrative remedies, proceed to D.4.b. below.

ii. **Yes**—If yes, then, under APA § 704, the plaintiff must exhaust administrative remedies prior to filing suit. You may wish to note here that the common law exceptions to exhaustion likely to do not apply because Congress did not codify them within APA § 704. Stop here.

b. Does the agency's own regulation expressly require the plaintiff to exhaust administrative remedies and stay its action pending administrative appeal?

i. **No**—If no, then APA § 704 does not require the plaintiff to exhaust administrative remedies. To determine whether the action is ripe, proceed to D.5. below.

ii. **Yes**—If yes, then, under APA § 704, the plaintiff must exhaust administrative remedies prior to filing suit. You may wish to note here that the common law exceptions to exhaustion likely to do not apply because Congress did not codify them within APA § 704. Stop here.

5. Ripeness—Is the case sufficiently developed for judicial review?

a. Does the case involve purely legal issues?

i. **No**—If no, then the case is not ripe, and the court should not hear it at this time. Stop here.

ii. **Yes**—If yes, then the case meets one of the ripeness elements. To determine whether the case meets both elements, proceed to D.5.b. below.

b. Will the plaintiff actually be harmed if judicial review is delayed?

i. **No**—If no, then the case is not ripe, and the court should not hear it at this time. Stop here.

ii. **Yes**—If yes, then the case is ripe for judicial review. To determine the appropriate standard of review the court will apply, proceed to Chapter 7.

ILLUSTRATIVE PROBLEMS

■ PROBLEM 6.1 ■

Environmental and other public interest groups can sue on behalf of their members' injuries. What must such a group show to establish standing?

Analysis

The issue in this problem is how to establish associational standing. Using the checklist above (C.), you should ask (1) whether the lawsuit relates to the purposes of the association; (2) whether the lawsuit can proceed without an individual's participation, meaning that the lawsuit is for injunctive or declaratory relief only; and whether one member would have constitutional standing, meaning injury in fact, causation, and redressability. The member's required injury need not be financial, but can involve injury to environmental, aesthetic, or recreational interests.

■ PROBLEM 6.2 ■

Assume that Congress authorized the Department of Education (DOE) to administer a new federal student loan program. The DOE promulgated regulations using notice-and-comment procedures that were in effect for twenty years. These original regulations defined student eligibility. DOE has decided to change the eligibility requirements, which will make it more difficult for students to obtain student loans in the future. Specifically, DOE plans to lower the amount of family income a student may have access to before that student may qualify for a loan. DOE issues the new regulation after notice-and-comment. All loans already awarded will continue in force. After the notice-and-comment period, the DOE promulgates the new regulation, which will take effect the following year.

A student received a loan under DOE's original regulations. That loan will continue without change. But if the student were to apply for another loan, the student would be denied because his family income would be too high to qualify. The student sues to enjoin the DOE from enforcing its new regulation, claiming that DOE has misinterpreted language in the statute. Would judicial review be available? The statute is silent regarding exhaustion, and there are no relevant agency rules on exhaustion.

Analysis

The issue in this problem is whether the student meets all of the availability requirements. Using the checklist above (A.1.), you should ask first whether a federal court would have jurisdiction over this particular claim. In this case, the relevant statute does not appear to grant the federal court jurisdiction, the APA does not grant jurisdiction; hence, jurisdiction must be found based on the federal question statute, 28 U.S.C. § 1331. The student is alleging a claim that arises under a statute of the United States, the federal student loan program; thus, the court would have jurisdiction.

Second, you should determine whether the enabling act gives the student the right to sue ("a cause of action") (B.). Here, the enabling act does not provide that anyone adversely affected by the agency's action may file an action challenging its validity or otherwise provide a cause of action; hence, you should turn to the APA to see if it provides the plaintiff with a cause of action. To determine whether the APA § 702 provides the student with a cause of action, you should determine that the agency acted in a discrete manner. You conclude it did so; it issued a regulation. Therefore, there was agency action. Next, you would note that there are no facts suggesting that the enabling act either explicitly or implicitly precludes judicial review. Finally, you would note that there are no facts suggesting that the act does not provide meaningful standards with which to measure the agency's action, meaning Congress did not commit this particular decision to the agency's discretion. Thus, the plaintiff likely has a cause of action under the APA.

Third, you must determine whether the student has standing to bring this claim: prudential, constitutional, and statutory (C.). The student is not an association, so associational standing requirements are not applicable, and the grievance is particularized.

As for constitutional standing, the student must demonstrate injury in fact, causation, and redressability. In this case, while the student has not yet been harmed by the regulation, were it to be enacted, the student would be economically harmed because the amount of his federal aid would likely be reduced. Injury in fact is thus met. Moreover, the student would likely be able to show that by changing the eligibility requirements, the DOE's allegedly illegal action will cause the harm and that a favorable decision would remedy the plaintiff's harm. The agency is causing the harm, not a third party. Hence, constitutional standing is likely met.

As for statutory standing, the student is likely able to demonstrate that he or she is *arguably* within the zone of interests of the federal student loan program statute. Hence, statutory standing is likely met.

Fourth, you must determine whether the student can bring this particular claim at this particular time (D.). The statute of limitations is not an issue because the student would be filing within the six-year window.

The student would be suing pursuant to the APA, so section 704's finality and exhaustion requirements apply (ripeness is a common law doctrine and also applies). Regarding finality, a final regulation is the culmination of the agency's decision making process and the change in the eligibility change is one from which rights will be determined or legal consequences will flow. Hence, finality is met. Regarding exhaustion, the statute does not require the student to exhaust administrative remedies, and there is no relevant administrative regulation. Hence, exhaustion is met.

Regarding ripeness, you must analyze (1) whether the plaintiff's claims are purely legal, and (2) whether the plaintiff would be harmed if judicial review were delayed. Here, the student's claims involve purely legal issues, namely the interpretation of language in the statute. No factual development is necessary to resolve that question. However, delay will not harm the student. This suit would involve pre-enforcement review because the regulation is not yet in effect. Here, the student has not yet applied for a loan and been denied. The student may never apply for the loan. Hence, the case is not yet ripe, and the court should not hear it at this time.

POINTS TO REMEMBER

- Judicial review is not always available, due to certain judge-made doctrines and constitutional limitations.
- Courts must have jurisdiction over the plaintiff's claim. Such jurisdiction comes from the agency's enabling act or from the federal question statute (28 U.S.C. § 1331). It does not come from the APA.
- The enabling act may provide plaintiff with a cause of action. If it does not include one, the APA does.
- Congress can preclude review, explicitly or implicitly.
- Congress may grant agencies complete discretion, in which case courts will have no "law to apply."
- Courts must have jurisdiction over the plaintiff, meaning that the plaintiff must have standing: constitutional, prudential, and statutory.
- For a plaintiff to have constitutional standing, the plaintiff must have an injury in fact, which is concrete and particularized, which is caused by the agency action challenged, and which is redressable by a favorable court decision.

- For a plaintiff to have prudential standing, the plaintiff must generally assert its own claims and those claims must be particularized.
- An association may assert claims on behalf of its members if one of its members has constitutional standing, the association's purpose are related to the issues, and the lawsuit seeks only declaratory or injunctive relief so that the individual member's participation is unnecessary.
- For a plaintiff to have statutory standing under the APA, the plaintiff must *arguably* be within the zone of interests of the relevant enabling act.
- The six-year default statute of limitations begins to run when the particular plaintiff suffers injury, not when the agency acts.
- Courts only review final agency actions, when administrative remedies have been exhausted (if required) and when the actions are ripe enough to present issues clear enough for judicial resolution.

CHAPTER 7

What Standard of Review Applies?

In the last chapter, you learned about the doctrines limiting a plaintiff's ability to obtain judicial review of an agency's action. In this chapter, you will learn what standard of review a court will apply to resolve a plaintiff's claims assuming the plaintiff is able to get into court. While I cannot guess in advance whether your professor will test you on rulemaking or adjudication, I can virtually guarantee that your professor will test you on the material in this chapter.

To determine the appropriate standard of review, you will need to determine what type of issue the court is reviewing: did the agency decide a question of fact, policy, law, or law application? If the question is one of fact, you must also determine how the agency resolved that issue: using formal or informal procedures.

After you have asked these two questions and determined the appropriate standard of review, you may then need to apply that standard of review to the facts of your case. This latter step is the one that students often omit on their exams. Do not make this mistake.

REVIEW

An agency's decision may be reviewed multiple times. When a court reviews a decision an agency reached as part of a formal adjudication process, for example, that decision may be reviewed three different times. First, the agency may review the administrative law judge's (ALJ) decision during an internal review process, using a *de novo* standard of review. Second, a court of appeals may review the agency's final decision, using any one of the standards of review identified below. Third, the Supreme Court may review the appellate court's decision. This chapter addresses the second step, when an appellate court reviews an agency's final administrative decision, whether that decision is an order or a rule.

The enabling act may provide the standard of review. Check there first. If the act does not include a standard of review, then APA § 706 contains default standard of review provisions. We will explore these provisions below.

As noted above, the applicable standard of review under § 706 depends on the issue, or question, the agency resolved. There are four such questions: (1) questions of fact; (2) questions of discretion or policy; (3) questions of law; and (4) mixed questions of law and fact (otherwise known as questions of law application).[1]

A. Defining Questions of Fact & Policy

1. Questions of Fact

A question of fact is one in which the resolution of the question does not require an application of or knowledge of the law. The finding "is an assertion that a phenomenon has happened or is or will be happening independent of or anterior to any assertion as to its legal effect."[2] Findings of fact answer questions about who did what, to whom, and with what effect.

Let's consider a finding of fact made in a non-agency setting: a car accident. Assume that during the investigation, the accident investigator noted that the skid marks on the pavement were forty-six feet long. This would be a finding of fact. The law is irrelevant.

Now let's turn to the agency setting. Agencies make factual determinations regularly. For example, an agency may have to determine whether a pesticide is dangerous. An agency may have to determine whether an employee was fired as she claimed or quit as her employer claimed. These are questions of fact. Agencies answer these questions by making findings.

What is the scope of review for a court reviewing an agency's finding of fact? APA § 706 provides the standards for judicial review. First, the reviewing courts shall hold unlawful *all* agency findings and conclusions that are arbitrary, capricious, an abuse of discretion, or otherwise not in accordance with law."[3] Additionally, for cases subject to APA § 556 or § 557 (formal rulemaking and adjudication), courts must determine whether the findings are supported by substantial evidence.[4] Hence, courts apply (1) the substantial evidence standard for findings of fact made during proceedings brought under § 556 and § 557, and (2) the arbitrary and capricious

---

1 APA § 706.

2 LOUIS L. JAFFE, JUDICIAL CONTROL OF ADMINISTRATIVE ACTION 548 (1965).

3 APA § 706(2)(A).

4 APA § 706(2)(E).

standard for findings of fact made during all other proceedings. Notice that the appropriate standard of review turns on the procedure the agency used to resolve the question of fact.

2. *Questions of Policy & Discretion*

A question of policy involves an agency's application of the law to facts, usually made during rulemaking. Questions of policy generally arise during rulemakings rather than during adjudications because the relevant facts are not judicial facts (*e.g.*, who said what, did what, and did it when); rather, the relevant facts are legislative in nature (*e.g.*, how much of a pesticide should be prohibited to make food safe?).

Often, policy questions involve complex and controverted scientific and technical issues. For example, suppose an agency must decide on the location for a new highway, must determine how many parts per million of a certain chemical will be injurious to human health, must identify what kinds of safety features should be required in passenger cars, or must indicate what level of protection should be afforded workers in factories. These questions are all policy questions, involving complex and controverted legislative facts. To resolve such policy questions, the agency must consider the relevant legislative facts in light of its delegated authority, *e.g.* "to make drinking water safe." Commonly, the legislative facts do not clearly point in one direction, so the agency must use its expertise and discretion to determine the best policy choice.

What is the scope of review for a court reviewing an agency's finding of policy? Courts apply the default standard regardless of the formality of the proceeding: arbitrary and capricious review.[5] The next section explains and compares the substantial evidence and arbitrary and capricious standards of review.

B. Standards of Review for Questions of Fact & Policy

1. *Substantial Evidence*

A reviewing court must use the *substantial evidence* standard to review the adequacy of an agency's findings of fact made during *formal* proceedings (adjudications or rulemakings required to be conducted on the record under APA § 556 and § 557).[6] Substantial evidence is commonly thought of as fairly deferential to the agency to recognize that the agency has expertise that the court does not.

---

5 APA § 706(2)(A).

6 APA § 706(2)(E).

Under the substantial evidence standard of review, a reviewing court should not substitute its judgment for that of the agency. The test has been defined as follows:

> [S]ubstantial evidence is more than a mere scintilla. It means such relevant evidence as a reasonable mind might accept as adequate to support a conclusion . . . . [I]t must do more than create a suspicion of the existence of the fact to be established. . . . [I]t must be enough to justify, if the trial were to a jury, a refusal to direct a verdict when the conclusion sought to be drawn from it is one of fact for the jury.[7]

Using this standard, a reviewing court should ask whether a reasonable person could make the same finding that the agency made after reviewing the evidence in the record (remember that formal agency proceedings must be "on the record"). The court should examine each of the agency's findings of fact to see if there is evidence in the record to support that finding. In doing so, the court must consider not only the evidence supporting the agency's findings but also any evidence that "fairly detracts" from that finding.[8] A reviewing court's job is to decide whether the agency's findings are well-reasoned, not whether those findings are correct.

2. *Arbitrary & Capricious*

Courts use substantial evidence standard to review the sufficiency of findings of fact made during *formal* proceedings. For reviewing the sufficiency of findings of fact made during *non-formal* proceedings and findings of policy made during either type of proceeding, the APA provides that the reviewing court shall hold unlawful and set aside agency findings that are "arbitrary, capricious, [or] an abuse of discretion."[9] These three terms do not have independent significance; rather, combined, they are understood to mean arbitrary and capricious review. An agency finding is arbitrary or capricious when it is not "reasonable and reasonably explained."[10] While a court cannot substitute its judgment for the agency, the court must ensure that the agency "has offered 'a satisfactory explanation for its action[,] including a rational connection between the facts found and the choice made.' "[11]

---

7 Universal Camera Corp. v. NLRB, 340 U.S. 474, 477 (1951) (internal citations omitted).

8 *Id.* at 487.

9 APA § 706(2)(A).

10 FCC v. Prometheus Radio Project, 592 U.S. 414, 423 (2021).

11 Ohio v. EPA, 144 S. Ct. 2040, 2053 (2024) (quoting Motor Vehicle Mfrs. Assn. v. State Farm Mut. Auto. Ins. Co., 463 U.S. 29, 43 (1983)).

Historically, the arbitrary and capricious standard of review was viewed as providing overwhelming deference to agency findings. However, the Supreme Court gave the standard unexpected teeth in *Citizens to Preserve Overton Park, Inc. v. Volpe,*[12] describing it in the following way:

> To make [a finding that the actual choice made was not "arbitrary, capricious, an abuse of discretion, or otherwise not in accordance with law"] the court must consider whether the decision was based on a consideration of the relevant factors and whether there has been a clear error of judgment. Although this inquiry into the facts is to be searching and careful, the ultimate standard of review is a narrow one. The court is not empowered to substitute its judgment for that of the agency.[13]

Thus, using arbitrary and capricious review, courts must review the administrative record that was before the agency when it made its findings to determine whether "the decision was based on a consideration of the relevant factors and whether there has been a clear error of judgment."[14]

In *Motor Vehicles Manufacturers Ass'n v. State Farm Mutual Automobile Insurance Co.*,[15] the Supreme Court reviewed an agency's policy findings (that air bags and automatic seatbelts would not save enough lives to justify their cost). In doing so, the Court further explained the arbitrary and capricious standard of review:

> [T]he agency must examine the relevant data and articulate a satisfactory explanation for its action including a rational connection between the facts found and the choice made. In reviewing that explanation, we must consider whether the decision was based on a consideration of the relevant factors and whether there has been a clear error of judgment. Normally, an agency rule would be arbitrary and capricious if the agency has relied on factors which Congress has not intended it to consider, entirely failed to consider an important aspect of the problem, offered an explanation for its decision that runs counter to the evidence before the agency, or is so implausible that it could not be ascribed to a difference in view or the product of agency expertise.[16]

---

[12] 401 U.S. 402 (1971).

[13] *Id.* at 416 (quoting APA § 706(A)(2)).

[14] *Id.*

[15] 463 U.S. 29 (1983).

[16] *Id.* at 43 (citations omitted).

In other words, "[the rule must be] the product of reasoned decisionmaking."[17]

Today, arbitrary and capricious review is also known as *hard look* review. Originally, hard look review focused on the competency of the agency's review of the record before it, not the appellate court's review of the agency's decision. As Judge Leventhal explained, hard look review meant that a court would overturn agency decisions "if the court [became] aware . . . that the agency ha[d] not really taken a 'hard look' at the salient problems and ha[d] not genuinely engaged in reasoned decisionmaking."[18] Today, as a result of *Overton Park* and *State Farm*, hard look review requires that a court ensure not only that the agency took a hard look at the problem but that the court itself take a hard look at the agency's resolution of that problem.

The Supreme Court recently sharpened the teeth of this standard. In *Ohio v. EPA*, the Court held that the EPA acted arbitrarily when it failed to offer a reasoned response to significant comments in the rulemaking proceeding.[19] The Court described this standard as follows:

> An agency action qualifies as "arbitrary" or "capricious" if it is not "reasonable and reasonably explained." In reviewing an agency's action under that standard, a court may not " 'substitute its judgment for that of the agency.' " But it must ensure, among other things, that the agency has offered "a satisfactory explanation for its action[,] including a rational connection between the facts found and the choice made." Accordingly, an agency cannot simply ignore "an important aspect of the problem."[20]

3. Arbitrary & Capricious Review v. Substantial Evidence Review

Both the substantial evidence and the arbitrary and capricious standards are framed in terms of the reasonableness of the agency's reasoning process. Hence, it is unclear whether these two standards reflect different levels of review. Indeed, while a circuit judge, former Justice Scalia claimed that the two standards were essentially identical because "it is impossible to conceive of a non-arbitrary

---

17 *Id.* at 52.

18 Greater Boston Television v. FCC, 444 F.2d 841, 851 (D. C. Cir. 1970).

19 *Ohio*, 144 S. Ct. at 2054 ("Although commenters posed this concern to EPA during the notice and comment period . . . EPA offered no reasoned response."); *accord* Perez v. Mortgage Bankers Ass'n, 575 U.S. 92, 96 (2015) ("An agency must consider and respond to significant comments received during the period for public comment.").

20 *Id.* at 18 (internal citations omitted).

factual judgment supported only by evidence that is not substantial in the APA sense."[21] While the Supreme Court has never clearly addressed whether the two standards differ, the Court applied arbitrary and capricious review in *State Farm* even though the relevant enabling act expressly provided that the agency's findings had to be supported by "[s]ubstantial evidence on the record considered as a whole."[22] Some scholars suggest that this choice shows that the Court does not believe that these standards differ at all.

Other scholars argue that the standards are different; substantial evidence requires the court to conduct a slightly more searching inquiry. There is support for this argument; after all, Congress specifically identified two different standards in the APA. Moreover, Congress sometimes requires the substantial evidence standard in an act when the arbitrary and capricious standard would be the default under the APA. In sum, we do not yet know whether the two standards truly reflect different intensity standards, but we do know the two standards are described differently. Be sure you use the correct description.

C. Defining Questions of Law & Mixed Questions

1. Questions of Law

Assuming the issue to be resolved is not a question of fact or a question of policy, then it must be either a question of law or a mixed question. A statement of law is an assertion about legal effect that can be advanced with no knowledge of the facts in a particular case. Thus, a pure question of law is one in which the resolution of the question does not require any knowledge of the facts.

Let's return to our non-agency example, a car accident. During the investigation, the accident investigator noted that the speed limit was thirty mph on the road where the accident took place. This would be a finding of law. The facts are irrelevant.

Now, let's return to agencies. Agencies often resolve questions of law, such as determining what language in a statute or regulation means. Assume that an agency must interpret language in its enabling act to determine the boundaries of the authority Congress delegated to it. For example, the Food and Drug Administration had to determine whether tobacco was a *drug* or *drug delivery device*, while the Treasury Department had to determine whether health

21 Ass'n of Data Processing Serv. Orgs. v. Bd. of Governors of Fed. Reserve Sys., 745 F.2d 677, 683 (D.C. Cir. 1984).

22 *State Farm*, 463 U.S. at 44 (quoting S. Rep. No. 1301, 89th Cong., 2d Sess., 8 (1966); H. R. Rep. No. 1776, 89th Cong., 2d Sess., 21 (1966)).

care exchanges *established by the federal government* can also be established by a state (true story). In both situations, the question to be answered was one of law. Facts were irrelevant.

In a moment, we will focus on the standards of review that courts apply when agencies resolve pure questions of law (you will not be surprised to learn that there is more than one standard). But we must first cover another type of question that agencies resolve, questions of law application, or mixed questions of law and fact.

2. *Mixed Questions/Questions of Law Application*

Mixed questions of law and fact, or application questions, occur during adjudication. Let's once again return to our car accident example. Assume the investigator concluded that the defendant must have exceeded the speed limit because the skid marks were unusually long. Such a question involves applying the relevant law (the speed limit) to the specific facts in a particular case (the unusually long skid marks) to reach a conclusion (the defendant was speeding). This question is a mixed question of law and fact.

Let's turn back to the world of agencies. During adjudications, agencies must determine whether a particular law applies to a given set of facts. For example, in one case, an agency had to determine whether people who deliver newspapers were employees of a particular newspaper or were independent contractors.[23] In another case, an agency had to decide whether the refusal of an employer to bargain with its employees constituted an unfair labor practice. These are mixed questions: the agency had to consider both the facts and the law to resolve the questions.

D. Standards of Review for Mixed Questions & Pure Questions of Law

1. *Mixed Questions of Law & Fact*

The appropriate standard applicable to mixed questions of law and fact is currently unclear. Some courts accept an agency's resolution of a mixed question if the resolution has "warrant in the record" and "a reasonable basis in the law."[24] Some courts treat the mixed question as a pure question of law,[25] while others treat mixed question as one of fact.[26] Finally, some courts break the mixed

---

[23] *See, e.g.*, NLRB v. Hearst Publ'n, Inc., 322 U.S. 111 (1944).

[24] *Id.* at 131.

[25] Packard Motor Car Co. v. NLRB, 330 U.S. 485, 493 (1947).

[26] *See, e.g.*, O'Leary v. Brown-Pacific-Maxon, Inc., 340 U.S. 504, 507 (1951) (treating as a question of fact the issue of whether the death of a federal worker "arose out of and in the course of employment.").

question into its component parts: part law and part fact. To the extent the courts treat the question as one of fact, the standards of review from the preceding section apply. To the extent the courts treat the question as a pure question of law, the standards of review discussed below apply.

2. *Questions of Law*

Agencies most commonly answer questions of law when they interpret statutory language, whether in a statute or a regulation. The appropriate standard courts apply to review agency interpretations has undergone a dramatic shift in the last decade.

For agency interpretations of statutory language, the Supreme Court recently "overruled" a forty-year-old case[27] whose methodology had become known as the *Chevron* doctrine (also the *Chevron* two-step and *Chevron* deference).[28] Hence, the discussion in this edition of this text has been significantly rewritten. However, the prior law is included because courts decided so many cases using the *Chevron* doctrine and because your professor will likely want you to know how the law changed so dramatically.

For agency interpretation of regulations, the Supreme Court in *Kisor v. Wilkie*[29] narrowed the broad deference it had given to agencies in the past. We cover both changes next, starting with agency interpretations of statutory language.

a. Agency Interpretations of Statutory Language

Prior to 2024, courts used two different standards to review agency interpretations of *ambiguous*[30] statutory language. Importantly, the statutory language had to be sufficiently ambiguous for the court to consider the agency's interpretation at all. If Congress was clear (however the court determined clarity), then there was no room for an agency to interpret the statute. This limitation has not changed. What changed is what happens when Congress is not clear.

The two standards courts used prior to 2024 were known as *Chevron* deference and *Skidmore* respect[31] based on the cases in

---

[27] Chevron v. Nat. Res. Def. Council, Inc., 467 U.S. 837 (1984). The word "overruled" is in quotes because the Court did not overrule the holding in the case, just the methodology used in the case.

[28] Loper Bright Enters. v. Raimondo, 144 S. Ct. 2244 (2024).

[29] 588 U.S. 558 (2019).

[30] The label *ambiguous* is inexact. The Court described step one as determining whether "Congress has directly spoken to the precise question at issue." *Chevron*, 467 U.S. at 482.

[31] Sometimes Courts use the term "*Skidmore* deference." But this term is a misnomer. *Skidmore* does not require courts to adopt interpretations with which it disagrees; rather, it instructs courts to respect some agency interpretations.

which the Supreme Court delineated each approach.[32] In 2024, in *Loper Bright Enterprises v. Raimondo*, the Supreme Court overruled *Chevron* deference, reasoning that the doctrine was inconsistent with APA § 706, which requires courts to use independent judgment to determine the meaning of statutory language.[33]

The next section will explain all three doctrines: *Skidmore, Chevron,* and *Loper Bright.* To understand *Loper Bright*, you must first understand *Chevron*, the deference approach *Loper* overruled, and *Skidmore*, the "deference" approach that *Loper Bright* seems to have reinvigorated.

Additionally, there are two other doctrines that may still be relevant despite *Chevron*'s overruling: the *Brand X* doctrine and the major questions doctrine. To understand all of these doctrines, you must first understand the very famous case, used for forty years, whose methodology is no longer valid: *Chevron*.

i. Chevron

Under *Chevron*, courts deferred (notice the use of the past tense here) to agency interpretations of *ambiguous* statutory language when the agency's interpretation was reasonable.[34] The Supreme Court described *Chevron* analysis as having two distinct steps. Pursuant to *Chevron*'s first step, a reviewing court should determine "whether Congress has directly spoken to the precise question at issue."[35] In other words, the court should determine whether congressional intent about the meaning of the language in the statute is clear. In doing so, the court must use the "traditional tools of statutory construction"; step one is not a simple search for textual clarity.[36] At step one, courts did not defer to agency interpretations at all. Rather, "[t]he judiciary [was] the final authority on issues of statutory construction . . . ."[37]

Assuming Congress's intent was not clear at step one, then, at step two, a court was to defer to any *reasonable* agency

---

[32] *Chevron* applied when agencies used *force of law* procedures to interpret statutory language, such as by engaging in formal rulemaking and adjudication and notice-and-comment rulemaking. In contrast, *Skidmore* applied when agencies did not use *force of law* procedures to interpret statutory language, such as by issuing guidance. Christensen v. Harris County, 529 U.S. 576, 587 (2000) (describing which actions received *Chevron* rather than *Skidmore* analysis); Am. Mining Cong. v. MSHA, 995 F.2d 1106, 1109 (D.C. Cir. 1993) (defining "force of law").

[33] *Loper Bright,* 144 S. Ct. at 2263 ("The deference that *Chevron* requires of courts reviewing agency action cannot be squared with the APA.").

[34] 467 U.S. 837 (1984).

[35] *Id.* at 842–43.

[36] *Id.* at 843 n.9.

[37] *Id.* at 843.

interpretation, even if the court believed a different interpretation (policy choice) would be better (hence the use of the term deference).[38]

The Supreme Court justified deferring to reasonable agency interpretations of unclear statutes for three reasons. First, agency personnel are experts in their field while judges are not.[39] Second, Congress cannot legislate every detail in a comprehensive regulatory scheme; thus, gaps and ambiguities are inevitable. By leaving these gaps and ambiguities, Congress impliedly delegated authority to the agency to resolve them.[40] Third, administrative officials, unlike federal judges, have a political constituency to which they are accountable.[41]

Deferring to reasonable agency interpretations at step two was known as *Chevron* deference. The Supreme Court never clearly identified when agency interpretations were *reasonable*. Sometimes, the Court suggested that to be reasonable, the agency's interpretation must not be arbitrary and capricious (the standard for reviewing agency findings of fact and policy).[42] This approach focused on the method the agency used to reach its interpretation. Other times, the Court focused on the correctness of the interpretation using the traditional tools of statutory interpretation.[43]

But it no longer matters whether an agency interpretation is reasonable because in *Loper Bright*, the Court overruled this aspect of *Chevron*.[44] To be precise, the Court rejected only *Chevron*'s second step. The Court did not reject *Chevron*'s first step regardless of what the Court said because *Chevron*'s first step is simply *de novo* review and the *Loper Bright* Court replaced *Chevron* with *de novo* review.[45] So let's turn to *Loper Bright*.

---

[38] *Id*; SAS Inst., Inc. v. Iancu, 584 U.S. 357, 369 (2018) "[Un]der *Chevron*, we owe an agency's interpretation of the law no deference unless, after 'employing traditional tools of statutory construction,' we find ourselves unable to discern Congress's meaning.").

[39] *Chevron*, 467 U.S. at 865.

[40] *Id.* at 843–44.

[41] *Id.* at 866.

[42] *See, e.g.*, Judulang v. Holder, 565 U.S. 42, 52 n.7 (2011) ("Were we to [apply *Chevron*], our analysis would be the same, because under *Chevron* step two, we ask whether an agency interpretation is 'arbitrary or capricious in substance.' ") (citations omitted); Mayo Found. for Med. Educ. & Rsch. v. United States, 562 U.S. 44, 58–60 (2011) (conflating step two and arbitrary and capricious review).

[43] *Chevron*, 467 U.S. at 859–66 (considering text, legislative history, and purpose).

[44] *Loper Bright*, 144 S. Ct. at 2272.

[45] *Id.* at 2261 ("The APA thus codifies for agency cases the unremarkable, yet elemental proposition reflected by judicial practice dating back to Marbury: that courts decide legal questions by applying their own judgment.").

ii. Loper Bright

In 2024, in *Loper Bright*, the Supreme Court held that courts must review agency interpretations of statutory language *de novo*, meaning courts should give no deference to agency interpretations. The Court reasoned that neither the APA nor the U.S. Constitution permits courts to defer to agency interpretations. Consequently, agencies no longer get a "finger[ ] on the scales of justice."[46]

Pursuant to *Loper Bright*, a court applies *de novo* review using the traditional tools of statutory interpretation to determine whether the statute is clear. This approach is required under APA § 706. Depending on the judge's approach to statutory interpretation, these tools include the statute's text, the linguistic and substantive canons, legislative history, and purpose.

As part of the *de novo* review process, the court will consider whether the agency's interpretation is the correct interpretation.[47] Agency "interpretations reached contemporaneously with the [enactment of the] statute at issue, and which have remained consistent over time, may be especially useful in determining the statute's meaning" and are more likely to persuade the court.[48] This approach comes from *Skidmore*, a case that predated *Chevron* and which is described in more detail next.

The Supreme Court in *Loper Bright* did not explain how or in what order a court should apply *de novo* review and the *Skidmore* factors. One possibility, and one that would seem to match the Supreme Court's final approach to *Chevron*'s two steps, is to apply *de novo* review first, then turn to the agency's interpretation if any ambiguity remains. With this approach, *Loper Bright* step one is *de novo* review, while *Loper Bright* step two is respect to persuasive interpretations. To be clear, in *Loper Bright*, the Supreme Court did not talk in step one and step two terms. Rather, the Court presented the analysis as though it were all one giant first step. However, for any analysis, there must be a place to start and a place to end. Conceptually, it makes sense to start with *de novo* review, then bring in the *Skidmore* factors for the hard cases, where Congress has not

---

46 Buffington v. McDonough, 143 S. Ct. 14, 14 (2022) (Gorsuch, J., dissenting).

47 *Loper Bright*, 144 S. Ct. at 2262 ("courts may—as they have from the start—seek aid from the interpretations of those responsible for implementing particular statutes. Such interpretations "constitute a body of experience and informed judgment to which courts and litigants may properly resort for guidance" consistent with the APA.") (quoting *Skidmore* 323 U.S. at 140).

48 *Id.* at 2262.

been clear. But whether the Court will agree with this approach given its similarity to *Chevron*, only time will tell.

We turn now to *Skidmore*'s power-to-persuade test.

iii. Skidmore

Pursuant to *Skidmore*, courts should respect (notice the use of the present tense) agency interpretations of ambiguous statutory language when the agency *persuades* the court that its interpretation is a good one.[49] This is known as the power-to-persuade test. Agency interpretations have the power to persuade when the agency thoroughly considered the issue (focus on the process the agency used), offered valid reasoning for its interpretation (focus on the answer the agency reached), and has consistently interpreted the language (focus on how often the agency has interpreted the language). And *Loper Bright* added two more considerations: the contemporaneousness of the interpretation and the relevance of the agency's expertise.

The Supreme Court called these factors ones "which give [the agency] power to persuade, if lacking power to control."[50] In short, an agency earns judicial respect under *Skidmore* by carefully, thoroughly, and consistently interpreting statutory language within the agency's wheelhouse, especially in close proximity to the statute's enactment. Note that "respecting" an interpretation is not the same as deferring to it. "Respecting" an agency's interpretation means taking it into account but not letting it "supersede . . . the judgment of the Judiciary."[51]

Be aware that *Skidmore*'s lifespan is not linear. It came into being in 1944, disappeared in 1984 when *Chevron* was decided, then reappeared in early 2000 with the Court's development of *Chevron* step zero.[52] Finally, it appears to have made a strong comeback in *Loper Bright*. Time will tell how much continued vitality *Skidmore* will have.

---

[49] Prior to 2024, courts applied *Skidmore* when agencies interpreted statutory language without using "force of law" procedures—for example, in a guidance document or during an informal adjudication. This limitation was colloquially known as *Chevron Step Zero*.

[50] Skidmore v. Swift, 323 U.S. 134, 140 (1944).

[51] *Loper Bright*, 144 S. Ct. at 2258 (" 'Respect,' though, was just that. The views of the Executive Branch could inform the judgment of the Judiciary, but did not supersede it. Whatever respect an Executive Branch interpretation was due, a judge 'certainly would not be bound to adopt the construction given by the head of a department.' ") (quoting Decatur v. Paulding, 39 U.S. 497, 14 Pet. 497, 515 (1840)).

[52] *Christensen*, 529 U.S. at 587. The term—*Chevron* step zero—was coined in a law review article. Cass R. Sunstein, Chevron *Step Zero*, 92 VA. L. REV. 187 (2006).

iv. Brand X

There may be another casualty of *Loper Bright*: the *Brand X*[53] doctrine. *Chevron* had applied when there were no pre-existing judicial interpretations of that same statute. The *Brand X* doctrine applies (or had applied) when a court had already interpreted the statutory language and the agency wanted to interpret the language differently.

Pursuant to *Brand X*, when a court interprets language in a statute before an agency interprets the same language, the agency must interpret the language identically only if the court reasoned that the statute was clear under *Chevron's* first step.[54] If the court held that congressional intent was not clear, then the agency remained free to adopt a different interpretation of that statute so long as its new interpretation was reasonable and its process was not arbitrary and capricious.

But *Brand X* is on shaky footing after *Loper Bright*. In *Loper Bright*, the Court said that *Brand X*'s approach "is the antithesis of the time-honored approach the APA prescribes."[55] Further, *Chevron* no longer applies, although the Court may apply a *Brand X* approach to its new *Loper Bright-Skidmore* test. Hence, it is unclear whether *Brand X* is still relevant.

v. Major Questions Doctrine

But before we leave this topic (judicial review of agency interpretations of statutes), there is one final doctrine we must discuss: the major questions doctrine.

Beginning in 2000, the Supreme Court created an exception to *Chevron* doctrine known as the *extraordinary case* exception. Pursuant to this exception, the Court would refuse to defer to an agency's interpretation of ambiguous statutory language in cases that were *too important* to the national economy.[56] The Court reasoned that in these cases it was unlikely Congress would have impliedly delegated to the agency at all.[57] The Court acknowledged

---

[53] This doctrine was developed in Nat. Cable & Telecoms. Ass'n. v. Brand X Internet Servs., 545 U.S. 967, 982 (2005) (hereinafter *Brand X*).

[54] *Id.* at 982.

[55] *Loper Bright*, 144 S. Ct. at 2265.

[56] FDA v. Brown & Williamson Tobacco Corp., 529 U.S. 120, 159 (2000) (finding the regulation of tobacco to be extraordinary). The Court never clearly explained which cases and topics were "too important" for agency resolution.

[57] King v. Burwell, 576 U.S. 473, 485 (2015) ("In extraordinary cases, however, there may be reason to hesitate before concluding that Congress has intended such an implicit delegation.") (quoting Util. Air Regul. Grp. v. EPA, 573 U.S. 302, 324 (2014)); Whitman v. Am. Trucking Ass'ns, Inc., 531 U.S. 457, 468 (2001) (noting that Congress

that were the case not extraordinary, *Chevron* would have applied. Importantly, this extraordinary case exception was rare: it applied in only a handful of cases for more than twenty years (from 2000 to 2022).

In 2022, however, the Supreme Court reimagined and toughened this doctrine, which is now known as the major questions doctrine. Whereas the Court had generally applied the extraordinary case exception while acknowledging *Chevron*'s applicability,[58] in the major questions cases, the Court ignored *Chevron* entirely. The Court explained that it had created and modified this doctrine to address "a particular and recurring problem: agencies asserting highly consequential power beyond what Congress could reasonably be understood to have granted."[59] In other words, agencies were stepping in to regulate because Congress was unable, and the Court was not pleased.

Like *Chevron*, the major questions doctrine includes two steps. At step one, the court will determine whether the subject matter of an agency's action is of "vast 'economic and political significance.' "[60] If so, then at step two, the court will look for a clear statement from Congress authorizing the agency to regulate (which the Court never seems to find).[61] Thus, when the doctrine applies, the agency's regulation is typically struck down.

The doctrine is a new favorite of the conservatives on the Court. The Supreme Court applied it in four cases in just the first two years of its reimagined existence.[62]

What is unknown at the time this book goes to press is how the major questions doctrine and *Loper Bright*'s *de novo* review will interact. When *Chevron* was still a valid methodology, the major questions doctrine displaced *Chevron* analysis entirely. Likely, courts

---

does not "hide elephants in mouseholes"); Gonzales v. Oregon, 546 U.S. 243, 267 (2006) (finding the regulation of physician-assisted suicide to be extraordinary).

[58] In *Brown & Williamson*, the Court turned to the extraordinary nature of the agency's asserted authority in *Chevron*'s first step. 529 U.S. at 159–60. In contrast, in *UARG*, the Court waited until *Chevron*'s second step to apply the exception. 573 U.S. at 322–24. And in *King*, the Court used the exception to replace both steps in *Chevron*. 576 U.S. at 485.

[59] West Virginia v. EPA, 597 U.S. 697, 724 (2022).

[60] *Id.* at 716 (quoting Util. Air Regul. Grp., 573 U.S. at 324.

[61] *Util. Air Regul. Grp.*, 573 U.S. at 324.

[62] *See, e.g.,* Biden v. Nebraska 600 U.S. 477 (2023) (invalidating the Department of Education's student loan forgiveness program); *West Virginia*, 597 U.S. at 734–35 (invalidating the Environmental Protection Agency's "Clean Power Plan"); Nat. Fed. of Indep. Bus. v. OSHA, 595 U.S. 109, 117–18 (2022) (invalidating Occupational Safety and Health Administration's nationwide vaccine requirement); Ala. Realtors Ass'n v. HHS, 594 U.S. 758, 765 (2022) (invalidating the Center for Disease Control and Prevention's eviction moratorium).

will take the same approach with *Loper Bright*, meaning for those agency interpretations that have "vast economic and political significance," a court will look for a clear statement giving the agency power to regulate. If none is found, the court will strike down the regulation without examining the statute further or considering the agency's regulation at all.

b. Agency Interpretations of Regulatory Language

The Supreme Court has been busy. It did not just alter judicial review of agency interpretations of statutory language. The Court also narrowed another judicial review doctrine: *Auer* deference. In 1945, the Supreme Court held that an agency's interpretation of its own regulation has "controlling weight unless it is plainly erroneous or inconsistent with the regulation."[63] In 1997, after the Court decided *Chevron*, the Court confirmed that the plainly erroneous" deference standard survived *Chevron*;[64] hence, deference to an agency's interpretations of its own regulations is called either *Seminole Rock* (the 1945 case) or *Auer* (the 1997 case) deference.

In 2019, the Supreme Court was poised to overrule *Auer*.[65] Instead, the Court *Chevronized* *Auer*, adding a two-step approach equivalent to *Chevron*'s two steps. First, *Auer* applies only when a regulation is *genuinely ambiguous*, meaning after a court has applied all the traditional tools of interpretation. Second, if ambiguity remains, the agency's interpretation controls only if it is "within the bounds of reasonable interpretation."[66]

Additionally, the Court cabined *Auer* by adding four deference prequalifications. Even reasonable agency interpretations of genuinely ambiguous regulations may not get deference. First, the interpretation must be the agency's authoritative, or official position, rather than an ad hoc statement by lower-level personnel. Second, the interpretation must implicate the agency's area of substantive expertise. Third, the interpretation must reflect the agency's fair and considered judgment; it cannot be advanced as a convenient litigating position or post hoc rationalization. Fourth, the interpretation cannot create *unfair surprise* to those being regulated.[67] Whether *Auer* deference will survive *Loper Bright*'s fallout is unclear.

---

63 Bowles v. Seminole Rock & Sand Co., 325 U.S. 410, 414 (1945).

64 Auer v. Robbins, 519 U.S. 452, 461–63 (1997).

65 The Court accepted certiorari on a case in which the only question the Court wanted argued was whether to overrule *Auer*. Kisor v. Wilkie, 588 U.S. 558 (2019).

66 *Id.* at 573, 576.

67 *Id.* at 573–79.

STANDARD CHECKLIST

A. **Type of Finding/Question:**

1. Is the court reviewing a finding of fact?

   a. **No**—If no, then then to determine whether the court is reviewing a question of policy, of law, or a mixed question, proceed to A.2. below.

   b. **Yes**—If yes, then ask whether the agency made its finding as a part of a *formal* adjudication or rulemaking.

      i. **Yes**—If yes, then the reviewing court will review the agency's finding using the substantial evidence standard. To determine whether the agency applied this standard correctly, proceed to B.1. below.

      ii. **No**—If no, then the reviewing court will review the agency's finding using the arbitrary and capricious standard. To determine whether the agency applied this standard correctly, proceed to B.2. below.

2. Is the court reviewing a finding of policy?

   a. **No**—If no, then to determine whether the court is reviewing a question of law or a mixed question, proceed to A.3. below.

   b. **Yes**—If yes, then the reviewing court will review the agency's finding using the arbitrary and capricious standard regardless of how the agency made its decision. To determine whether the agency applied this standard correctly, proceed to B.2. below.

3. Is the court reviewing a finding of law?

   a. **No**—If no, then the court is reviewing a mixed question. Proceed to A.4. below.

   b. **Yes**—If yes, then ask the following:

      i. Is the agency interpreting language in a constitution or contract?

         (a). Yes—If yes, then the reviewing court will review the language *de novo*, giving the agency's interpretation no extra weight. Stop here.

(b). **No**—If no, then then the reviewing court may give the agency's interpretation some weight. To determine whether the agency applied this standard correctly, proceed to A.3.b.ii.

ii. Is the agency interpreting language in its own regulation?

(a). **Yes**—If yes, then to determine whether the *Auer* doctrine applies, proceed to B.5. below.

(b). **No**—If no, then the agency must be interpreting statutory language. To determine whether the agency's interpretation receives deference, proceed to A.3.b.iii. below.

iii. Is the agency interpreting language in a statute that the agency administers?

(a). **No**—If no, then the reviewing court will review the language *de novo*, giving the agency's interpretation no deference. Stop here.

(b). **Yes**—If yes, then apply the major questions analysis to see whether the court will give the agency's interpretation any weight. Proceed to B.3. below.

4. Is the court reviewing a mixed finding of law and fact (law application)?

a. **No**—If no, then return to A.1. You have made an error.

b. **Yes**—If yes, then follow the analysis for findings of fact (A.1.) for that portion of the finding and follow the analysis for findings of law (A.3.) for that portion of the finding.

B. **Standards of Review:** Apply the appropriate standard of review to determine the validity of the agency's finding.

1. If the **substantial evidence** standard of review applies, then ask whether the evidence in the record would allow a reasonable person to make the same finding that the agency made. Substantial evidence is defined as such relevant evidence as a reasonable mind might accept as adequate to support a conclusion.

a. **No**—If no, then the court will reject the agency's finding. Stop here.

b. **Yes**—If yes, then the court will uphold the agency's finding. Stop here.

2. If the **arbitrary and capricious** standard of review applies, ask the following: was the agency's decision (1) based on a consideration of all the relevant factors (including responding to all substantial comments), and (2) free of clear error? (Both elements must be satisfied). A non-arbitrary and capricious decision is one that considers all the relevant factors and has no clear errors of judgment.

   a. **No**—If no, then the court will reject the agency's finding. Stop here.

   b. **Yes**—If yes, then the court will uphold the agency's finding. Stop here.

3. If the **major questions doctrine** applies, ask first whether the agency's action is one that will have "vast economic and political significance."

   a. **No**—If no, then the court will apply *Loper Bright*. Proceed to B.4. below.

   b. **Yes**—If yes, then ask whether there is a clear statement from Congress giving the agency the power to act in the way it did.

      i. **Yes**—If yes (which will be rare), then the court will apply *Loper Bright*. Proceed to B.4. below.

      ii. **No**—If no, then the agency had no power to act, and the regulation (or possibly an order) is invalid. Stop here.

4. If ***Loper Bright*** applies, then using *de novo* review (and the traditional tools of statutory interpretation), ask whether the statutory language has a clear meaning?

   a. **Yes**—If yes, then the agency's interpretation is invalid if it contradicts that clear meaning. Apply the alternative interpretation to the problem's facts. Stop here.

   b. **No**—If no, then ask whether the agency's interpretation is persuasive using the *Skidmore* factors: (1) the thoroughness evident in the agency's consideration of the issue, (2) the validity of the agency's reasoning for its interpretation, (3) the consistency of the agency's interpretation over time, (4) the contemporaneousness of the interpretation, (5) the relevance of the agency's expertise, and (6) all other factors that show persuasiveness.

i. **No**—If no, then the court will reject the agency's interpretation as unpersuasive. Apply the alternative interpretation to the problem's facts. Stop here.

ii. **Yes**—If yes, then the court will respect the agency's interpretation because the agency was persuasive. Apply the agency's interpretation to the problem's facts. Stop here.

5. If ***Auer*** analysis applies, then ask the following questions:

a. Is the interpretation the agency's authoritative position?

i. **No**—If no, then no deference is due. Apply the alternative interpretation to the problem's facts. Stop here.

ii. **Yes**—If yes, then to determine whether the interpretation implicates the agency's areas of substantive expertise, proceed to B.5.b. below.

b. Does the interpretation implicate the agency's areas of substantive expertise?

i. **No**—If no, then no deference is due. Apply the alternative interpretation to the problem's facts. Stop here.

ii. **Yes**—If yes, then to determine whether the interpretation reflects the agency's fair and considered judgment, proceed to B.5.c. below.

c. Does the interpretation reflect the agency's fair and considered judgment and is not one advanced as a litigating position or post hoc rationalization?

i. **No**—If no, then no deference is due. Apply the alternative interpretation to the problem's facts. Stop here.

ii. **Yes**—If yes, then to determine whether the interpretation creates unfair surprise to those being regulated, proceed to B.5.d. below.

d. Does the interpretation create unfair surprise to those being regulated?

i. **Yes**—If yes, then no deference is due. Apply the alternative interpretation to the problem's facts. Stop here.

ii. **No**—If no, then to determine whether the agency is interpreting genuinely ambiguous regulatory language, proceed to B.5.e. below.

e. Is the regulatory language "genuinely ambiguous"?

i. **No**—If no, then no deference is due. Apply the alternative interpretation to the problem's facts. Stop here.

ii. **Yes**—If yes, ask whether the agency's interpretation is "within the bounds of reasonable interpretation."

(a). **No**—If no, then no deference is due. Apply the alternative interpretation to the problem's facts. Stop here.

(b). **Yes**—If yes, then the court will defer to the agency's interpretation of its own regulation. Apply the agency's interpretation to the problem's facts. Stop here.

ILLUSTRATIVE PROBLEMS

■ PROBLEM 7.1 ■

Assume that the Department of Education (DOE) administers a program known as Children Are Exceptional ("CARE"). CARE implements the president's policy of "decreasing drug use, teenage pregnancy, and domestic violence through education." To this end, under CARE, the DOE provides federal funds to schools that meet certain criteria. The enabling act authorizes DOE to promulgate rules "after hearing." Assume, the DOE published a notice of proposed rulemaking (NPRM) and invited comments on how DOE could best meet the program's objectives.

To decrease teenage pregnancy, the DOE proposed in its NPRM that public school sex education classes address abstinence-only options. The American Academy of Pediatrics commented that there were no studies that supported the proposition that abstinence-only education decreased teenage pregnancy. Similarly, the American Public Health Association cited multiple studies finding that comprehensive sex education programs that include a discussion of abstinence are more effective in decreasing teenage pregnancy than abstinence-only education programs. And the American Medical

Association sent the DOE a copy of the numerous studies conducted, none of which supported the agency's proposed rule. A group called Mom's Against Teenagers Having Sex wrote to support the proposed rule, arguing that teens should not have sex.

Assume that the DOE promulgates the final rule and makes no changes after the notice-and-comment period has ended. The DOE ignores the comments that run counter to its preferred rule. If the American Medical Association files suit, what standard of review should the reviewing court apply and how will the court likely rule?

Analysis

Note that the issue of whether the agency should have used formal rulemaking rather than notice-and-comment rulemaking is not at issue for this chapter, although it might be an issue your professor would expect you to address. See Chapter 3 for how to resolve this issue.

The issue here is what standard of review the court will apply to the DOE's decision to require abstinence only education, which was made during a notice-and-comment rulemaking. Using the checklist above (A.2.), you should first conclude that this decision (or finding) is a policy decision. Courts review policy decisions using the arbitrary and capricious standard of review in APA § 706(2)(A).

Now you must explain how a court would rule after applying that standard. Using the checklist above (B.2.), you know that a court applying arbitrary and capricious review should ask the following questions: (1) whether the agency's decision was based on a consideration of all the relevant factors (as identified in the statute), and (2) whether the judgment was free of clear error. Further, for policy decisions, reviewing courts will look to see whether there was a rational connection between the facts in the record and the policy decision. Finally, the agency must respond to all substantive comments.

Here, the act is not provided, so we do not know whether the agency was directed to consider specific factors. However, the overwhelming factual evidence in the record does not support the DOE's policy finding, including the American Academy of Pediatrics' comment that no studies supported the proposition that abstinence-only education decreased teenage pregnancy; the studies cited by the American Public Health Association, finding that comprehensive sex education programs that include a discussion of abstinence are more effective in decreasing teenage pregnancy than abstinence-only education programs; and the studies sent by the American Medical

Association, none of which supported the agency's proposed rule. Moreover, the agency failed to respond to these significant comments.

The only evidentiary support for the agency's position came from the views of Mom's Against Teenagers Having Sex. Thus, the decision does not appear to be free of error. Moreover, there was no rational connection between the facts in the record and the agency's policy decision. Hence, the court would likely find the DOE's policy decision to be arbitrary and capricious.

■ PROBLEM 7.2 ■

The Social Security Act directs the Social Security Administration (SSA) to pay disability insurance benefits to individuals with disabilities. The Act defines an individual with a disability as follows (emphasis added):

> An individual shall be determined to be under a disability only if his physical or mental impairment or impairments are of such severity that he is not only unable to do his previous work but cannot . . . engage in any other kind of substantial gainful work *which exists in the national economy*.

The year after the Act was enacted, the SSA promulgated a rule interpreting the modifying phrase "which exists in the national economy" to modify only the phrase "any other kind of substantial gainful work." Under SSA's interpretation, someone who applies for disability benefits must prove both (1) that she could not preform the previous job because of her physical or mental impairment, and (2) that she could not perform any other substantial gainful work *that exists in the national economy* because of her physical or mental impairment. Thus, according to the SSA's rule, it is irrelevant whether the claimant's prior job exists in the national economy when she applies for disability; the only questions are whether she could still perform her prior job and whether she can perform any other job that is available.

The SSA rejected an interpretation in which the modifying phrase applied to both "his previous work" and "any other kind of substantial gainful work." Under this interpretation, whether the claimant's prior job exists in the national economy when she applied would be very relevant. Thus, the questions would be whether her current job still exists, whether she could perform it, and whether she can perform any other job. This is a much friendlier interpretation for claimants. Although the SSA acknowledged that this interpretation better furthered the Act's purpose, the agency felt constrained to interpret the language as it did by the doctrine of last antecedent.

Ellen is an individual who has heart disease and cervical and lumbar radiculopathy. She worked as microfilm document preparer. When microfilm became less commonly used, her job was eliminated, so she was let go. Microfilm document preparer jobs no longer exist in the national economy. She applied for disability benefits, alleging that she was disabled. An Administrative Law Judge (ALJ) applied the SSA's definition and found that because Ellen's impairments did not prevent her from performing her prior job, she was not disabled, even though that job no longer existed anywhere and she could not perform any other jobs. Ellen appealed. The SSA denied Ellen's appeal.

Assume that Ellen appeals the SSA's decision in federal court. What standard of review will a court apply to determine the validity of the SSA's interpretation of the Social Security Act, assuming the agency's interpretation was made during notice-and-comment rulemaking? Assume that there is no relevant legislative history, the statute is remedial, and its purpose is to aid the disabled.

Analysis

The issue in this problem is to identify and apply the appropriate standard of review to the SSA's interpretation of its enabling act. First, let's identify the appropriate standard of review. Using the checklist above (A.1.–A.3.), you should determine that the court is not reviewing a finding of fact or policy; rather, the court is reviewing an agency's interpretation of language in a statute, specifically the SSA's interpretation of language in the Social Security Act. Thus, the court would be reviewing an agency's finding of law. The major questions doctrine is the first place to start (B.3.).

[Major Questions Doctrine]: So, let's apply the major questions doctrine to the problem. Pursuant to this doctrine, a court will first ask whether the agency's action will have "vast economic and political significance." Likely, the agency's interpretation that someone applying for SSA benefits must not be able to perform their current job even if it no longer exists will not significantly impact the national economy because this interpretation will only affect a small number of claimants. Only a few jobs disappear from the national economy over time. Assuming this analysis is correct, then the second step of major questions doctrine does not apply; a court will instead apply the *Loper Bright* analysis (B.4.).

However, and arguing in the alternative, if the interpretation would have a significant impact, then the next step would be to determine whether the enabling act provides a clear statement from Congress that it wanted the agency to interpret the language in the way it did. Here, there is no clear statement; hence, a court would likely reject the agency's interpretation if it was different from the interpretation the court reached using *de novo* review. However, it is more likely a court would find that agency's action did not have a significant impact on the economy.

Applying *Loper Bright*, a court will use *de novo* analysis by applying the traditional tools of statutory interpretation, including text, linguistic and substantive canons, legislative history, and purpose. The court will also consider the persuasiveness of the agency's reasoning by balancing the *Skidmore* factors: (1) the thoroughness evident in the agency's consideration of the issue, (2) the validity of the agency's reasoning for its interpretation, (3) the consistency of the agency's interpretation over time, (4) the contemporaneousness of the interpretation, (5) the relevance of the agency's expertise, and (6) all other factors that show persuasiveness.

As noted above, the Court in *Loper Bright* did not explain how or in what order a court should apply *de novo* review and the *Skidmore* factors. Below is the possibility mentioned above, which assume the court applies *de novo* review first, then turns to the agency's interpretation if ambiguity remains. To be clear, avoid using the step one and step two terms unless your professor uses them.

[Loper Bright Step One]: The Act provides that a claimant is not eligible for disability benefits if "he [1] is not only unable to do his previous work but [2] cannot . . . engage in any other kind of substantial gainful work *which exists in the national economy*." The issue is whether the modifying phrase "which exists in the national economy" modifies both descriptions [1] and [2] or just the description in [2]. The text is ambiguous, so the court will turn to the other tools of interpretation.

First, the absurdity doctrine. Recall that the SSA concluded that the modifying phrase modifies both descriptions [1] and [2]. A court would likely find the SSA's interpretation absurd. Under the SSA's interpretation, Ellen is not disabled because she can still perform her prior job, even though that job no longer exists anywhere and she cannot perform any jobs that do exist. In short, she has no way to make a living; yet she is considered non-disabled. The absurdity doctrine supports Ellen's interpretation.

Second, the linguistic canons. Pursuant to doctrine of last antecedent, the modifying phrase modifies only description [2] because there is no comma before the modifying phrase. This canon supports the SSA's interpretation.

Third, legislative history. There is no relevant legislative history pointing in either direction even were the court willing to consider legislative history.

Fourth, the substantive canons. The Social Security Act is a remedial act that should be interpreted to further its remedial purpose. The Act's purpose is to help individuals with disabilities who cannot otherwise find work. The SSA's interpretation does not further that remedial purpose; it thwarts it.

Arguably, the doctrine of last antecedent conflicts with the remedial canon, the purpose of the statute, and the absurdity doctrine. Indeed, the SSA noted that it felt constrained by the doctrine of last antecedent.

After applying *de novo* review, a court would likely conclude that questions remain about the statute's meaning. Hence, the court should consider the persuasiveness of the agency's interpretation, using the *Skidmore* factors.

[Loper Bright Step Two]: The first factor is how thoroughly the SSA considered its interpretation. To reach its interpretation, the SSA used notice-and-comment rulemaking (even though it could have used publication rulemaking under APA § 553(b)(4)(A) for this interpretive rule). The agency's decision to use the more procedurally prescribed process suggests the SSA's decisionmaking process was thorough, although more facts would help. This factor suggests respect for the SSA's interpretation.

The second factor is the validity of the agency's reasoning. The SSA applied both the doctrine of last antecedent and the remedial canon yet concluded the doctrine of last antecedent controlled. Given the current judicial focus on the text of the statute rather than its purpose, this reasoning seems very valid. This factor also suggests respect for the SSA's interpretation.

The third and fourth factors are the consistency of the agency's interpretation over time and the contemporaneousness of its promulgation. While this is the first time the SSA has interpreted the statute, the interpretation was contemporaneous. This factor also suggests respect for the SSA's interpretation

Finally, the fifth and final factor (ignoring the catch-all "all other factors that show persuasiveness") is the relevance of the agency's expertise to the issue. Here, the SAA's expertise might be relevant if the issue related to disability and how it affects a person's ability to work, but the SSA interpreted the language as it did not because of its unique expertise with disability issues but because the SSA believe it was constrained to do so because of the rule of last antecedent. Courts are experts at interpreting statutory language, not agencies. Hence, this factor does not suggest that the agency's interpretation should be respected.

Because *de novo* review did not point to a clear answer and, on balance, the *Skidmore* factors weigh in favor of respect, a court will likely respect the SSA's interpretation and find it valid.

The final step in the analysis is for you to apply the agency's interpretation to the facts of the case (this step is often missed on exams). This is generally a quick step. Here, because the SSA's interpretation is likely valid, Ellen will lose her appeal. She is still able to perform her prior work. It does not matter that no one will employ her to do that job anymore.

As we conclude this topic, remember that it is still very much in flux and developing. Whether the Court will agree with the approach above is unclear. Most importantly, listen to your professor. He or she may have a different understanding of how these doctrines relate to each other.

POINTS TO REMEMBER

- After determining that a court will review an agency's action (reviewability from Chapter 6), you need to determine the appropriate standard of review and then apply that standard.
- The appropriate standard of review depends on the type of finding the agency made.
- Courts review agency findings of fact made during formal rulemaking and formal adjudication using the substantial evidence standard. A court applying that standard would determine whether the agency relied on "such relevant evidence as a reasonable mind might accept as adequate to support a conclusion."
- Courts review agency findings of fact made during informal rulemaking, non-legislative rulemaking, and informal adjudication using the arbitrary and capricious standard. A court applying that standard would determine "whether the decision was based on a consideration of the relevant factors and whether there has been a clear error of judgment." Additionally, reviewing courts will look to see whether there was a rational connection between the facts in the record and the policy decision made.
- Courts also review agency findings of policy, however made, using the arbitrary and capricious standard.

- Agency interpretations that have vast economic and political significance must be clearly authorized by Congress in a clear statement. Assuming no clear statement exists, courts review these interpretations *de novo*. This is the major questions doctrine.
- Courts review agency interpretations of statutory language that do not have "vast economic and political significance" using *de novo* review under *Loper Bright*.
- In applying *de novo* review, a court may respect an agency's interpretation if has the power-to-persuade pursuant to the *Skidmore* factors: how thoroughly the agency considered the issue, how valid the agency's reasoning is, how consistent the agency has been, how close in proximity to the statute's enactment the interpretation was promulgated, and the relevance of the agency's expertise to the issue.
- Courts review agency interpretations of language in the agency's own regulations using *Auer* analysis. Before applying *Auer*, the court will first ensure that the interpretation is authoritative, implicates the agency's substantive area of expertise, is fair and considered, and does not create undue surprise to those being litigated. A court applying *Auer* will defer to an agency interpretation when the regulation is genuinely ambiguous and the agency's interpretation is reasonable.

CHAPTER 8

The Big Picture

THE ENTIRE CHECKLIST

In this chapter, all of the checklists from the prior chapters have been joined into one, large checklist. After the checklist, a long exam question with various subparts is included to test your understanding of the topic and your ability to use the checklist to answer a typical exam question. Finally, brief answers to the subparts are included to guide your analysis, not to provide you with canned answers—trust me when I say that prepared answers are always a bad way to write your exam answer.

Further, the answers raise and dismiss non-issues quickly to show you how to work through the checklist, but not because non-issues should always be addressed. Some professors prefer that students do not waste time addressing non-issues, while others will give students points for raising and dismissing them quickly. You would do well to figure out which type of professor you have. In addition, you will need to augment these brief answers substantially if you wish to do well on your exam. The answers do not include cases, full explanations, or complete analysis and counter-analysis. However, the sample answers provide you with a plan of attack: a way to use the checklist to be sure that you do not miss important issues or apply the wrong analysis. The rest is up to you!

I. IS THERE AGENCY ACTION? (CHAPTER 1)

A. ***Agency* Action**—Is the actor an authority of the United States government, such as an administration, commission, corporation, board, department, division, or agency?

1. **No**—If no, then the actor is not an agency, and the APA does not apply. The president, Congress, a federal court, a state or territorial government, a military commission or court martial, and specifically exempted authorities under

APA § 551(1)(A)–(H) are not agencies. But if this is an essay question, this answer is likely wrong. Stop here.

2. **Yes**—If yes, then the actor is a federal agency, and administrative law applies. Proceed to I.B. below.

B. **Agency *Action***—Did the agency act, fail to act, or unreasonably delay acting?

1. **No**—If the agency did not act and was not required to act or if the agency did not unreasonably delay acting, then the APA does not apply. Stop here.

2. **Yes**—If the agency unreasonably delayed acting, then the APA applies. To determine whether the agency's delay was reasonable, a reviewing court will apply the TRAC factors: [1] whether the applicable statute contains a timetable, [2] whether delay will impact human welfare, [3] how forcing a decision would affect higher agency priorities, and [4] how all the interests are affected. Stop here.

3. **Yes**—If the agency acted or failed to act when legally required, the APA applies. Proceed to I.C. below.

C. **Agency *Action***—How did the agency act?

1. **Rulemaking**—Did the agency promulgate a general rule with future application?

   a. **No**—If no, then the agency may have acted using adjudicatory or investigative powers. Proceed to I.C.2. below.

   b. **Yes**—If yes, then the agency acted via rulemaking, and the APA applies. Proceed to II below.

2. **Adjudication**—Did the agency issue an order that applies to specific parties and their past actions?

   a. **No**—If no, then the agency may have acted using investigative powers. Proceed to I.C.3. below.

   b. **Yes**—If yes, then the agency acted using adjudication, and the APA applies. Ask whether a party was substantially penalized for abiding by prior policy.

      i. **Yes**—If yes, then the agency's choice to use adjudication is invalid, and any order should be set aside. Stop here.

      ii. **No**—If no, then the agency's choice is valid. Proceed to II below.

3. **Investigation and Disclosure**—Did the agency seek information through an inspection, through a request for information, or through a subpoena?

   a. **No**—If no, then you have reached a wrong answer at some point in your analysis. Start over.

   b. **Yes**—If yes, then the agency acted using executive power and administrative law applies (such as FOIA), but the APA does not apply. Proceed to II below.

II. DID THE AGENCY HAVE AUTHORITY TO ACT? (CHAPTER 2)

A. ***Statutory Authority***—Does the agency have *statutory* authority to act?

1. Does the enabling or another act authorize the agency to conduct rulemaking, adjudication, or investigation, as applicable?

   a. **No**—If no, then the agency has no legal authority to act. Stop here. *Caveat*: Note that an agency does not need statutory authority to announce what its policy is or how it interprets a statute or regulation because such actions do not make law.

   b. **Yes**—If yes, then to see if the agency complied with hybrid procedures, proceed to II.A.2. below.

2. Did the agency comply with all additional requirements in the enabling act, other relevant acts, and relevant executive orders (*e.g.*, the Regulatory Flexibility Act and E.O. 12,866)?

   a. **No**—If no, then the agency must go back and follow these procedures. Stop here.

   b. **Yes**—If yes, then to see whether the agency has constitutional authority to act, proceed to II.B. below.

B. ***Constitutional Authority***—Is the agency's structure constitutional? (Warning, the law in this area is far from settled and does not lend itself to a simple checklist answer).

1. **Appointment**—Is the relevant actor a principal officer (typically heads of agencies), an inferior officer (those working closely with the heads of agencies), or an employee? Officers hold *continuing* positions established by law and exercise *significant authority*. Inferior officers have supervisors.

a. **Principal Officer**—If the officer is a principal officer, does the enabling act provide that the president will appoint the officer and the Senate must confirm him or her?

   i. **No**—If no, then the structure is unconstitutional under U.S. CONST. art. II, § 2, cl. 2, and the agency has no authority to act. Stop here.

   ii. **Yes**—If yes, then the structure is constitutional under U.S. CONST. art. II, § 2, cl. 2. Proceed to II.B.2. below.

b. **Inferior Officer**—If the officer is an inferior officer, does the enabling act vest the appointment power in the president, the courts of law, or in the head of a department?

   i. **No**—If no, then the structure is unconstitutional under U.S. CONST. art. II, § 2, cl. 2, and the agency has no authority to act. Stop here.

   ii. **Yes**—If yes, then the structure is constitutional under U.S. CONST. art. II, § 2, cl. 2. Proceed to II.B.2. below.

c. **Employee**—If the officer is an employee, there are no constitutional requirements relating to appointment. Congress can limit the appointment and removal of employees as it wishes. Proceed to II.B.2. below.

2. **Removal**—Is there any limit on the president's power to remove the relevant actor, such as a for-cause restriction?

   a. **No**—If no, then the structure is constitutional because there are no limits on the president's power to remove. Proceed to II.C. below.

   b. **Yes**—If yes, then ask whether the relevant actor is a principal officer, an inferior officer, or an employee? (See above for definitions).

      i. **Principal Officer**—If the actor is a principal officer, ask whether the officer is a single director of an independent agency and whether the officer performs purely executive acts.

         (a). **Single Director**—If the officer is a single director of an independent agency, then any removal restriction is likely unconstitutional under *Seila Law*. Stop here.

(b). **Not a Single Director**—If the officer is not a single director of an independent agency, then the constitutionality of any restriction turns on the types of acts that the officer performs. <u>Proceed to II.B.2.b.i.(c). below</u>.

(c). **Purely Executive Acts**—If the officer performs purely executive acts, then any removal restriction is likely unconstitutional under *Myers*. <u>Stop here</u>.

(d). **Quasi-Legislative/Adjudicatory Acts**—If the officer performs quasi-legislative/ adjudicatory acts, then the removal restriction may be constitutional under *Humphrey's Executor*. This area is unclear so you should argue in the alternative that it is unconstitutional. Then, <u>proceed to II.C. below</u>.

ii. **Inferior Officer**—If the actor is an inferior officer, then ask whether the president can perform his or her constitutional duty to ensure that the laws are faithfully executed with the removal restriction in place. (Generally, single for-cause removal restrictions are constitutional, while dual for-cause removal restrictions are unconstitutional.).

(a). **No**—If no, then any restriction is likely unconstitutional under *Free Enterprise*. <u>Stop here</u>.

(b). **Yes**—If yes, then any restriction is likely constitutional under *Free Enterprise*. <u>Proceed to II.C. below</u>.

iii. **Employee**—If the actor is an employee, then the individual is constitutionally removable under the Constitution. Congress can limit the appointment and removal of employees as it wishes. <u>Proceed to II.C. below</u>.

C. ***Constitutional Authority***—Does the agency have *constitutional* authority to act?

1. **For Rulemaking**—Did Congress provide an *intelligible principle* to guide the agency's decision making? Examples of intelligible principles include "requisite to protect the public health," "necessary to avoid an imminent hazard to

the public safety," "adequately assures . . . that no employee will suffer any impairment of health," and "[not] unduly or unnecessarily complicate[d]."

a. **No**—If no, which is highly unlikely, then the statute is unconstitutional, and the agency has no legal authority to act. Stop here.

b. **Maybe**—If maybe, then consider whether the court should apply the constitutional avoidance doctrine to avoid interpreting the statutory language in a way that would raise the constitutional question. If so, proceed to III below.

c. **Yes**—If yes, then the statute is constitutional. Proceed to III below.

2. **For Adjudication**—Determine whether you think the court will apply the public rights doctrine or the *Schor* factors, being sure to apply the other test in the alternative.

a. **Apply the Public Rights Doctrine**—Does the issue involve public rights—meaning an issue arising between the government and another, or private rights—meaning an issue arising between individuals and entities other than the government?

i. **Private Rights**—If the issue involves only private rights, then the delegation is likely unconstitutional. To argue the *Schor* factors in the alternative, proceed to II.C.2.b. below.

ii. **Public Rights**—If the issue involves public rights—defined as rights so closely integrated into a public regulatory scheme as to be a matter appropriate for agency resolution with limited involvement by the Article III judiciary—then the delegation is likely constitutional. To argue the *Schor* factors in the alternative, proceed to II.C.2.b. below.

b. **Apply the *Schor* Factors**—Does the balance of the factors suggest that Article III courts should hear the controversy? The factors are: [1] the extent to which the essential attributes of judicial power are reserved to Article III courts, and, conversely, the extent to which the non-Article III forum exercises the range of jurisdiction and powers normally vested only in Article III courts; [2] the origins and importance of the right to be adjudicated; and [3] the concerns that drove

Congress to depart from the requirements of Article III.

i. **Yes**—If yes, then the delegation is likely unconstitutional. Proceed to II.C.2.a. above if you have not analyzed the public/private rights doctrine already, otherwise stop here.

ii. **No**—If no, then the delegation is likely constitutional. If so, proceed to II.C.2.a. above if you have not analyzed the public/private rights doctrine already, otherwise proceed to IV below.

3. **For Investigation and Disclosure**—The agency likely has constitutional authority. Proceed to V. below.

III. DID THE AGENCY FOLLOW APPROPRIATE RULEMAKING PROCEDURES? (CHAPTER 3)

A. **Initiating Rulemaking**—Who initiated rulemaking?

1. Did a citizen petition to issue, amend, or repeal a rule?

a. **No**—If no, then the agency initiated the rulemaking, and you will need to evaluate the agency's choice of rulemaking procedure. Proceed to III.B. below.

b. **Yes**—If yes, then to determine what the agency did with the petition, proceed to III.A.2. below.

2. Did the agency grant the petition and initiate rulemaking?

a. **No**—If no, then the agency either denied or delayed acting on the petition. Proceed to III.A.3. below.

b. **Yes**—If yes, then you will need to evaluate the agency's choice of rulemaking procedure. Proceed to III.B. below.

3. Did the agency delay acting on the petition?

a. **No**—If no, then the agency must have denied the petition. Proceed to III.A.4. below.

b. **Yes**—If yes, then the agency's delay is subject to judicial review under TRAC's rule of reason test. Evaluate (1) whether Congress provided a timetable for the agency action; (2) whether the delay would negatively affect human health and welfare; (3) whether expediting the delay would lead to negative effects on issues of higher priority for the agency; and (4) whether the nature and extent of other interests would be unduly prejudiced by the delay. Courts are very deferential of agency decisions to delay. Stop here.

4. Did the agency deny the petition?

   a. **No**—If no, then the agency must have either granted the petition or delayed acting on it. Return to III.A.2. and III.A.3. above.

   b. **Yes**—If yes, then the denial is agency action subject to judicial review. To determine whether judicial review is available and whether the agency's decision was valid, proceed to VI and VII below.

B. **Choice of Rulemaking Procedure**—Did the agency use the appropriate procedure: formal rulemaking, notice-and-comment rulemaking, or publication rulemaking?

1. Was the agency required to use formal rulemaking? Did the enabling act include the phrase "on the record after a hearing" or similar words??

   a. **No**— If no, then the agency could choose to use formal rulemaking procedures but was not required to do so under the APA. To see whether the agency was required to use notice-and-comment rulemaking, proceed to III.B.2. below.

   b. **Yes**—If yes, then the agency was required to use formal rulemaking procedures. If the agency used formal rulemaking procedures, then to see whether the procedures were proper, proceed to III.C.3.below. And if the agency did not do so its decision is invalid. Stop here.

2. Was the agency required to use notice-and-comment rulemaking procedures?

   a. Does the rule relate to (1) to military and foreign affairs; (2) to agency management and personnel, or (3) to public property, loans, grants, benefits, and contracts?

      i. **No**—If no, then the rule may still be exempt from notice-and-comment rulemaking procedures. To see whether the agency has good cause to avoid notice-and-comment procedures, proceed to III.B.2.b. below.

      ii. **Yes**—If yes, then the agency was not required to use notice-and-comment rulemaking procedures, including publication. The choice to use publications procedures is valid. Stop here.

b. Did the agency have *good cause* to believe that notice would be impracticable, unnecessary, or contrary to the public interest?

   i. **No**—If no, then the rule may still be exempt from notice-and-comment rulemaking procedures. To determine whether the rule is a valid procedural rule exempt from notice-and-comment rulemaking, proceed to III.B.2.c. below.

   ii. **Yes**—If yes, then the agency was not required to use notice-and-comment rulemaking procedures because it has *good cause* to skip those procedures. The choice to use publication procedures is valid. To see whether the procedures were proper, proceed to III.C.1. below.

c. Does the rule relate only to procedure?

   i. **No**—If no, then the rule may still be exempt from notice-and-comment rulemaking procedures. To determine whether the rule is a valid policy statement exempt from notice-and-comment rulemaking, proceed to III. B.2.d. below.

   ii. **Yes**—If yes, then ask whether the rule has a substantial impact on the rights of the people affected by it (or, if in D.C., whether it encodes a substantial value judgment).[1]

      (a). No—If no, then the agency was not required to use notice-and-comment rulemaking procedures. The choice to use publication procedures is valid. To see whether the procedures were proper, proceed to III. C.1. below.

      (b). Yes—If yes, then the agency's choice to use publication procedures is invalid. Stop here.

d. Does the rule *prospectively* advise the public and agency personnel on the way in which the agency plans to exercise *discretionary* power in the future?

---

1 Remember, the D.C. Circuit applies a different test. It examines whether the rule encodes a substantive value judgment and substantially alters the rights of the parties; if so, notice-and-comment procedures are necessary. JEM Broad. Co., Inc. v. FCC, 22 F.3d 320, 328 (D.C. Cir. 1994).

i. **No**—If no, then the rule is not a policy statement but may still be exempt from notice-and-comment rulemaking procedures. To see whether the rule is a valid interpretive rule exempt from notice-and-comment procedures, proceed to III.B.2.e. below.

ii. **Yes**—If yes, then the rule is a non-legislative rule, specifically a policy statement, for which the agency was not required to use notice-and-comment rulemaking so long as the rule does not impose rights and obligations or restrict the agency's ability to exercise its discretion (the binding effects test). The choice to use publication procedures is valid. To see whether the procedures were proper, proceed to III.C.1. below.

e. Does the rule interpret language in an existing statute or regulation?

i. **No**—If no, then either you made a mistake or the rule is a legislative rule, and the agency was required to use notice-and-comment rulemaking procedures. The choice to use publication procedures is invalid. Stop here.

ii. **Yes**—If yes, then determine whether the agency intended to exercise legislative rulemaking authority. Determine whether any of the *intent to exercise* factors are present: (1) must the agency refer to an existing legislative rule to enforce the new rule; (2) is the new rule published in the Code of Federal Regulations; (3) did the agency invoke its legislative rulemaking authority to issue the new rule; or (4) is the new rule inconsistent with a prior legislative rule. Are any of the four *intent to exercise* factors present?

(a). **No**—If no, then the rule is a non-legislative, interpretive rule, for which the agency was not required to use notice-and-comment rulemaking. The choice to use publication procedures is valid. To see whether the procedures were proper, proceed to III.C.1. below.

(b). **Yes**—If yes, then the agency likely intended to use its legislative rulemaking authority and should not have used publication procedures. The choice to use publication procedures is invalid. Stop here.

C. **Rulemaking Procedures**—Did the agency follow the appropriate procedures?

1. Did the agency use publication procedures?

   a. **No**—If no, then the agency used either notice-and-comment rulemaking or formal rulemaking procedures (with hybrid procedures). Proceed to III.C.2. below.

   b. **Yes**—If yes, and the agency published the rule or provided personal notice to the relevant entity, the rule is valid under the APA. Stop here.

2. Did the agency use notice-and-comment rulemaking procedures?

   a. **No**—If no, then the agency likely used formal rulemaking procedures. Proceed to III.C.3. below.

   b. **Yes**—If yes, did the *notice* include the time, place, and nature of any public proceedings; the legal authority for the rule; and either the substance of the proposed rule or a description of the subjects and issues involved? Was the notice "sufficient to fairly apprise interested persons of the issues involved, so that they may present responsive data or argument"?[2]

      i. **No**—If no, then the notice was insufficient, and the rule is invalid. Stop here.

      ii. **Yes**—If yes, then the notice was sufficient, and the rule may be valid. To determine whether the agency engaged in improper *ex parte* communications, proceed to III.C.2.c. below.

   c. Did the agency engage in improper *ex parte* communications during the rulemaking process? Generally, *ex parte* communications are not prohibited for notice-and-comment rulemaking.

      i. **No**—If no, then the rule may be valid. To determine whether the comment process was sufficient, proceed to III.C.2.d. below.

[2] The D.C. Circuit also requires the notice contain all the scientific data and methodology on which the agency relied. Portland Cement Ass'n v. Ruckelshaus, 486 F.2d 375, 394 (D.C. Cir. 1973).

ii. **Yes**—If yes, then ask whether the rulemaking proceeding involved "conflicting private claims to a valuable privilege," like a license.

(a). **Yes**—If yes, then the *ex parte* communications violated the Due Process Clause of the Fifth Amendment, and the rule is invalid. Stop here.

(b). **No**—If no, then the rule may be valid. To determine whether the comment process was sufficient, proceed to III.C.2.d. below.

d. Did the agency allow interested parties to submit *written data, views, or arguments* on the proposed rule?

i. **No**—If no, then the commenting process was insufficient, and the rule is invalid. Stop here.

ii. **Yes**—If yes, then the commenting process was sufficient, and then the rulemaking process may be valid. To determine whether the agency properly followed any required hybrid procedures, proceed to III.C.2.e. below.

e. Did the agency follow any hybrid procedures as required by the enabling act, the agency's regulations, or other acts? Note that a court cannot require additional procedures under *Vermont Yankee.*

i. **No**—If no, then the rulemaking process was insufficient, and the rule is invalid. Stop here.

ii. **Yes**—If yes, then the rule may be valid. To determine whether the notice was sufficient, proceed to III.C.2.f. below.

f. Can the final rule be characterized as a *logical outgrowth* of the proposed rule, meaning that the final rule did not materially alter the issues involved in the rulemaking and the final rule did not substantially depart from the substance of the proposed rule (there were no surprise switcheroos)?

i. **No**—If no, then the notice was insufficient, and the rule is invalid. Stop here.

ii. **Yes**—If yes, then the notice was sufficient, and the final rule was validly promulgated (meaning the rule is valid). To see if the substance of the rule is valid and can be challenged in court, proceed to VI and VII below.

3. Did the agency use formal rulemaking procedures?

   a. **No**—If no, then you have reached a wrong answer at some point in your analysis. Start over.

   b. **Yes**—If yes, then to determine whether the agency correctly followed the formal rulemaking procedures, proceed to IV below.

IV. DID THE AGENCY FOLLOW APPROPRIATE ADJUDICATION (AND FORMAL RULEMAKING) PROCEDURES? (CHAPTER 4)

A. **Choice of Adjudication Procedure**—Was the agency required to use formal adjudication procedures? Does the enabling act include the phrase "on the record after a hearing" or similar words?

1. **No**—If no, then the agency was allowed to proceed using informal procedures. To determine whether the agency used the proper information procedures, proceed to IV.C. below.

2. **Yes**—If yes, then did the agency use formal procedures?

   a. **Yes**—If yes, then the agency's choice of procedure was valid. To determine whether the agency correctly used formal procedures, proceed to IV.B. below.

   b. **No**—If no, then the agency's choice of procedure was unlawful, and the adjudication is invalid. Stop here.

B. **Formal Adjudication Procedures**—Did the agency use appropriate procedures?

1. Did the agency notify "persons entitled to notice of an agency hearing" regarding when and where the hearing would occur, the matters of fact alleged, the relevant law, and the agency's legal authority to hold the hearing? Was the notice sufficient to inform the regulated entity of what it did wrong?

   a. **No**—If no, then notice was insufficient, and any ensuing order or rule would be invalid under APA § 554(b). Stop here.

   b. **Yes**—If yes, then notice was sufficient to fairly apprise the interested parties of the allegations. To determine whether the APA's separation of functions provision was violated, proceed to IV.B.2. below.

2. Did the agency allow officials who performed investigative or prosecutorial functions to supervise or oversee the ALJ who presided over the hearing?

   a. **No**—If no or if the agency head presided over the hearing, then there was no violation of the APA's separation of functions provision. To determine whether the allocation of the burden of proof was proper, proceed to IV.B.3. below.

   b. **Yes**—If yes, then any ensuing order or rule would be invalid under APA § 554(d)(2) (the APA's separation of functions provision). Stop here.

3. Did the proponent of the order or rule, usually the agency, have the burden of proof?

   a. **No**—If no, then any ensuing order or rule would be invalid under APA § 556(d). Stop here.

   b. **Yes**—If yes, then the burden was correct. To determine whether the hearing procedures were sufficient, proceed to IV.B.4. below.

4. Did the parties have the ability to present their cases personally or through counsel, to present rebuttal evidence, and to conduct cross-examination *if necessary*?

   a. **No**—

      i. If no and the proceeding was not one seeking benefits, one seeking an initial license, or a formal rulemaking, then any ensuing order or rule would be invalid. Stop here.

      ii. If no and the proceeding was one seeking benefits, one seeking an initial license, or a formal rulemaking, then the agency may limit oral testimony and require all relevant information be submitted in writing under APA § 556(d). To determine whether improper *ex parte* communications occurred, proceed to IV.B.5. below.

   b. **Yes**—If yes, then to determine whether improper *ex parte* communications occurred, proceed to IV.B.5. below.

5. Did any communications occur that were not on the public record and to which notice to all parties was not given, other than status reports?

a. **No**—If no, then no improper *ex parte* communications occurred as defined in APA § 551(14). To determine whether the agency applied the appropriate standard when the case was appealed to the agency, proceed to IV.B.8. below.

b. **Yes**—If yes, then prohibited *ex parte* communications may have occurred. To determine whether the *ex parte* communications were prohibited, proceed to IV.B.6. below.

6. Did the ALJ (but not the agency or agency head) discuss a *fact in dispute* with anyone while not in the presence of all the parties in a proceeding other than one involving an application for an initial license or one challenging the validity or application of rates for public utilities and carriers? (Note that the agency and agency head are allowed to make such communications under APA § 554(d)(2)(A)–(C)).

   a. **No**—If no, then to determine whether other prohibited *ex parte* communications took place, proceed to IV.B.7. below.

   b. **Yes**—If yes, then the ALJ engaged in prohibited *ex parte* communications under APA § 554(d)(1). To determine the remedy, ask whether the prohibited communication was discovered while the action was pending before the agency.

      i. **No**—If no, then the reviewing court will consider whether to void the order by considering the following factors: (1) the gravity of the *ex parte* communications; (2) whether the *ex parte* communications may have influenced the agency's decision; (3) whether the party making the *ex parte* communications ultimately benefited from making them; (4) whether the contents of the *ex parte* communications were known to the other side, who would thus have had an opportunity to respond; and (5) whether vacating the agency's decision would serve a useful purpose. If the order or rule must be voided, stop here. If the order or rule is not voided for this reason, then to consider whether other prohibited *ex parte* communications took place, proceed to IV.B.7. below.

ii. **Yes**—If yes, then the agency must cure the violation by placing the communication on the public record and must consider whether to sanction the violator under APA § 557(d)(1)(C)(i)–(ii). To consider whether other prohibited *ex parte* communications took place, proceed to IV.B.7. below.

7. Did the decision maker (the ALJ, agency, or agency head) discuss *the merits of the case* with *interested persons outside the agency* while not in the presence of all the parties?

   a. **No**—If no, then no prohibited *ex parte* communications occurred. To determine whether the agency applied the appropriate standard when the case was appealed to the agency, proceed to IV.B.8. below.

   b. **Yes**—If yes, then the decision maker engaged in prohibited *ex parte* communications under APA § 557(d)(1). To determine the remedy, ask whether the prohibited communication was discovered while the action was pending before the agency?

      i. **No**—If no, then the reviewing court will consider whether to void the order or rule by considering the following factors: (1) the gravity of the *ex parte* communications; (2) whether the *ex parte* communications may have influenced the agency's decision; (3) whether the party making the *ex parte* communications ultimately benefited from making them; (4) whether the contents of the *ex parte* communications were known to the other side, who would thus have had an opportunity to respond; and (5) whether vacating the agency's decision would serve a useful purpose. If the order or rule must be voided, stop here. If the order or rule is not voided for this reason, then to determine whether the agency applied the appropriate standard when the case was appealed to the agency, proceed to IV.B.8. below.

      ii. **Yes**—If yes, then the agency must cure the violation by placing the communication on the public record and consider whether to sanction the violator under APA § 557(d)(1)(C)(i)–(ii). To determine whether the agency applied the appropriate standard when the issue was appealed to the agency, proceed to IV.B.8. below.

8. On appeal to the agency, in applying *de novo* review, did the agency defer to the ALJ's testimonial findings but not the derivative findings?

   a. **No**—If no, then a reviewing court may reverse the agency's decision as not supported by substantial evidence unless the agency had a good reason for rejecting the testimonial findings. To determine whether the substance of the order or rule is valid and whether the plaintiff can sue, proceed to VI and VII below.

   b. **Yes**—If yes, then a reviewing court is less likely to reverse the agency's findings as not supported by substantial evidence. To determine whether the substance of the order or rule is valid and whether the plaintiff can sue, proceed to, proceed to VI and VII below.

C. **Informal Adjudication Procedures**—Did the agency follow appropriate procedures?

1. Did the agency promptly decide the issue and notify the affected party?

   a. **No**—If no, then the agency violated the APA § 552(e), and the order is invalid. Stop here.

   b. **Yes**—If yes, then the agency complied with all procedures required by the APA but may also have to follow additional procedures to comply with the U.S. Constitution or the enabling act. Proceed to IV.C.2. below.

2. To determine whether Due Process applies, ask whether the regulated entity has a constitutionally protected interest at stake.

   a. Does the regulated entity have more than a *unilateral expectation* or abstract need for the interest being deprived?

      i. **No**—If no, then the regulated entity does not have a protected property interest. To determine whether the regulated entity has a protected liberty interest, proceed to IV.C.2.b. below.

      ii. **Yes**—If yes, then the regulated entity has a protected property interest, and the agency must provide some form of a hearing. To determine what hearing procedures are necessary, proceed to IV.C.3. below.

b. Will the regulated entity suffer both reputational harm (stigma) and future harm as a result of the deprivation (plus)?

i. **No**—If no, then the regulated entity does not have a protected liberty interest and, assuming the regulated entity did not have a protected property interest, has no right to any procedures other than that required by the APA (prompt notice of the decision). To determine whether the substance of the order is valid and whether the plaintiff can sue, proceed to the VI and VII below.

ii. **Yes**—If yes, then the regulated entity has a protected liberty interest. To determine whether the regulated entity has a right to a hearing, ask whether the regulated entity disputes the underlying facts leading to the reputational injury.

(a). **No**—If no, then under *Codd v. Velger*[3] the regulated entity has no right to a hearing. Stop here.

(b). **Yes**—If yes, then the agency must provide some form of a hearing. To determine what type of hearing is necessary, proceed to IV.C.3. below.

3. To determine what hearing procedures are required when Due Process applies, ask the following questions.

a. Do exigent circumstances prevent the agency from providing some form of a pre-deprivation hearing?

i. **No**—If no, then the agency must provide some form of a pre-deprivation hearing.

(a). If the agency failed to do so, the order is invalid. Stop here.

(b). If the agency did so, then to determine whether the procedures provided were constitutionally sufficient, proceed to IV.C.3.b. below.

---

[3] 429 U.S. 627 (1977).

ii. **Yes**—If yes, then the agency may provide a post-deprivation hearing rather than a pre-deprivation hearing. To determine whether the procedures provided were constitutionally sufficient, proceed to C.3.b. below.

b. Ask the following question for each specific procedure the regulated entity wants, such as the right to the assistance of counsel or the ability to conduct cross-examination: Does the seriousness of the harm to the individual and the risk of erroneous deprivation if the procedure is not used outweigh the administrative and fiscal burden on the agency if it is?

i. **No**—If no, then the agency need not provide that procedure under *Mathews v. Eldridge*,[4] and the order is procedurally valid. To determine whether the substance of the order is valid and whether the plaintiff can sue, proceed to the VI and VII below.

ii. **Yes**—If yes, then the agency must provide the relevant procedure and any order resulting from a hearing that did not include the procedure would be invalid. Stop here.

V. DID THE AGENCY FOLLOW APPROPRIATE INVESTIGATION AND DISCLOSURE PROCEDURES? (CHAPTER 5)

A. Information Gathering—Did the agency seek or disclose information?

1. **No**—If no, then return to I above. You have made a mistake in identifying the type of agency action at issue.

2. **Yes**—If yes, then ask whether the agency sought or disclosed information.

   a. If the agency sought information, proceed to V.B.1. below.

   b. If the agency disclosed information, proceed to V.C.1. below.

B. Information Flowing to the Agency—

1. Did the agency seek information in documentary or testimonial form?

4 424 U.S. 319, 335 (1976).

a. **No**—If no, then the agency likely inspected a regulated entity. Proceed to V.B.2. below.

b. **Yes**—If yes, then ask whether the regulated entity voluntarily provided the information.

   i. **Yes**—If yes, then stop here. The agency can ask for information and the regulated entity can voluntarily provide that information. There is no constitutional violation.

   ii. **No**—If no, then to determine whether the agency constitutionally obtained the information, proceed to V.B.1.c. below.

c. **Involuntary Production**—Did the agency go to court to compel compliance with an agency subpoena (for testimony) or subpoena *duces tecum* (for documents)?

   i. **No**—If no, stop here. The agency has no independent power to enforce its subpoena and must go to federal court to seek the information.

   ii. **Yes**—If yes, then to determine whether the regulated entity can quash the subpoena, proceed to V.B.1.d. below.

d. **Quashing a Subpoena**—Check to see if the agency has both statutory and constitutional authority to issue the subpoena.

   i. Did the agency prove that it has statutory authority to issue the subpoena?

      (a). **No**—If no, then stop here. The court should quash the subpoena because the agency does not have statutory authority to issue it.

      (b). **Yes**—If yes, then to determine whether the agency has constitutional authority to issue the subpoena, proceed to V.B.1.d.ii. below.

   ii. **Fourth Amendment**—Did the agency prove that (1) the subpoena was issued for a congressionally authorized purpose, (2) the information sought was relevant to an authorized purpose, and (3) the information sought was adequately described?

      (a). **No**—If no, then stop here. The court should quash the subpoena because enforcing it would violate the Fourth Amendment of the U.S. Constitution.

(b). **Yes**—If yes, then to determine whether enforcing the subpoena would violate the Fifth Amendment to the U.S. Constitution, proceed to V.B.1.d.iii. below.

iii. **Fifth Amendment**—Did the person moving to quash the subpoena prove that complying with it would compel an individual, not a business, to testify *orally* against himself or herself and that testifying would lead to criminal prosecution?

(a). **No**—If no, then to determine whether the subpoena would require an individual to produce voluntarily created documents, proceed to V.B.1.d.iv. below.

(b). **Yes**—If yes, then stop here. The court should quash the subpoena because it violates the Fifth Amendment of the U.S. Constitution.

iv. **Fifth Amendment**—Did the person moving to quash the subpoena prove that complying with it would compel an individual, not a business, to produce voluntarily created documents, not involuntarily created documents, and that the very act of production could serve as proof that a crime occurred?

(a). **No**—If no, then the court should not quash the subpoena, and the regulated entity must comply. Stop here.

(b). **Yes**—If yes, then stop here. The court should quash the subpoena because it violates the Fifth Amendment of the U.S. Constitution. But this is likely the wrong answer because the act of production doctrine is so narrow you have likely missed one of the elements.

2. Did the agency seek to inspect a regulated entity?

a. **No**—If no, then you have made a mistake. Return to V.A.1.

b. **Yes**—If yes, then ask whether the regulated entity voluntarily allowed the inspection.

i. **Yes**—If yes, then stop here. The agency can ask to inspect without a warrant and the regulated entity can voluntarily allow the inspection.

ii. **No**—If no, then to determine whether a warrant was required, proceed to V.B.2.c. below.

c. **Involuntary Production**—Does the agency need a warrant to conduct the inspection?

i. Is the location to be searched in plain view?

(a). No—If no, then to determine whether an emergency justifies the search without a warrant, proceed to V.B.2.c.ii. below.

(b). Yes—If yes, then stop here. A warrant is not needed under the Fourth Amendment to the U.S. Constitution. The search is valid.

ii. Is there an emergency that justifies a search without a warrant?

(a). No—If no, then to determine whether the search was conducted pursuant to informed consent, proceed to V.B.2.c.iii. below.

(b). Yes—If yes, then stop here. A warrant is not needed under the Fourth Amendment to the U.S. Constitution. The search is valid.

iii. Is the search conducted pursuant to informed consent?

(a). No—If no, then to determine whether the search is of a closely regulated business, proceed to V.B.2.c.iv. below.

(b). Yes—If yes, then stop here. A warrant is not needed under the Fourth Amendment to the U.S. Constitution. The search is valid.

iv. Is the search of a closely regulated business, such as a liquor dealer, weapon dealer, stone quarries, or dismantling junkyard?

(a). No—If no, then stop here. A warrant is required under the Fourth Amendment to the U.S. Constitution. However, the agency need only show administrative probable cause, meaning the statute or regulation allows periodic inspections and this inspection falls within the statutory parameters.

(b). Yes—If yes, then stop here. A warrant is not needed under the Fourth Amendment to the U.S. Constitution. The search is valid.

C. Information Flowing from the Agency—

1. Did a requester seek information from the agency?

   a. **No**—If no, then FOIA does not apply. To see if the Sunshine Act applies, proceed to V.C.2. below.

   b. **Yes**—If yes, then FOIA applies. To see if an exception allows the agency to withhold the information, proceed to V.C.1.c. below.

   c. Does one of the nine exceptions in APA § 552(b)(1)–(9) apply?

      i. **No**—If no, then stop here. FOIA applies, and the information must be disclosed. The requester can sue in federal court; if the requester substantially prevails, the court may award costs and attorneys' fees.

      ii. **Yes**—If yes, then stop here. The agency is allowed to withhold the information.

2. Did an independent agency hold a meeting with a quorum of its members, to deliberate, which resulted in the disposition of official agency business that was not open to the public?

   a. **No**—If no, then the Sunshine Act does not apply, and the meeting did not need to be open to the public. To see whether FACA applies, proceed to V.C.3. below.

   b. **Yes**—If yes, then the Sunshine Act applies. To see if an exception allows the agency to keep the meeting closed, proceed to V.C.2.c. below.

   c. Does one of the ten exceptions in APA § 552b(c)(1)–(10) apply?

      i. **No**—If no, then stop here. The Sunshine Act applies, and the meeting should have been open to the public. If the meeting has not yet occurred, anyone can sue to have the meeting opened. If the meeting already occurred, the only judicial remedy is likely to be a transcript of the illegally closed meeting, costs, and attorneys' fees.

      ii. **Yes**—If yes, then stop here. The agency is allowed to conduct a closed meeting.

3. Did the agency hold a meeting with "any committee, board, commission, council, conference, panel, task force, or other similar group, or any subcommittee . . . established by

statute or reorganization plan, . . . established or utilized by the President, or . . . established or utilized by one or more agencies" that was not open to the public?

a. **No**—If no, then FACA does not apply, and the meeting did not need to be open to the public. Stop here.

b. **Yes**—If yes, then the FACA applies. To see if an exception allows the agency to keep the meeting closed, proceed to V.C.3.c. below.

c. Does one of the exceptions in FACA §§ 10(b) & (d) apply?

   i. **No**—If no, then stop here. FACA applies, and the meeting should have been open to the public. However, FACA does not provide for judicial review, so there is no remedy.

   ii. **Yes**—If yes, then stop here. The agency is allowed to conduct a closed meeting.

VI. IS JUDICIAL REVIEW OF THE AGENCY'S ACTION AVAILABLE? (CHAPTER 6)

A. Jurisdiction—

1. Does the enabling act give federal courts jurisdiction?

   a. **No**—If no, then jurisdiction must be found based on the federal question statute, 28 U.S.C. § 1331. The APA does not provide jurisdiction. To determine whether the federal question statute applies, proceed to VI.A.1.2. below.

   b. **Yes**—If yes, then the court has jurisdiction. To see if the plaintiff has a cause of action, proceed to VI.B. below.

2. Does the plaintiff allege a claim that "aris[es] under the Constitution, law, or treaties of the United States"?

   a. **No**—If no, then the court does not have jurisdiction. Stop here. But this answer is likely wrong because most challenges to agency action will involve questions about federal law.

   b. **Yes**—If yes, then the court has jurisdiction. To see if the plaintiff has a cause of action, proceed to VI.B. below.

B. Cause of Action—

1. Does the enabling act provide that "anyone adversely affected by the agency's action may file an action challenging its validity" or otherwise provide a cause of action?

   a. **No**—If no, then the enabling act does not provide a cause of action. To see if the APA provides a cause of action, proceed to VI.B.2. below.

   b. **Yes**—If yes, then the plaintiff has a cause of action. To see if the plaintiff has standing, proceed to VI.C. below.

2. Does APA § 702 provide the plaintiff with a cause of action?

   a. **Agency Action**—Did the agency either act in a discrete manner or fail to act when required to act?

      i. **No**—If no, then there is no agency action. The court cannot hear the case. Stop here.

      ii. **Yes**—If yes, then there was agency action. To determine whether the statute precludes review implicitly or explicitly, proceed to VI.B.2.b. below.

   b. **Statutory Preclusion—**

      i. Does the statute explicitly preclude the court from reviewing plaintiff(s)'s claim?

         (a). No—If no, then Congress did not explicitly preclude review. To determine whether Congress implicitly precluded review, proceed to VI.B.2.b.ii. below.

         (b). Yes—If yes, then the court cannot hear the case. Stop here. But this answer is likely wrong because Congress rarely precludes review explicitly.

      ii. Does the statute implicitly preclude the court from reviewing plaintiff(s)'s claim by providing for appellate review after agency proceedings of some claims?

         (a). No—If no, then Congress did not implicitly preclude review. To determine whether the issue is committed to agency discretion, proceed to VI.B.2.c. below.

         (b). Yes—If yes, then ask (1) would a finding of preclusion foreclose all meaningful judicial review, (2) is the federal suit wholly collateral to a statute's review provisions, and (3) are the claims outside of the agency's expertise?

— **Yes**—If you answered yes to any of these questions, then Congress likely did not implicitly preclude review, although whether meeting one factor is sufficient to overcome preclusion is currently unclear. To determine whether the issue is committed to agency discretion, proceed to VI.B.2.c. below.

— **No**—If you answered no to all the questions, then Congress precluded review, and the district court cannot hear the case. Stop here.

c. **Committed to Agency Discretion**—Does the act provide meaningful standards with which to measure the agency's action?

i. **No**—If no, then Congress committed this particular decision to the agency's discretion, and the court cannot hear the case (assuming that is the only challenge). Stop here. But this answer is likely wrong because judicial review is preferred.

ii. **Yes**—If yes, then the plaintiff has a cause of action that the court can hear. To determine whether the plaintiff(s) has standing, proceed to VI.C. below.

C. **Standing**—

1. **Prudential Standing**—Is the plaintiff an association suing on behalf of the public rather than for its own personal injury?

a. **No**—If no, then plaintiff must be suing directly (whether it is the association suing for its own harm or a plaintiff suing for his/her/its own harm). Associational standing is irrelevant. To determine whether the plaintiff has constitutional standing, proceed to VI.C.2. below.

b. **Yes**—If yes, then the plaintiff must meet the associational standing requirements. Proceed to VI.C.1.c. below.

c. **Associational Standing—**

i. Assuming an association is suing, does the lawsuit relate to the purposes of the association?

(a). **No**—If no, then the association has no prudential standing. Stop here. But this answer is likely wrong because associations generally only sue for issues related to their mission.

(b). **Yes**—If yes, then the association meets one element of associational standing. To see if the association meets the other elements, proceed to VI.C.1.c.ii. below.

ii. Assuming an association is suing, can the lawsuit proceed without an individual's participation, meaning that the lawsuit is for injunctive or declaratory relief only?

(a). **No**—If no, then the association has no standing pursuant to prudential standing. Stop here. But this answer is likely wrong because associations generally only sue for declaratory and injunctive relief.

(b). **Yes**—If yes, then the association meets another element of associational standing. To see if the association meets the remaining element, proceed to VI.C.1.c.iii. below.

iii. Assuming an association is suing, does one member have constitutional standing, meaning injury in fact, causation, and redressability? (You will need to work through VI.C.2. below, then return here).

(a). **No**—If no, then the association has no standing pursuant to prudential standing, and the court cannot hear the case. Stop here.

(b). **Yes**—If yes, then the association meets the prudential standing requirements. To see if the plaintiff meets the statutory standing requirements, proceed to VI.C.3. below.

2. **Constitutional Standing—**

a. **Injury in Fact—**

i. Does the plaintiff allege that he or she would be directly injured economically (*e.g.*, by a fine) or physically by the agency?

(a). **No**—If no, then the plaintiff must be alleging an indirect injury. Proceed to C.2.a.ii. below.

(b). **Yes**—If yes, the plaintiff has an injury in fact that is concrete and particularized, which is one element of constitutional standing. To determine whether plaintiff can show causation, proceed to C.2.b. below.

ii. Does the plaintiff allege only that he or she suffered a procedural injury, meaning the agency failed to follow a legally required procedure?

(a). **No**—If no, then plaintiff must be alleging a different indirect injury. Proceed to VI.C.2.a.iii. below.

(b). **Yes**—If yes, then the plaintiff does not have injury in fact, which is one element of constitutional standing, and the court cannot hear the case. Stop here.

iii. Does the plaintiff allege that he or she suffered an informational injury, meaning the agency failed to disclose information *it was required* to disclose to this plaintiff?

(a). **No**—If no, then to see if plaintiff must be alleging a different indirect injury, proceed to VI.C.2.a.iv. below.

(b). **Yes**—If yes, then plaintiff has injury in fact. To determine whether plaintiff can show causation, proceed to VI.C.2.b. below.

iv. Does the plaintiff allege that he or she suffered a recreational, aesthetic, or environmental injury?

(a). **No**—If no, then the plaintiff does not have injury in fact, which is one element of constitutional standing. Stop here. This answer is likely wrong; plaintiff must be alleging one of the injuries above.

(b). Yes—If yes, then ask whether the plaintiff can show concrete plans to visit the location or see the area to be harmed in the near future?

— **No**—If no, then the plaintiff does not have injury in fact, which is one element of constitutional standing, and the court cannot hear the case. Stop here.

— **Yes**—If yes, then plaintiff has injury in fact. To see if the plaintiff can show causation, proceed to VI.C.2.b. below.

b. **Causation**—Can the plaintiff show that the alleged illegal action by the agency caused the plaintiff's harm?

i. **No**—If no, then the harm was likely caused by a third party, and plaintiff cannot show causation, which is one element of constitutional standing, and the court cannot hear the case. Stop here.

ii. **Yes**—If yes, then the plaintiff can show causation. To determine whether plaintiff can show redressability, proceed to VI.C.2.c. below.

c. **Redressability**—Can the plaintiff show that a favorable decision will remedy the plaintiff's harm?

i. **No**—If no, then the harm cannot be remedied by the agency, and the plaintiff cannot show redressability, which is one element of constitutional standing. The court cannot hear the case. Stop here.

ii. **Yes**—If yes, then the plaintiff can show redressability, which is one element of constitutional standing. To determine whether plaintiff meets statutory standing requirements, proceed to VI.C.3. below.

3. **Statutory Standing (Zone of Interests)**—Is plaintiff suing pursuant to APA § 702?

a. **No**—If no, then the plaintiff must be suing pursuant to the enabling act, the zone of interest requirement does not apply because the plaintiff must be within the protection of the relevant act. To determine whether plaintiff's lawsuit meets the timing requirements, proceed to VI.D. below.

b. **Yes**—If yes, then the plaintiff must demonstrate that he/she/it is "arguably" within the zone of interests the specific statute was meant to protect. Can plaintiff meet this burden?

i. **No**—If no, then the plaintiff cannot meet statutory standing requirements. The court cannot hear the case. Stop here.

ii. **Yes**—If yes, the plaintiff can meet the statutory standing requirements. To determine whether plaintiff's lawsuit meets the timing requirements, proceed to VI.D. below.

D. **Timing**—

1. Assuming the enabling act does not include a limitations period, ask whether the plaintiff's action is barred by the six-year statute of limitations in 28 U.S.C. § 2401(a)? (Consider whether the plaintiff was harmed in the preceding six years, not whether the agency's action occurred in the last six years.).

a. **No**—If no, then to determine whether now is the appropriate time for a court to hear the plaintiff's claim, proceed to VI.D.2. below.

b. **Yes**—If yes, then the statute of limitations bars the case from being heard, and the court must dismiss it. Stop here.

2. Is the plaintiff suing pursuant to APA § 704?

a. **No**—If no, then the *common law* doctrines of finality, exhaustion, and ripeness may apply. Stop here and apply those doctrines. But in an Administrative Law course, it is more likely that you will be tested on these doctrines as codified in APA § 704.

b. **Yes**—If yes, then to determine whether now is the appropriate time for a court to hear the plaintiff's claim, proceed to VI.D.3. below.

3. **Finality**—Has the agency completed its consideration of the issue?

a. Is the action the culmination of the agency's decision making process?

i. **No**—if no, then the agency's action is not final, and the court cannot hear the case at this time. Stop here.

ii. **Yes**—If yes, then the agency's action meets one of the finality elements. To determine whether the case meets both elements, proceed to VI.D.3.b. below.

b. Is the agency action one from which "rights or obligations have been determined,' or from which 'legal consequences will flow?' "

i. **No**—if no, then the agency's action is not final, and the court cannot hear the case at this time. Stop here.

ii. **Yes**—If yes, then the agency's action is final. To see if the plaintiff meets the exhaustion requirements, proceed to VI.D.4. below.

4. Exhaustion—If the plaintiff is suing under the APA, must the plaintiff appeal to the agency before suing?

a. Does the enabling act expressly require the plaintiff to exhaust administrative remedies?

i. **No**—If no, then APA § 704 does not require the plaintiff to exhaust administrative remedies. To determine whether a regulation requires the plaintiff to exhaust administrative remedies, proceed to VI.D.4.b. below.

ii. **Yes**—If yes, then, under APA § 704, the plaintiff must exhaust administrative remedies prior to filing suit. You may wish to note here that the common law exceptions to exhaustion likely to do not apply because Congress did not codify them within APA § 704. Stop here.

b. Does the agency's own regulation expressly require the plaintiff to exhaust administrative remedies and stay its action pending administrative appeal?

i. **No**—If no, then APA § 704 does not require The plaintiff to exhaust administrative remedies. To determine whether the action is ripe, proceed to VI.D.5. below.

ii. **Yes**—If yes, then, under APA § 704, the plaintiff must exhaust administrative remedies prior to filing suit. You may wish to note here that the common law exceptions to exhaustion likely to do not apply because Congress did not codify them within APA § 704. Stop here.

5. **Ripeness**—Is the case sufficiently developed for judicial review?

   a. Does the case involve purely legal issues?

      i. **No**—If no, then the case is not ripe, and the court should not hear it at this time. Stop here.

      ii. **Yes**—If yes, then the case meets one of the ripeness elements. To determine whether the case meets both elements, proceed to VI.D.5.b. below.

   b. Will the plaintiff actually be harmed if judicial review is delayed?

      i. **No**—If no, then the case is not ripe, and the court should not hear it at this time. Stop here.

      ii. **Yes**—If yes, then the case is ripe for judicial review. To determine the appropriate standard of review the court will apply, proceed to VII. below.

VII. WHAT STANDARD OF REVIEW APPLIES? (CHAPTER 7)

A. Type of Finding/Question:

1. Is the court reviewing a finding of fact?

   a. **No**—If no, then to determine whether the court is reviewing a question of policy, of law, or a mixed question, proceed to VII.A.2. below.

   b. **Yes**—If yes, then ask whether the agency made its finding as a part of a *formal* adjudication or rulemaking.

      i. **Yes**—If yes, then the reviewing court will review the agency's finding using the substantial evidence standard. To determine whether the agency applied this standard correctly, proceed to VII.B.1. below.

      ii. **No**—If no, then the reviewing court will review the agency's finding using the arbitrary and capricious standard. To determine whether the agency applied this standard correctly, proceed to VII.B.2. below.

2. Is the court reviewing a finding of policy?

   a. **No**—If no, then to determine whether the court is reviewing a question of law or a mixed question, proceed to VII.A.3. below.

b. **Yes**—If yes, then the reviewing court will review the agency's finding using the arbitrary and capricious standard regardless of how the agency made its decision. To determine whether the agency applied this standard correctly, proceed to VII.B.2. below.

3. Is the court reviewing a finding of law?

a. **No**—If no, then the court is reviewing a mixed question. Proceed to VII.A.4. below.

b. **Yes**—If yes, then ask the following:

i. Is the agency interpreting language in a constitution or contract?

(a). **Yes**—If yes, then the reviewing court will review the language *de novo*, giving the agency's interpretation no extra weight. Stop here.

(b). **No**—If no, then the reviewing court may give the agency's interpretation some weight. To determine whether the agency applied this standard correctly, proceed to VII.A.3.b.ii. below.

ii. Is the agency interpreting language in its own regulation?

(a). **Yes**—If yes, then to determine whether the *Auer* doctrine applies, proceed to VII.B.5. below.

(b). **No**—If no, then the agency must be interpreting statutory language. To determine whether the agency's interpretation receives deference, proceed to VII.A.3.b.iii. below.

iii. Is the agency interpreting language in a statute that the agency administers?

(a). **No**—If no, then the reviewing court will review the language *de novo*, giving the agency's interpretation no deference. Stop here

(b). **Yes**—If yes, then apply the major questions analysis to see whether the court will give the agency's interpretation any weight. Proceed to VII.B.3. below.

4. Is the court reviewing a mixed finding of law and fact (law application)?

    a. **No**—If no, then return to VII.A.1. You have made an error.

    b. **Yes**—If yes, then follow the analysis for findings of fact (VII.A.1.) for that portion of the finding and follow the analysis for findings of law (VII.A.3.) for that portion of the finding.

B. **Standards of Review:** Apply the appropriate standard of review to determine the validity of the agency's finding.

1. If the **substantial evidence** standard of review applies, then ask whether the evidence in the record would allow a reasonable person to make the same finding that the agency made. Substantial evidence is defined as such relevant evidence as a reasonable mind might accept as adequate to support a conclusion.

    a. **No**—If no, then the court will reject the agency's finding. Stop here.

    b. **Yes**—If yes, then the court will uphold the agency's finding. Stop here.

2. If the **arbitrary and capricious** standard of review applies, ask the following: was the agency's decision (1) based on a consideration of all the relevant factors, and (2) free of clear error? (Both elements must be satisfied). A non-arbitrary and capricious decision is one that considers all the relevant factors and has no clear errors of judgment.

    a. **No**—If no, then the court will reject the agency's finding. Stop here.

    b. **Yes**—If yes, then the court will uphold the agency's finding. Stop here.

3. If the **major questions doctrine** applies, ask first whether the agency's action is one that will have "vast economic and political significance."

    a. **No**—If no, then the court will apply *Loper Bright*. Proceed to VII.B.4. below.

    b. **Yes**—If yes, then ask whether there is a clear statement from Congress giving the agency the power to act in the way it did.

i. **Yes**—If yes (which will be rare), then the court will apply *Loper Bright*. Proceed to VII.B.4. below.

ii. **No**—If no, then the agency had no power to act, and the regulation (or possibly an order) is invalid. Stop here.

4. If ***Loper Bright*** applies, then using *de novo* review (and the traditional tools of statutory interpretation), ask whether the statutory language has a clear meaning?

a. **Yes**—If yes, then the agency's interpretation is invalid if it contradicts that clear meaning. Apply the alternative interpretation to the problem's facts. Stop here.

b. **No**—If no, then ask whether the agency's interpretation is persuasive using the *Skidmore* factors: (1) the thoroughness evident in the agency's consideration of the issue, (2) the validity of the agency's reasoning for its interpretation, (3) the consistency of the agency's interpretation over time (4) the contemporaneousness of the interpretation, (5) the relevance of the agency's expertise, and (6) all other factors that show persuasiveness.

i. **No**—If no, then the court will reject the agency's interpretation as unpersuasive. Apply the alternative interpretation to the problem's facts. Stop here.

ii. **Yes**—If yes, then the court will respect the agency's interpretation because the agency was persuasive. Apply the agency's interpretation to the problem's facts. Stop here.

5. If ***Auer*** analysis applies, then ask the following questions:

e. Is the interpretation the agency's authoritative position?

i. **No**—If no, then no deference is due. Apply the alternative interpretation to the problem's facts. Stop here.

ii. **Yes**—If yes, then to determine whether the interpretation implicates the agency's areas of substantive expertise, proceed to VII.B.5.b. below.

f. Does the interpretation implicate the agency's areas of substantive expertise?

i. **No**—If no, then no deference is due. Apply the alternative interpretation to the problem's facts. Stop here.

ii. **Yes**—If yes, then to determine whether the interpretation reflects the agency's fair and considered judgment, proceed to VII.B.5.c. below.

g. Does the interpretation reflect the agency's fair and considered judgment and is not one advanced as a litigating position or post hoc rationalization?

i. **No**—If no, then no deference is due. Apply the alternative interpretation to the problem's facts. Stop here.

ii. **Yes**—If yes, then to determine whether the interpretation creates unfair surprise to those being regulated, proceed to VII.B.5.d. below.

h. Does the interpretation create unfair surprise to those being regulated?

i. **Yes**—If yes, then no deference is due. Apply the alternative interpretation to the problem's facts. Stop here.

ii. **No**—If no, then to determine whether the agency is interpreting genuinely ambiguous regulatory language, proceed to VII.B.5.e. below.

e. Is the regulatory language "genuinely ambiguous"?

i. **No**—If no, then no deference is due. Apply the alternative interpretation to the problem's facts. Stop here.

ii. **Yes**—If yes, ask whether the agency's interpretation is "within the bounds of reasonable interpretation."

(a). **No**—If no, then no deference is due. Apply the alternative interpretation to the problem's facts. Stop here.

(b). **Yes**—If yes, then the court will defer to the agency's interpretation of its own regulation. Apply the agency's interpretation to the problem's facts. Stop here.

ILLUSTRATIVE PROBLEMS

■ LONG ESSAY PROBLEM 8.1 ■

Climate change has been in the news lately, as more and more scientific studies suggest that humans are causing the changes in climate seen in recent decades. Shrinking polar ice caps, changes in global weather patterns, increases in atmospheric carbon dioxide, and rising average temperatures worldwide suggest there is a very real problem. The scientific evidence is by no means conclusive, but there is a growing public consensus in the United States that climate change is an issue the federal government should no longer ignore.

After a particularly hot summer and autumn, last January, Congress enacted legislation addressing climate change: Congress overwhelmingly passed the "Handling Environmental Adjustments in Temperature Act" ("the HEAT Act"). Sensing the public mood and reassured by the bill's sponsor during the floor debates that the bill was not intended to target any specific industry, the President signed the bill in February. The law became effective on December 31 of that same year.

The HEAT Act provides, in relevant part, as follows:

Section 1: Findings. The Congress makes the following findings:

(a) Scientific studies have documented that average temperatures are increasing globally due to carbon dioxide and other noxious emissions;

(b) This phenomenon, popularly known as *climate change*, is a significant danger to world environmental stability and is the cause of severe hurricanes, tornadoes, floods, and other catastrophic events;

(c) The United States, as leader of the free world, has a moral and ethical duty to combat the adverse effects of climate change;

(d) At the same time, continued growth of the U.S. economy is of paramount importance so no one industry should bear the burden of remedying this threat to our nation.

Section 2: In light of these findings, the U.S. Environmental Protection Agency (EPA) shall have the power, after opportunity for a full public hearing in which all interested parties may participate, to issue rules and regulations to reduce emissions of any industry that contributes to climate change to protect the general welfare of the Nation consistently with the findings in Section 1.

Section 3: The EPA may also seek enforcement individually against any person who does not comply with regulations promulgated by the EPA pursuant to the HEAT Act. Such enforcement actions shall be undertaken only after opportunity for an agency hearing on the record in which interested parties may participate.

Section 4: Any violation of this Act shall be punishable by a fine not exceeding $50,000, imprisonment not exceeding 3 years, or both.

* * *

The HEAT Act does not define "any industry that contributes to climate change" in Section 2. Nor does the lengthy legislative history contain any discussion of which industries Congress intended would be covered. As noted above, the bill's sponsor said during the House floor debates, "No one industry will bear this burden alone." Further, the legislative history makes repeated mention of Congress's concern with both carbon dioxide and methane gasses and with the effect of those pollutants on climate change.

In April of the year immediately after the HEAT Act was signed into law, the EPA drafted new regulations to implement the HEAT Act's provisions. As part of this process, the EPA reviewed existing scientific evidence on climate change. The EPA's research revealed that while there was general scientific agreement that climate change was occurring, there was no scientific consensus as to the *cause*. That is, while many relevant scientific studies suggested that climate change was at least partly caused by human industrial activity, a smaller number of studies concluded that climate change was a cyclical climate change pattern that had nothing to do with human factors.

Furthermore, even those scientific studies that concluded that human factors were contributing to climate change did not fully agree on exactly which human factors were involved. In other words, while most of the scientific studies suggested that *carbon dioxide* emissions by industries were the most significant human-caused factor in climate change, there were a few isolated studies that suggested that *methane* gas emissions by agricultural activities were another significant human-caused factor in climate change.

In the U.S., meat production relies on concentrated forms of agriculture such as cattle feedlots, hog feedlots, and poultry farms (for chickens and turkeys). These forms of agribusiness are admirably efficient in producing low-cost meat for consumers, but they produce enormous amounts of animal waste. Animal waste, of course, produces large amounts of methane gas as it decomposes. And the decomposition of large amounts of waste causes a lot of heat, impacting climate change.

The EPA issued a detailed Notice of Proposed Rulemaking (NPRM) on May 1 (the year after the HEAT Act was enacted). The NPRM, which was over 200 pages long, contained the following relevant language:

> **The EPA finds** that available scientific evidence irrefutably points to climate change as being caused largely by human activity. Carbon dioxide and methane scrubbers are the most efficient at lowering both carbon dioxide and methane gas emissions. The evidence is also clear that such emissions must be no more than 50 parts per billion for climate change to be reduced. Accordingly, the EPA proposes to promulgate the following "Geo-Atmospheric Standards" ("GAS") Regulation:
>
> > **GAS section 1:** All companies whose manufacturing or production activities produce carbon dioxide or methane gas shall install carbon dioxide and methane scrubbers at their own expense as part of their air ventilation systems, to capture carbon dioxide and methane gasses within their facilities and reduce emissions of these gasses from these facilities to no more than 50 parts per billion.
>
> The EPA will accept comments on these regulations from interested parties until July 1. Comments should be submitted to [the NPRM lists the name and address where comments should be submitted].

The potential breadth of this proposed rule resulted in a flurry of comments to the EPA. Various industries—notably those involved in carbon dioxide emissions such as car manufacturers—vociferously objected to the proposed regulations. There were a few comments from the poultry and pork industries objecting to the strict requirements. These industries were concerned that the cost of implementing the regulation would put them out of business compared to the small impact on the environment. Some commentators felt the regulation did not go far enough.

In contrast, no beef producers submitted comments to the EPA about the proposed regulation. In the words of one beef producer, "the scientific data on methane gas and climate change is pretty weak, and we're not wasting our time or money on submitting comments to the EPA even though the proposed regulation might impact our industry."

On September 1, the EPA issued a comprehensive Notice of Final Rulemaking and "Statement of Basis and Purpose" (collectively, the "SOBP") explaining its *final* GAS Regulation. The SOBP is 300 pages long and contains a detailed statement regarding the background of the proposed rule, summaries of the public comments received on the NPRM, and the EPA's responses to these comments. The SOBP contains the following relevant language regarding the GAS Regulations being adopted by the EPA:

> **The EPA finds** that available scientific evidence irrefutably suggests that the primary contributor to climate change is methane gas emissions by cattle, especially in large feedlots. Methane scrubbers are an efficient method to lower methane gas emissions; additionally, keeping cattle indoors will also lower emissions. The evidence is also clear that such emissions must be no more than 50 parts per billion for climate change to be reduced. Accordingly, the EPA issues the following "Geo-Atmospheric Standards" ("GAS") Regulation:
>
> > **Section 1:** All U.S. cattle feedlots shall keep their cattle in indoor facilities that have been rendered appropriately airtight to prevent the escape of methane gasses into the atmosphere.
> >
> > **Section 2:** All U.S. cattle feedlots shall install methane scrubbers as part of their air ventilation systems to capture methane gasses within their facilities and reduce methane emissions to no more than 50 parts per billion.
> >
> > **Section 3:** To allow cattle feedlots to come into compliance with this regulation, it shall take effect beginning in September (the year following the regulation's enactment). No enforcement actions shall commence before that date. After that date, any cattle feedlot found to be in violation of this regulation will be fined $10,000 per day of violation.

The EPA offered no data to support any of its findings. There are no other relevant regulations.

Needless to say, beef producers, who own cattle feedlots, are upset about this regulation. You are a junior associate in the law firm of Huey, Duey, & Luey. Your firm has been hired as counsel for the Beef Producers of America ("BPA"), which wants to challenge the validity of the final GAS Regulation. How would you answer the following questions?

QUESTION 1

Steve Duey and David Luey are two senior partners in your firm. One Friday at 4:45 p.m. they walk into your office. Duey says, "I hear you took Administrative Law in law school. That's good, because we didn't. So we need a memo about the BPA matter on our desks by Monday at 9:00 a.m. Have a great weekend!"

The specific questions Duey and Luey want you to address in the memorandum are as follows:

(a) Does the HEAT Act unconstitutionally delegate authority to the EPA? Why or why not?

(b) If BPA wished to bring suit challenging the constitutionality of the delegation to the EPA before the rule takes effect, would the case survive a *reviewability* challenge? Please explain. Assume the BPA is seeking only injunctive and declaratory relief.

QUESTION 2

You work all weekend on the memo and get it to Duey and Luey Monday morning. The memo then sits on their desks all week until the following Friday at 4:52 p.m., when David Luey walks into your office and says, "Great work on the first BPA memo. But now Duey and I have some more questions. We've got golf plans for the weekend, so you'll need to take care of this for us."

This time, the partners have the following questions about how BPA might challenge the EPA's final GAS Regulations. Your answers are of course due by 9:00 a.m. Monday.

(a) Should the EPA have proceeded by formal rather than informal rulemaking? Please explain.

(b) Assuming the action is subject to judicial review, would the EPA's decision to limit the final GAS Regulation to cattle feedlots only survive a *procedural* challenge? Please explain.

QUESTION 3

You worked all weekend (again) and finished the second memo after an all-nighter on Sunday. The next Friday, senior partner Lisa Huey walks into your office at 4:59 p.m. and says, "Great work on the BPA matter. Got one more question for you. I need an answer by Monday at 9:00 a.m. sharp. I'm going to the beach for the weekend." Huey's questions are as follows:

(a) Assuming this action is subject to judicial review, would the EPA's *factual* findings in its final rule survive a legal challenge? Please explain, being sure to identify the appropriate standard of review.

(b) Assuming this action is subject to judicial review, would the EPA's *interpretation* that "any industry that contributes to climate change" provides the agency with the power to regulate only one industry, specifically, cattle feedlots, survive a legal challenge? Please explain, being sure to identify the appropriate standard of review.

Analysis[5]

Before answering the individual questions, 1–3, you should begin by asking yourself whether the question involved an agency and agency action (Checklist I.A. and I.B.) and, if so, what kind of agency action was involved (Checklist I.C.). These questions are foundational and must precede every question you analyze, even if you do not include your analysis in your answer (although you may win some brownie points by doing so).

Here, the EPA is an authority of the United States government, and it issued a regulation; thus, an agency and agency action were involved. Because the EPA promulgated a regulation, the APA's rulemaking procedures apply. So, turn to Chapter 2's checklist (or II above) for Question 1.

ANALYSIS FOR QUESTION 1

1(a): Does the HEAT Act unconstitutionally delegate authority to the EPA? Why or why not?

The issue here is whether the HEAT Act unconstitutionally delegates legislative power to the agency. Turning to II.C.1. in the checklist above, you need to analyze whether Congress provided an *intelligible principle* to guide the EPA's decision making. The Supreme Court has upheld many broad delegations as including intelligible principles. Some examples include "requisite to protect the public health," "necessary to avoid an imminent hazard to the public safety," "adequately assures . . . that no employee will suffer any impairment of health," and "[not] unduly or unnecessarily complicate[d]."

5 Be aware that the answers below are necessarily succinct and do not cite relevant case law or the APA. The purpose is to show you how to use the checklist not how to draft a perfect answer. Hence, be sure to expand these arguments much more fully and cite relevant law.

Here, section 2[6] of the HEAT Act authorizes the EPA to issue rules to reduce emissions of industries that contribute to climate change "to protect the general welfare of the nation." This intelligible principle is sufficiently like those intelligible principles that have survived Supreme Court scrutiny in this area in the past. Hence, the HEAT Act likely is constitutional under the delegation doctrine.

1(b): If BPA wished to bring suit challenging the constitutionality of the delegation to the EPA before the rule takes effect, would the case survive a *reviewability* challenge? Please explain. Assume the BPA is seeking only injunctive and declaratory relief.

The issue here is whether the BPA would be able to seek judicial review at this time (pre-enforcement review). Turning to VI.A.1. in the checklist above, you should ask first whether a federal court would have jurisdiction over this particular claim. In this case, the HEAT Act does not appear to grant the federal courts jurisdiction. Because the APA does not grant jurisdiction, jurisdiction must be found based on the federal question statute, 28 U.S.C. § 1331. The BPA is alleging a claim that arises under an act of the United States (specifically, the HEAT Act); thus, the court would have jurisdiction.

Second, you should determine whether the enabling act gives the BPA the right to sue ("a cause of action") (VI.B.). Here, the enabling act does not provide that anyone adversely affected by the agency's action may file an action challenging its validity or otherwise provide a cause of action (VI.B.1.a.); hence, you should turn to the APA to see if it provides the BPA with a cause of action (VI.B.2.).

To determine whether APA § 702 provides the BPA with a cause of action, you must evaluate the three things: (1) whether there was agency action, (2) whether the enabling act precludes judicial review, and (3) whether the enabling act commits the decision of how to correct climate change entirely to the agency's discretion. Here, the EPA acted in a discrete manner—it issued a regulation, which is agency action (VI.B.2.a.). The HEAT Act does not explicitly preclude judicial review because there are no statements to that effect in the Act. Nor does the Act impliedly preclude review by providing appellate review for some claims (VI.B.2.b.). Finally, there are no

---

[6] In analyzing this question, be sure that you correctly identify the section of the act that applies. Here, the action is rulemaking, so Section 2 of the HEAT Act is the relevant section. The question does not ask about adjudication. Some professors will not want you to analyze this provision of the HEAT Act. Others will want you to raise the concerns but dismiss them quickly. To see if you can do so, use the checklist above to see if you can determine (1) whether the adjudication provision is constitutional (consider whether a jury must hear the claim), (2) whether formal adjudication is required, and (3) what standard of review would apply to the EPA's findings.

facts suggesting that the HEAT Act does not provide meaningful standards with which to measure the EPA's action, meaning Congress did not commit this this particular decision to the agency's discretion (VI.B.2.c.). The Act does not mention the word "discretion," for example.

Third, you must determine whether the BPA has standing to bring this claim: prudential, constitutional, and statutory standing (VI.C.). As for prudential standing, the BPA is an association suing on behalf of its members; thus, the BPA must meet the three associational standing requirements (VI.C.1.c.): (1) the lawsuit must relate to the purpose of the organization (VI.C.1.c.i), (2) the lawsuit must be able to proceed without an individual's participation (VI.C.1.c.ii.), and (3) one member of the organization must have constitutional standing (VI.C.1.c.iii.).

Here, the lawsuit relates to the purposes of the organization: the organization represents beef producers generally and this regulation affects beef producers. Moreover, the lawsuit seeks declaratory and injunctive relief only, so an individual member's participation is not required. The final associational standing question is whether one of the BPA's members has constitutional standing (VI.C.2.), meaning one member would have injury in fact (VI.C.2.a.), causation (VI.C.2.b.), and redressability (VI.C.2.c.).

Here, one of BPA's members, a beef producer, would be able to demonstrate that it has constitutional standing. First, a beef producer would have injury in fact because it would likely be fined if the regulation takes effect. Such an injury would be sufficiently concrete, particularized, and imminent (VI.C.2.a.i.). So, injury in fact is met. Second, there is causation and redressability. The alleged illegal action is by the agency and not a third party, the regulation will cause the member's harm, and that the harm will be redressed if the regulation is not issued. Thus, causation and redressability are met. Thus, BPA has prudential and constitutional standing.

As for statutory standing, the BPA would be suing pursuant to APA § 702 (recall that the HEAT Act did not provide a cause of action); hence, the BPA must show that its members are within the zone of interest the HEAT Act was designed to protect (VI.C.3.). Here, the BPA is likely to be able to demonstrate that its members are "arguably" within the zone of interests of the HEAT Act because they are in an industry that contributes to climate change and Congress expressed concern that all industries be equally impacted by any regulation. Hence, statutory standing is likely met.

Fourth, you must determine whether the BPA can bring this particular claim at this time (VI.D.). The statute of limitations (28

U.S.C. § 2401(a)) does not bar the action because it is being brought within six years of both the agency's action and the potential harm to the BPA members.

Further, because the BPA would be suing pursuant to the APA, APA § 704's finality and exhaustion doctrines apply (VI.D.3. & 4.). Additionally, the common law doctrine of ripeness applies (VI.D.5.).

Regarding finality (VI.D.3.), the BPA must show that the EPA's rule is the culmination of the agency's decision making process and that the action is one from which legal consequences will flow (VI.D.3.a. & b.). Here, the EPA's regulation is final; it was issued after the notice comment process. When there is a final rule, finality is not an issue. Further, the regulation is one from which legal consequences will flow because the cattle feedlots will have to comply or risk $10,000 per day fines. Hence, finality is met.

Regarding exhaustion (VI.D.4.), the BPA must show that neither the HEAT Act (VI.D.4.i.) nor a regulation requires the association to appeal to the agency first (VI.D.4.ii.). Here, the HEAT Act does not require anyone to exhaust administrative remedies before filing suit (the Act is silent on exhaustion), and there is no relevant administrative regulation provided. Hence, exhaustion is not required in this case.

Regarding ripeness (VI.D.5.), the BPA must show (1) that the claims are purely legal (VI.D.5.i.), and (2) that BPA members will be harmed if judicial review is delayed (VI.D.5.ii.). Here, the BPA's challenge relates only to the constitutionality of the delegation. This question is purely legal and no further factual development would be necessary. Additionally, the cattle lots may well be harmed if judicial review is delayed. Every day that they fail to comply with the regulation, they are subject to $10,000 fine. Yet compliance will be very costly. Thus, because BPA members must spend significant sums to comply or risk significant fines, they will be harmed if review is delayed (VI.D.5.a.ii.). Hence, the case is likely ripe for review, and the court should hear it at this time.

ANALYSIS FOR QUESTION 2

2(a): Should the EPA have proceeded by formal rather than informal rulemaking? Please explain, being sure to identify the appropriate standard of review.

The issue here is whether the EPA correctly chose to use notice-and-comment rulemaking rather than formal rulemaking. Turning to III.B.1.a. in the checklist above, you need to analyze whether the EPA was required to use formal rulemaking. Typically, courts will look to see whether the enabling act includes the phrase "on the record after a hearing" or a similar phrase. If those words are not included, then the agency is not required to use formal rulemaking.

Here, Section 2 of the HEAT Act authorized the EPA to issue rules "after opportunity for a full public hearing in which all interested parties may participate." This language is not identical to "on the record after a hearing;" however, the statutory language is not simply "after hearing," which is often found in enabling acts and is not sufficient to require formal rulemaking. Likely, a court would determine that the included language was not sufficient to trigger formal rulemaking. However, you may wish to include counter-analysis: that the language suggests Congress intended to allow for more participation than the more typical "after hearing" phrase would indicate.

2(b): Assuming the action is subject to judicial review, would the EPA's decision to limit the GAS Regulation to Beef producers survive a *procedural* challenge? Please explain.

The issue here is whether the EPA followed the notice-and-comment rulemaking procedures the APA requires. Turning to III.C.2. in the checklist above, you need to first analyze whether the notice included the time, place, and nature of the public proceedings (if any); the legal authority for the rule; and either the substance of the proposed rule or a description of the subjects and issues involved. Ask: Was the notice sufficient to fairly apprise interested persons of the issues involved so that they may present responsive data or argument? (III.C.2.b.).

In this case, it is likely that the NPRM was "sufficient to fairly apprise interested persons of the issues involved." While the NPRM noted that climate change "is largely caused by human activity" and seemed focused on carbon dioxide emissions, the NPRM mentioned methane gas and the 50 parts per million standard. Moreover, the poultry and pork industries submitted comments that objected to the extreme effects those requirements would have on their industries. While the beef producers did not believe it was necessary to comment, their failure to comment relates less to their conclusion that the rule would not apply to them and more to their belief the data was so weak that their industry would not be regulated. These facts suggest that the beef producers had sufficient notice.

Returning to the checklist, you should work your way through the next few questions and conclude that no prohibited *ex parte* occurred (III.C.2.c.), the agency allowed interested parties to submit "written data, views, or arguments" on the proposed rule (III.C.2.d.), and that no hybrid procedures were ignored (III.C.2.e).

You should note, however, that the final rule differed significantly from the proposed rule (III.C.2.f.). Thus, you will need to determine whether the final rule can be characterized as a *logical outgrowth* of the proposed rule or whether the EPA pulled a "surprise switcheroo." To do so, ask whether the final rule materially altered the issues involved in the rulemaking and whether the final rule substantially departed from the substance of the proposed rule.

In this case, the *proposed* rule did not target any specific industry, focused on human causes of climate change, targeted companies whose manufacturing or production activities produced carbon dioxide *and* methane gas, and only discussed the implementation of scrubbers. Airtight buildings and masks were not mentioned, and all industries, rather than one specific industry, were targeted. The final rule differed from the proposed rule in all these aspects. Hence, it is likely that the final rule was not a logical outgrowth of the proposed rule, and the EPA should begin the notice-and-comment rulemaking process again if it wishes to promulgate the final rule.

ANALYSIS FOR QUESTION 3

3(a): Assuming this action is subject to judicial review, would the EPA's *factual* findings in its final rule survive a legal challenge? Please explain, being sure to identify the appropriate standard of review.

The issue here is whether the EPA's factual findings would be upheld after judicial review. To answer this question, you need to identify and then apply the appropriate standard of review. To identify the appropriate standard of review, you should turn to VII.A.1. in the checklist above and conclude that the court is reviewing findings of fact made during a notice-and-comment rulemaking; hence, the court will review the agency's finding using the arbitrary and capricious standard (VII.A.1.b.ii.).

To apply the arbitrary and capricious standard of review, courts ask the following: was the agency's decision (1) based on a consideration of all the relevant factors, and (2) free of clear error? (Both elements must be satisfied) (VII.B.2.).

You must first identify the factual findings the EPA made in its final rule. Here, the EPA determined that (1) "the primary contributor to climate change is methane gas emissions by cattle, especially in large feedlots;" (2) "methane scrubbers are an efficient method to lower methane gas emissions;" (3) "keeping cattle indoors will also lower emissions;" and (4) "[methane] emissions must be no more than 50 parts per billion for climate change to be reduced."

(SOBP). Importantly, EPA offered no evidence to support any of these findings.

Now, to determine whether the agency's decision was based on a consideration of all the relevant factors, check the enabling act to see what factors, if any, Congress included. The HEAT Act identifies a number of findings in Section 1 and directs the EPA to consider these findings when promulgating regulations. One finding that is inconsistent with the HEAT Act is the EPA's finding that one industry, specifically cattle feedlots, are the primary cause of climate change. Congress, both in the findings section of the HEAT Act and in Act's legislative history, made clear that no one industry should bear the burden of addressing climate change on its own. Yet, that appears to have happened here. Hence, the EPA's finding—(1) "the primary contributor to climate change is methane gas emissions by cattle, especially in large feedlots"—is likely arbitrary and capricious. You should evaluate the other findings similarly.

Now, to determine whether the agency's decision was free of clear error, look to see if the evidence the agency relied on supports its factual findings. In this case, the EPA did not provide any evidentiary support for its findings; hence, the EPA's findings (2) "methane scrubbers are an efficient method to lower methane gas emissions;" (3) "keeping cattle indoors will also lower emissions;" and (4) "[methane] emissions must be no more than 50 parts per billion for climate change to be reduced" are all arbitrary and capricious.

3(b): Assuming this action is subject to judicial review, would the EPA's *interpretation* that "any industry that contributes to climate change" provides the agency with the power to regulate only one industry, specifically, cattle feedlots, survive a legal challenge? Please explain, being sure to identify the appropriate standard of review.

The issue here is whether the EPA's decision would be upheld after judicial review. To answer this question, you need to identify and then apply the appropriate standard of review. To identify the standard of review, you must first identify the language in the enabling act that the agency interpreted as well as the agency's interpretation. Here, the question tells you that the language in the act is "any industry that contributes to climate change," and the EPA interpreted that language to apply to one industry: cattle feedlots.

To identify the appropriate standard of review to apply, you should turn to VII.A. in the checklist above and conclude that the court is reviewing a question of law: specifically, the interpretation of language in the HEAT Act, an act that the EPA administers (VII.A.3.b.iii).

The next step is to apply the major questions analysis by asking whether the agency's action is one that will have "vast economic and political significance" (VII.B.3.). Likely, the regulation of the economy to reduce carbon and methane emissions will have vast economic and political significance. Although the EPA chose to interpret the Act to apply to only one industry (making it less costly), the BPA should argue that if the HEAT Act is applied to all industries (as it likely should have been), it would be very costly to implement. Moreover, whether climate change exists and the best way to address it is politically debated. Assuming that the EPA's action is one that will have vast economic and political significance even if applied just to the cattle industry, then Congress must provide a clear statement in the HEAT Act to allow the EPA to regulate in the way it did (VII.B.3.b.). Clear statements are rarely found, and there is no clear statement in the HEAT Act for the EPA to regulate just the cattle industry in this way; hence, the EPA's regulation is invalid.

Alternatively, if the EPA's action is not one that would have vast economic and political significance, then the *Loper Bright* analysis applies (VII.B.3.a.). Applying *Loper Bright*, a court will apply *de novo* review and use the traditional tools of interpretation to evaluate the meaning of the language. (VII.B.4.). Starting with the text of the HEAT Act, you should note that the Act addresses "*any* industry," not one industry. The dictionary defines "any" to mean "to one or some of a thing or number of things, no matter how much or many." This definition suggests that the EPA had authority to target just one industry, as it did, although the definition creates some ambiguity.

Assuming this language is ambiguous, you need to turn to the other tools of interpretation, such as the findings clause. That clause specifically states, "[N]o one industry should bear the burden of remedying this danger." And even were ambiguity to remain, the bill's sponsor noted during the House floor debates that "No one industry will bear this burden alone." In addition, Congress noted concern with both carbon dioxide and methane emissions, not just methane. So the EPA's interpretation seems contrary to congressional intent.

The EPA may respond that the dictionary is clear that "any industry" can mean just one industry; hence, because the text is unambiguous, there is no need for the court to consider the findings clause or legislative history. In any event, statements made during floor debates and statements from sponsors are not persuasive indicators of congressional intent.

Likely, a court would find the language to be ambiguous from the language alone. If the court is willing to consider legislative history and purpose, then the EPA's interpretation is invalid.

Alternatively, if the meaning of the Act is not clear from a *de novo* review alone, a court might consider whether the agency's interpretation is entitled to respect using the *Skidmore* factors: (1) the thoroughness evident in the agency's consideration of the issue, (2) the validity of the agency's reasoning for its interpretation, (3) the consistency of the agency's interpretation over time, (4) the contemporaneousness of the interpretation, (5) the relevance of the agency's expertise, and (6) any other persuasive factors (VII.B.4.b.).

Here, consistency is not relevant because this is the first time the EPA has interpreted the HEAT Act. Instead, thoroughness, validity, contemporaneousness, and expertise are relevant. Regarding thoroughness, the EPA's interpretation was made after notice and comment procedures and significant industry comment. As for contemporaneousness, the interpretation was made shortly after the enactment of the HEAT Act. As for expertise, the EPA's expertise with the climate is highly relevant for questions regarding climate change. The analysis of these factors suggest that the EPA's interpretation is entitled to respect.

But let's turn to validity. The EPA's interpretation did not reflect any consideration of the comments made during the rulemaking process. Also, the EPA's regulation will not further the statutory purpose because it targets only one industry and only one congressionally identified cause. And it is inconsistent with the legislative history. The EPA did not explain why it targeted one industry. The analysis of this factor suggests that the EPA's interpretation is not entitled to respect.

In sum, under the major questions doctrine and *Loper Bright*, the EPAs' interpretation is likely invalid, but it is a close call.